RUSSIA AND AMERICA:
The Roots
—— of ——
Economic
Divergence

COLIN WHITE

CROOM HELM
London • New York • Sydney

© 1987 Colin White
Croom Helm Ltd, Provident House,
Burrell Row, Beckenham, Kent BR3 1AT
Croom Helm Australia, 44–50 Waterloo Road,
North Ryde, 2113, New South Wales

Published in the USA by
Croom Helm
in association with Methuen, Inc.
29 West 35th Street
New York, NY 10001

British Library Cataloguing in Publication Data
White, Colin
  Russia and America: the roots of economic
  divergence.
  1. Soviet Union — Economic conditions —
  To 1861 2. United States — Economic
  conditions — To 1865
  I. Title
  330.947'04   HC334
  ISBN 0-7099-5246-5

Library of Congress Cataloging-in-Publication Data
White, Colin (Colin M.)
  Russia and America.

  Bibliography: p.
  Includes index.
  1. Soviet Union—Economic conditions. 2. United
  States—Economic conditions. 3. National characteristics,
  Russian-History. 4. National characteristics, American
  —History. I. Title.
  HC333.W46   1987   330.947   87-13646
  ISBN 0-7099-5246-5

For Sandra

Printed and bound in Great Britain
by Billing & Sons Limited, Worcester.

Contents

Preface and Acknowledgements

Books are much like children, requiring long and careful nurturing. Significant stages in the process of maturation cannot be skipped. Throughout infancy both books and children display an unreasonable degree of independence, their individual personality continuously reasserting itself, often against the wishes of the parent. This book is recognisably my product, but not at all what I intended at its inception.

In this book two influences project themselves. All good economic history is the birthchild of a creative tension between the economist and the historian, the hard exacting father and the soft, sympathetic mother. Because the economic historian has to blend the unique and the general, he is advantaged by an academic training in both disciplines — I was fortunate in this respect. The writing of history is a genuinely interdisciplinary endeavour. For the writing of this book the skills of not only economist and historian, but geographer, anthropologist, sociologist, demographer, political scientist, legal studies specialist, statistician, even linguist, were relevant.

In yet another way the book has two personalities. In the first place it is a comparative study of Russia and America, an attempt to illuminate in a new light each other's history. In the second it attempts to establish the framework of a theory of economic development. Such a theory can only be fully fleshed out after a long series of such comparisons.

My intellectual debts are many and varied. A healthy scepticism about the validity of neoclassical economics was instilled in me by Cambridge economics, a scepticism which has influenced my attitude to the new economic history; a useful tool but marginal to the pursuit of the proper discipline. Cambridge history, and in particular Cambridge economic historians such as David Joslin, gave me a rather broader view. A brief excursion into the abstract realms of planning theory aroused my interest in Russia.

At the University College of Swansea, the venue of my first appointment, Max Cole in the economic history department presented the model of a rigorous, analytical mind while my colleagues in the Russian centre, headed by Roger Pethybridge, encouraged a more literary and interdisciplinary approach, sometimes unconsciously promoting the latter against their own intellectual beliefs.

Later at La Trobe University a growing awareness of long-run

1

change as a significant topic of interest was given focus by Eric Jones. My interest in the comparative method has been further exercised in discussions with my colleagues, John Anderson, Ian Watt and Geoff Raby.

Readers will recognise some of the ideas set out initially in Eric Jones' work, particularly in *The European Miracle*, but given more formal treatment in my book. Many other influences are only acknowledged in the bibliography; some are unrecognised even by myself. I have been reading and thinking about Russia since the early 1960s and America since the 1970s — in that time a veritable flood has passed beneath the bridge. The relevant literature, straddling long periods in the history of the two major powers and a number of different disciplines, is enormous.

As with any book this one could be improved by further work but there are diminishing returns. Over the years the major themes have developed slowly. The stress on the desire for security, on cooperation rather than conflict, on the subtle interplay between resources, institutions and technology has emerged with glacial speed. There were occasional spurts. A critical turning point was the discovery that even in the era of rapid industrialisation risk was something to be avoided, induced by Strassman's criticism of Schumpeter's vision of innovational waves as gales of creative destruction and description of the painstaking management of risk by the not-so-heroic entrepreneur.

There are still major areas within the general theory needing to be researched carefully. For example, the aggregate level of risk confronting a given society is emphasised but more work needs to be done on the social mechanisms for distributing that risk. Clearly different comparisons would demand the clarification of different specific relationships within the whole.

I started my research on the narrowly economic topic of the criteria for the choice of technique adopted under Soviet planning. The present work could be interpreted as an explanation of the distant origins of the 'cold war'. The pathway between these widely differing topics was marked by unexpected changes of direction.

I have tried hard to make the book as readable as possible within the constraints of analytical respectability. References are placed in the text and kept to a minimum. A bibliographical review explores my intellectual debts. To avoid long and clumsy, if accurate, repetition the terms Russia and America are used as shorthand for the changing geographical areas, although Russia is today only one of the constituent republics of the Soviet Union and America might refer to a continent.

My greatest debts — practical rather than intellectual — are to those who have assisted in the preparation of the book, the typists, Sylvia Perkins, Helen Cook, Sandra Barnes and Lorraine Chai, and to my family who probably believed the final product would never be completed but spurred me on to prove them wrong. Without a secure and comfortable family life writing must be sheer hell.

Part 1
Theory and Practice

1

Coverage and Concepts

To a family that lives on the margin of subsistence, failure means hunger, probably death. So regarded risk is not something to be accepted casually. Among the very poor, risk aversion, as it is called by economists, is very high — and for reasons that are wholly rational.

Galbraith

In the end they [the Americans] came to love enterprises in which chance played a part.

de Tocqueville

Since the second world war the cold-war stereotypes of Russia and America juxtapose two contrasting societies, allegedly organised on diametrically opposed principles, particularly in the economic sphere, and enjoying significantly different standards of living, although, it must be added, both belong to the small group of developed economies. A centrally-planned, state-dominated economy is compared with a highly decentralised market economy, free from significant government intervention. A society of high mass consumption is compared with one which has a set of priorities which emphasise communal consumption and the conspicuous symbols of successful national pride. As always reality does not quite accord with the stereotypes but divergence there has been and still is.

It is often implicitly assumed, where not explicitly stated, that the divergence originated with the Russian Revolution of 1917 and its aftermath, in particular Stalin's Great Turn of 1929, which introduced the collectivisation of agriculture and the First Five-Year Plan. In practice divergence began well before, its determining features lying in the interaction between physical and human environments rather than in a single political upheaval. The forces of continuity, or of social inertia, as we shall call them, have perpetuated the main features of a divergence already established at a much earlier date.

As a consequence the book is mainly concerned with the early modern period in the history of both Russia and America, well before the advent of significant factory industrialisation, a period during which the relevant economies were for the first time seriously penetrated by the market.

The book is genuinely comparative, not simply a combination of two discrete case studies. Firstly a comparative perspective helps pose interesting questions. More significantly the comparative method lends itself particularly well to the discipline of economic history; it allows generalisation about the experience of economic development with full account taken of the uniqueness of each experience. In particular it has great potential for revealing previously neglected features of historical change. Sometimes the obvious is ignored because historians are either standing too close to the relevant society or alternatively distancing themselves too far, analysing that society only through current concepts. Moreover the comparative method makes a comparison between two real experiences, not between a real and a hypothetical or counterfactual experience. For the large or important historical questions the construction of counterfactual worlds is a matter of fiction, not history, such an approach having validity only for what economists call marginal cases.

The comparative method has its ultimate justification in hypothesis testing (Sewell 1967). The hypothesis to be tested in this book asserts that the divergence in pattern and structure of economic development in Russia and America is to be explained by their different endowment with resources and, more particularly, their different levels of exposure to risk.

However the comparative approach demands sufficient points of similarity to make the comparisons valid, otherwise the number of variables is too great. There are sufficient similarities of development between Russia and America to provide grounds for such a comparison of the two histories. These similarities make even more intriguing the eventual divergence in organisation of economy. They can be grouped under three headings; similarities of starting point, of process and of terminal point.

The similarities of starting point largely comprise geographical congruences. At least superficially these similarities are compelling. The territories of North America and the Soviet Union are roughly equal in area and fall within the same latitudes. Of course, the removal of

Canada reduces the territory of America, excluding largely wasteland within northerly latitudes. In both cases high land-to-labour ratios, within territories of continental dimension, generally conditioned the nature of economic advance. Vegetational belts are similar, although these run in an east-west direction in Russia and north-south in America. The main distinction between forest and steppe or prairie divides both territories into distinct natural environments. A whole series of similar export staples reflected a broadly similar resource endowment — fur, naval stores, textile fibres, grain. Both continents also showed a potentially high degree of self-sufficiency.

The similarities of process arise from a parallel chronology of development. Both countries contained significant areas of new settlement for most of the relevant period and therefore developed within the context of various moving frontiers. There is a considerable literature on so-called settler societies or regions of recent settlement which almost completely ignores the Russian case. In fact Russia represents a success story in permanent settlement to rival the American experience.

The growth of the two societies was therefore accompanied by a rapid rate of territorial expansion and population growth, factors which contributed to a high rate of extensive economic growth. Moreover foreign trade peaked in its relative importance at an early date and then declined in importance with the opening up of the full resources of the two continents. Both territories lying on the periphery represented for a period part of the 'ghost' acreage of the west European metropolis. Each then developed its own metropolis and periphery.

Movement into the industrial phase defined in terms of factory industry came relatively late, at least relative to western Europe, but extremely fast. The same lateness and speed characterised the process of urbanisation.

Both nations also experienced similar episodes in their advance to political maturity. Paul Dukes has pointed to political events of parallel significance — the assertion of political independence, the emancipation of servile labour, the occurrence of revolution and civil war.

Finally the similarities of terminal point arise from successful economic development, still a phenomenon limited to a small number of countries, moreover an economic development within the social context of a multinational empire, predominantly European and of comparable population size.

If strict chronological time is used as our standard of comparison there is always a problem of comparing like with like, that is, of choosing moments of time at which the two economies are at similar stages of economic development. Do we have criteria for recognising such stages?

There has been a long historical tradition of stages analysis running from the German historical school to W.W. Rostow, who offered his analysis as an alternative to the Marxist scheme. It has been established that there are certain minimum requirements of a valid stages approach (Kuznets 1965). A rigorous treatment would demand that each stage be characterised by distinct, that is, distinct from those of other stages, empirically testable features, and stand in a definite analytical relationship to both the preceding and succeeding stages; in other words there must be specified a particular evolutionary mechanism by which the economy is moved from one stage to another. Finally the particular world to which the stages construct applies must be delineated. Unhappily none of these analyses fully satisfies the minimum requirements, although the Marxist scheme possibly comes closest.

The Marxist approach identifies historical stages by their characteristic mode of production. The key modern transition is from feudalism to capitalism. Russian historians have made great play with this transition, said to have been achieved in Russia with the emancipation of the serfs in 1861. Some western commentators, most notably Perry Anderson, have taken up this periodisation, in Anderson's case even arguing that the state in Russia remained feudal until 1917. On this account it might be said that a central difference between early America and Russia is that they were at a different stage of development, Russia feudal and America already at first settlement beyond this stage.

It is also necessary to reject this example of the stages approach. Russia was never truly feudal in the west European sense of the term.

Although there are many definitions of feudalism, a reasonable definition would follow Rushton Coulborn in defining feudalism as primarily a method of government rather than an economic or social system, although the latter clearly modify and are in their turn modified by the former (Coulborn 1965: 4). The feudal method of government involves the exercise of political authority on a personal rather than an institutional basis. The essential relations in such a system are not between ruler and subject or state and citizen but between lord and vassal. Therefore feudalism is most effective at the local level, or as J.S. Critchely asserts, 'as a political concept, feudalism means above all the decentralisation of power'.

Coulborn sees feudalism as likely to occur as a series of responses to a particular kind of challenge, notably the decay or weakening of a highly organised political system with the breakdown of economic unity and the concomitant need for individual protection. In the west European case, the fall of the Roman Empire was the appropriate context. Control over military power is a key aspect of this process.

In applying this definiton to Russia Marc Szeftel quite rightly rejects the description of feudalism as fitting either Russia in its medieval age with its *de jure* right to, and *de facto* frequency of, mobility by both lord and peasant, or the Muscovite period with its characteristic centralisation of political authority. Szeftel puts the case concisely and cogently: 'all Muscovite institutional changes were results of the action from above of a "liturgical" state; they represent not stepping stones in the direction of a feudal system, but as many measures leading from it towards an extreme centralisation of all rational life' (Szeftel 1965: 182). In so arguing Szeftel had a respectable ancestry. Peter Struve had already described Russia as 'a kind of state feudalism, but in its legal aspect . . . in some ways the direct opposite of classical western feudalism', justifying this argument by the imposed requirement of service and the notable absence of the voluntary feudal contract with its reciprocal obligations, which is said to define the nature of the feudal bond (*Cambridge economic history of Europe*, 1, Cambridge, 1941: 419).

Analogously the parallel between the benefice and the *pomestye*, both estates granted on some form of service tenure, usually military, is more apparent than real. In Muscovy the pomestye was granted as a reward for service required of the subject by the state and in fact promoted the centralisation of political and economic life. In Western feudalism the benefice was associated with the decentralisation of political authority.

Such a conclusion could only be rejected if the emphasis on the political factor in the definition is replaced by an emphasis on the economic factor. Marxists stress the non-economic extraction of the surplus, that is, its extraction outside the market place, as the key element of a feudal system. Such a broad definition would empty the term of any real content since feudalism would then become almost universal, at least in the pre-capitalist world.

Unless the term is allowed to lose its historical concreteness it should be limited to western Europe during a particular historical period. Rieber has put the point rather well, ' . . . a preoccupation with general models of social change derived from Western European experience and fed by domestic political conflicts in late Imperial Russia has long obscured the real dimensions of Russia's social structure' (Rieber 1982: xix). An historical approach which attaches a label to a particular political or social structure and then initiates an interminable debate about the meaning of the label offers little of real insight into the historical process. We need from the beginning to free the analysis from such preconceptions. In Russia it is the very absence of a feudal background of decentralised power which makes autocratic centralisation easier to achieve.

A further approach, based implicitly on stages, sees the key transition as the beginning of modernisation, often conceived of in the economic area as industrialisation within the factory system, urbanisation and the conversion of the independent agricultural into a dependent sector. However this book avoids the use of the term modernisation for two reasons; firstly, because the term is inadequate to describe the process of change occurring before periods which could legitimately be called modern, and secondly, because the term is teleological, prejudging the significance of the activities it analyses.

In the spirit of a healthy, if speculative, empiricism we can conceptualise the process of economic development as divided into its phases. Such a phases approach is purely a heuristic device. The description of 'speculative empiricism' (Hirst 1975) need not be pejorative since there are alas no generally accepted 'covering laws' to explain the process of historical change.

There are four phases of economic development. First, during opening up or pioneer phase, an area is settled for the first time. This period sees the conversion of acquisition, or indeed initial exploitation, into permanent settlement. The second phase, the commercial phase, involves the penetration of the economy, principally the domestic economy, by market operations. Next the industrial phase sees the separation of activities involving manufacture; that is, industrialisation involves the satisfaction of economic needs by specialised industrial production and their location within the factory. Finally the planning phase has as its central feature the direct application of human reason to economic activity, involving a significant suspension of market activity. These are ideal-type phases rather than strictly chronological periods through which all economies must pass. This book is mainly concerned with the first two phases.

However, it is wise to make explicit what is already implicit in our earlier remarks. A key concept is that of a formative period, a period during which the basic principles of institutional organisation are established in a society, leaving a strong legacy for the future. The phases comprised within the formative period are then an even greater influence on future development.

12

It is helpful at this point to date the formative periods in the two societies and to justify this choice. The closing dates for the formative period adopted here are the 1780s for America and the 1580s for Russia. There are a number of signficant defining features of this closure period.

First, the United States gained a lasting constitution in 1789 which protected the important institutions of the market, of land held in fee simple and of free labour (with, it is true, one glaring exception) and defined the economic role of the government. In 1580 Russia sees a significant step in the establishment of the service state based on serfdom, the imposition of the so-called forbidden years when peasants could no longer move freely. There may be some case for choosing 1649 since the law code of that year finally completed this process of enserfment, or put more aptly, 'enservicement'.

Secondly, the 1780s saw the rejection of the Proclamation line restricting settlement beyond the Appalachians, and therefore the first significant movement across this major geographical barrier. In Russia in the 1580s the Russians crossed the Urals into Siberia; however, perhaps more significantly the first movement into the steppe, albeit slowly, occurred around the middle of the seventeenth century.

The area controlled at the end of the formative period defines the core area and the area outside the core is referred to as the periphery. Core Russia, or Muscovy, lacked clear boundaries; its vulnerability to incursion constituted one of the significant moulding influences. Bordered in the north by the White Sea and Arctic Ocean and in the east by the Urals, Muscovy lay open in the south and south-east, where the lower Volga and the wooded steppe represented vague frontier areas, and in the west by a completely imaginary line running from Kiev to the eastern corner of the Baltic.

Colonial America had a much better defined territory; to the east lay the sea, to the west the Appalachians. It consisted of thirteen self-contained colonies strung along the Atlantic coast.

There are two conceptual frameworks in the context of which economic history is usually written in America and the Soviet Union. The neo-classical world in which economic agents are rational economic men, maximisers to the core, prevails along the 'new economic historians' of America; the marxist world of power relations based on economic class prevails in the Soviet Union. In both, economic agents are seen as operating in the environment of conflict or competition. In an appropriate social context either viewpoint may be deemed valid, but not generally.

A more universal goal, although never completely universal, is

13

the desire for security. Deviant individuals or even societies may temporarily depart from this objective but they can only survive in exceptional circumstances. Individuals commonly seek to dissipate ignorance, to remove uncertainty and to reduce risk. Most would exchange at least some satisfaction or income to achieve security. Cooperative action is often engaged in to meet such uncertainties. Anglo-Saxon societies in particular have been adept at forming clubs, societies, institutions of a formal or informal kind, evolving a context favourable to problem solving. An environment of cooperation is therefore as common as an environment of conflict or competition.

Economists and economic historians often talk as if their smooth growth paths were not merely mental constructs but in some sense depicted the reality of social change. In practice economic man takes his decisions in a world perpetually in motion, in the midst of an endless chain of apparently arbitrary events and changing circumstances. Change is the normal state of affairs; disequilibrium rather than equilibrium is the norm. Survival in the short-run was more important than the advantageous secular trend. Man's life was, and continues to be, punctuated by a stream of unexpected and in exact terms unpredictable fluctuations. Disasters and shocks were the stuff of life. Out of this continuous flux men sought to create stability and continuity. Social institutions were either deliberately constructed or evolved unconsciously to preserve that stability and perpetuate continuity.

In this book the terms uncertainty and risk could be used interchangeably. Theoretically there is a distinction. Risk is a calculable chance of a certain event occurring or failing to occur, a specific magnitude, more particularly, a probability distribution of known possible returns; uncertainty is a more general ignorance, especially about the profile of possible returns. To an economist uncertainty means you do not know what will happen; risk means you do not know the precise outcome but can place probabilities on all of the possible outcomes (Thurow 1983: 162). Paradoxically risk rather than uncertainty carries connotations of meaning which more dramatically suggest a threat to security. The term is, therefore, preferred. In practice the two are so closely liked that this preference is not significant, nor therefore misleading.

The attitude, and later response, to uncertain returns on the part of an economic agent can be described as risk-inclined or risk-averse. Such attitudes depend on the level of income or consumption. Risk or uncertainty is a luxury good, certainty or security a subsistence good. A very high price will be paid for security at low income

14

levels. However, some security is desirable at any income level.

We could talk of the elimination of risk or in Easterbrook's terminology the 'conservation of certainty', as being a basic principle or law of history, if such laws really exist. Certainly some element of insurance against risk is inherent in the organisation of every social institution, although these elements differ in significance. One of the great achievements of modern economic development has been to conquer many sources of risk. Risk reduction has been an important result of industrialisation and economic diversification. Freedom from risk has allowed economic agents enormous space to pursue the goals of income or profit maximisation. Insurance itself has become a market commodity like any other. Moreover in extremis we know that the government will bail us out. The problem of the author, and therefore the reader, is both an imaginative one, projecting oneself back into a very much more unstable world; and analytical, classifying the different types of instability. The effort would not be worthwhile if a risk-minimising strategy invariably coincided with a growth-maximising strategy; at least in the Russian case this is not so.

Easterbrook, in an early but ignored treatment of risk, distinguishes between specific uncertainties, which threaten the security of the entrepreneur directly, and primary uncertainties, which threaten the stability of the larger setting in which the enterprise operates. Only in exceptional circumstances are primary uncertainties of minor importance; the United States is offered as an example. In a sense this classification is simply a distinction between the macro and micro; in theory the large uncertainties can be reduced to smaller uncertainties for the enterprise.

Koopmans distinguishes in a different way between primary and secondary uncertainty: the first involving changes unpredictable even in an ideal economic world, changes in the natural environment, in tastes or technology; the second uncertainty resulting from the operation of atomistic economic agents acting in ignorance of each others' intentions within a market context, and therefore, after the transfer of the appropriate information, avoidable.

Such approaches offer some clue to an effective incorporation of uncertainty, or risk, in a theory of economic development. The key idea is, again in Easterbrook's words, that 'the dynamics of change may be found in responses, generally group responses, to uncertainties both primary and specific'. The major problem is to analyse the changing nature of risk or uncertainty.

The most useful classification of risk is by historical phase. To each phase corresponds a particular kind of risk, which could be said to characterise that phase despite the co-existence of other types. During the opening up of an area, the characteristic kind of risk is pioneer risk, which arises in the context of the economic shocks to which the pioneers are exposed. Such shocks include flood, fire and famine, disease, war and animal depredation. Commercial risk arises from unexpected changes in supply and/or demand in any particular market, and from the ignorance of market conditions on the part of purchaser and supplier. Commercial risk is therefore indicated by unforeseen fluctuations in price. Industrial risk follows from the unforeseen changes in taste or technology which threaten the value of industrial capital.

We must also distinguish conceptually between a threshold level of risk and an actual level. Entry into a particular phase can only occur when actual risk is below the threshold level. The threshold is defined by the particular economic context, the main feature of which is the resource endowment expressed most often in terms of income per head. Higher returns compensate for higher risk — or more accurately, those who can more easily satisfy their subsistence requirements are more likely to take risks. Under these circumstances the threshold is higher.

An important question to ask is, who takes or bears the risk? Risk can be shared or passed on. Such a sharing or passing on involves both market operations and power relations in society. On the one hand there is deliberate and voluntary risk sharing which may be systematic or *ad hoc*, market or non-market; on the other hand there is involuntary risk sharing ordained by law or custom or simply the exercise of arbitrary power. Since security is a highly desired, if scarce, commodity its allocation and consumption reflects power relations in society. Individuals can be constrained to act in a way which will not minimise their own risk. An economic agent is therefore influenced by both the general risk environment and the actual distribution of aggregate risk.

These considerations lead us to make a distinction between primary and secondary risk. In theory the latter is defined as the risk to which economic agents are exposed as a result of other agents seeking to pass on the primary risk to which they themselves are exposed. In the context of this book secondary risk refers in particular to the risk generated by government attempts to pass on primary risk. It is recognised that this is only one kind of secondary risk, but in the context of our particular comparison a very important one.

The desire for security involves accommodation to an existing level of income, possibly even to an accustomed rate of increase in that level. Individual economic agents also accommodate to the fluctuations around that level inherent in any risk environment. A threat to expected welfare leads to adjustments to restore that level. The tenacity with which accommodation is made lends to social institutions a degree of inertia which is perhaps surprising, if the desire for security is ignored.

The institutional organisation of societies differs according to the nature of risk and changes, albeit slowly, according to phase movement. Security is derived from the known institutional patterns themselves. Vested interests develop in the existing distribution of risk. A desire for security, a leaning towards the known, vested interests — all comprise elements of the social inertia which affects institutional structures.

The importance of the book is, like its basic perspective, twofold. First, it offers a comparative analysis of the particular historical evolution of two societies. Implicitly it goes further than this: it suggests that the basic principles of institutional organisation, the main lines of economic advance, were already established in the two societies at an early date.

Secondly, it offers a theoretical framework for analysing historical change in terms of uncertainty or risk. Both the pace and pattern of change are influenced significantly by the level and nature of risk. Vital social institutions are organised to help mitigate or manage risk. Both power relations in society and the role of the government influence the distribution of risk.

The book is divided into four sections. First there is an introductory section, whose second chapter sets out the 'stylised facts' relating to the economic development of America and Russia.

The pith of the book consists in the two middle sections. The first of these looks at the relative impact of the natural environment on the evolution of the two economies. The second considers the relationship between the human environment and the development of the two economies. The main theme threading its way through both sections is the changing nature of risk and its influence on phase movement.

The concluding chapter seeks to broaden the argument into a general model of an uncertain and insecure world.

2

'Stylised Facts' and Questions

NATIVE POPULATIONS

> Incapable of conquering true wilderness, the Europeans were highly competent in the skill of conquering other people, and that is what they did. They did not settle a virgin land. They invaded and displaced a resident population.
>
> F. Jennings on the settlement of America

> With the conquest of Bashkiria, these gates were closed and the ancient threat to Europe ended.
>
> A.S. Donnelly

Opening up did not occur in a vacuum in either America or Russia. In both continents there already existed societies of varying size. From the perspective of this book, the native populations were an active element of an alien environment to which the new settlers had to accommodate. The nature of the relationship between settler and native varied greatly and had an important influence on the economic activities integral to opening up. The key factors determining the nature of this relationship were the size of the native population and their mode of economic organisation at the time of the intrusion of the new settlers, which itself largely set the limits on native population density.

In the past there has been a tendency to assume a native population of sparsely distributed hunters and gatherers who represented a temporary but insignificant obstacle to settlement. The history of new settlement, inevitably a piece of conscious or unconscious propaganda, stressed the movement into a largely empty land whose nomadic inhabitants lacked any attachment to a particular place and gained from contact with a culturally and technically superior civilisation. Recently revisionist historians have strikingly rewritten the story of America. There has been a general tendency to magnify native population numbers, to stress agricultural rather than nomadic pursuits and to devote equal attention to the influences flowing from native to settler as from settler to native. Explicit or implicit propagandising has been rejected.

It has always been recognised that a two-way process of acculturation occurred where the Russians confronted a relatively dense and settled population. The mutuality of the relationship with the Tartars has frequently been noted. Subjugation by the Russians of the Bashkirs or Crimean Tartars was a process of centuries rather than decades, a process of divide and rule, of mutual accommodation and assimilation as well as bloody conflict.

In both continents the statistics for the native populations are totally inadequate but some kind of estimate is crucial. The first carefully calculated estimate, by James Mooney, of the aboriginal population in America north of Mexico at the time of the initial European contact suggested a total of a little over one million. Such a figure is now recognised as a minimum estimate, because the native population probably declined precipitately before the date of estimation. For example, Mooney's estimate of 25,000 for New England in 1600 is inconsistent with later estimates. Russell's recent book on the Indians of New England suggests the total may have approached 75,000.

The critical difficulty is to calculate the relevant depopulation ratios. Cook argued for a reduction of 80 per cent in the Indian population as a whole during the first century of European settlement, concentrated particularly in the possibly plague years of 1616–19 and the smallpox epidemic of 1633–4. According to Cook there were 36,000 Indians in New England in 1620 and virtually none by 1750. Of this decline, 28.5 per cent was attributed to the results of warfare; most of the rest to the ravages of disease.

Recent estimates for North America as a whole reach as high as 12.25 million, in a total hemisphere population exceeding one hundred million. The maximum possible extent of the decline is suggested by an Indian population of just over 0.8 million in the 1790 census, itself a slight underestimate according to Jacobs. A conservative estimate for the whole of North America puts the pre-contact population at 4.4 million.

The statistical picture for Russia is even less clearcut. According to the 1897 census the Tartars constituted 1.9 per cent of the total population, at 2.3 million, the Finnic peoples, including the Finns

19

proper and Karelians, at 2.9 million, 2.3 per cent. At that time both groups were growing at an annual rate of just under one per cent, a rate significantly below the average Russian rate, which suggests they accounted for a larger proportion of the population at an earlier date. Some isolated statistics exist for earlier dates.

It seems likely that the Bashkir population was at least 100,000 in the seventeenth century. Casualties of over 30,000 are referred to as a result of the 'pacification' of Bashkiria by the Russians. According to Rychkov, in 1760 there were 200,000 male Russians, 400,000 Tartars and 100,000 Bashkirs in Orenburg province, which at least gives a good idea of relative numbers on the frontier. Again the imposition of Russian taxation and recruitment for the army on the Crimea in the 1780s is said to have caused an emigration *en masse* of 100,000 from a population of 150,000.

Except for the tribes of the far east, such as the Tunguses, or the nomadic Tartars of the Asian steppe, the peoples of non-European Russia were much less densely settled than those of European Russia. In 1662 the scattered aborigines of Siberia were said to number 200,000. Vulnerable because of their isolation, some groups experienced rapid depopulation as a result of disease. The native Aleut population of the Aleutian Islands is said to have been halved between the middle and end of the eighteenth century as a consequence of Russian contact. The Kolashes of Alaska were never really properly subjugated, although decimated by disease. For example, about one third of Kodiak's natives was killed by an epidemic in 1819.

Clearly the denser the population, the greater the likelihood that the population would have to support itself by agricultural activities. There is little doubt that during the pre-contact period, large, settled populations existed in both America and European Russia. Such large populations could act either as an indispensable help to settlers in accommodating to a new environment or as an obstacle to expansion. Whether the relationship was a positive or a negative one depended on the nature of the 'shadow' frontier which existed between first contact and permanent settlement, and on differences in the military technology of settlers and natives.

The nature of pre-settlement contact varied. Russia was confronted by three significantly different kinds of relationship. First, it interacted with European neighbours of at least an equal military or economic standing, who governed subject Russian populations, principally Lithuania, Poland and Sweden. Secondly, it dealt with the remants of the Tartar horde, initially centred on Kazan, Astrakhan and the Crimea, whose overall military control had only been rejected late in the fifteenth century. Thirdly the Russians absorbed isolated native populations, tribally fragmented and technically backward. American pre-settlement contact was predominantly of this third kind.

The nature of contact reflected differences in military technology. Russia had to fight with different methods on her two main military frontiers. In the west, the conventional confrontation in set-piece battles with an increasing emphasis on fire power was the norm; in the south there was stress on the mobility of the horse in the steppe and on fortified lines of control to exclude raiding parties from the steppe. Military superiority over isolated natives grew over time, so that the later the confrontation the less equal it was likely to be.

Ahead of settlement there moved new diseases, new trading patterns, even new techniques of production, transport or fighting. The demands of trade engendered frictions in the old societies which were already highly fragmented. However disease had the most destructive impact when it entered virgin soil populations. Diseases to which the Europeans were accustomed decimated previously isolated populations. Potential opposition to new settlement was thereby removed.

It is ironic that the diseases which could be such a potent element in the risk environment of the white population, made a direct positive contribution to white settlement in America by decimating the native population. In Siberia and Alaska there may have been a negative indirect impact on settlement through the reduction in the supply of labour.

In a number of ways the Indians of America had a very positive role to play in white settlement. They contributed foodstuffs, agricultural technology, furs and cleared lands. Weeden is right in asserting that the Indians never ceased to be a strong element in colonial life — either helping it forward or threatening it with disaster. Some recent historians have argued that without Indian help more early white settlements would have failed. The provision of foodstuffs by the Indians was at vital moments during the starving years the difference between life and death.

The clearing of land by the Indian represented a major investment of labour, and therefore a considerable saving for the white man. Moreover the new settlers were guided to areas where soil was good and transport easy. Russell argues that the extreme sensitivity of the main Indian crops to frost in both spring and autumn guided them to coastal and river valleys where the stabilising influence of substantial bodies of water lengthened the growing season from about 100 to 130 days. It is certainly the case that the high relative income levels of early America reflect partly the substitution of output produced

21

by white settlers for that previously produced by the Indians.

A Department of Agriculture pamphlet of 1934 pointed out that more than half of the agricultural production of the USA, measured in farm values, consisted of economic plants domesticated by the Indian and taken over by the white man, whether directly or indirectly. In short in the process of accommodation to a new environment, the white man learned a great deal from the Indians. By contrast the early contribution of the aboriginals of Russia to opening up was meagre, heavily outweighed by the negative elements.

The Red Indian was never assimilated, indeed was never allowed to assimilate, into white settler society. Negro slave labour was preferred. Russian natives on the other hand provided their labour as the major positive contribution in a long process of assimilation. In this respect Russia was more truly a melting pot.

OPENING UP

But of the many forces helping to create a distinct American culture, none was more important than the existence of a frontier during the three hundred years needed to settle the continent.

Billington

Throughout Russian history one dominating theme has been the frontier; the theme of the struggle for the mastering of the natural resources of an untamed country, expanded into a continent by the ever-shifting movement of the Russian people and their conquest and intermingling with other peoples.

Sumner

The process of opening up is not a simple one. The frontier can be viewed as a pattern or condition — unused resources awaiting exploitation; a process, of recurring stages of development; or a specific place. Analysis of the process is rather more than the tracing of the movement of a clearly demarcated frontier on an appropriate map. Usually opening up is deemed to have been achieved when a threshold density of population is achieved, say two per square mile. The information comprised in such a frontier line has even been reduced to a series of dots representing the centres of gravity of population. This is an oversimplification. In fact there exist a multitude of frontiers; frontiers of acquisition and exploration; of exploitation, embodied in different economic activities, in fur, mining, grazing or ranching; of settlement, and of political organisation. The present account is intended to trace the movement of the early frontier and to evaluate, provisionally, its significance.

In the modern period there can have been no more impressive achievement than the exploration, assimilation, both military and political, and settlement by the American and Russian peoples of areas continental in dimension. Especially striking are the extent and speed of the original acquisition.

The maximum rate occurred relatively early in Russia, during the first half of the seventeenth century, and much later in America, during the second quarter of the nineteenth century. Russia was acquiring territory earlier and at a faster absolute, if not proportional, rate. Moreover the process was very much more protracted in Russia, with a secondary spurt in the nineteenth century.

It is evident that in both extent and speed of acquisition Russia conceded nothing to the United States. However formal acquisition did not necessarily remove all obstacles to permanent settlement.

Table 2.1: Rate of territorial acquisition by Russia and America

	Russia			America	
Year	Total area (million square km) rounded to nearest 0.5m	Rate of addition per decade (thousand square km) rounded to nearest 100,000	Year	Total area (million square km)	Rate of addition per decade (thousand square km)
1533	3				
		400			
1598	5.5		1607	0	
		1,500			
1630	10				
		1,000			100
1688	15.5				
		100			
1800	17.5		1790	2.5	
					800
			1820	4.5	
		500			1,000
			1850	8.0	
					300
1900	22.5		1900	9.5	

Sources: Cole 1967: 55; *Historical statistics*: 8

The figures in the table show that in both America and Russia the decadal rate of acquisition was, at its peak, greater than 20 per cent of existing territory.

Before 1550 the expansion of Muscovy was contained within the forested area of European Russia and occurred within the context of a number of competing principalities during the so-called appanage period. The most significant event, apart from the assertion of independence from Mongol sovereignty, was the forcible assimilation of Novgorod and its lands, at the end of the fifteenth century. The destruction of the one principality with both a tradition of urban self-government and, as a member of the Hanse, a maritime orientation, had great symbolic significance. The immense growth of population before 1550 led to the filling in of this forested area, with a frontier of settlement moving progressively outwards from Moscow, mainly to the north and east, but even at this date slowly to the south.

The next major breakthrough came with the capture of Kazan and Astrakhan in the 1560s, which gave the Muscovites control over the Volga river and for the first time over significant numbers of non-Russians. Such a move not only allowed a further eastward movement of the frontier of settlement but also improved transport access to a large area of potential economic significance.

The pioneer spirit, an amalgam of missionary and mercenary motives, carried the Russians across Siberia to the Pacific in little more than half a century (1580s–1650), into Kamchatka by the end of the seventeenth century, and in the course of the eighteenth century across the Aleutians into Alaska. The lure was fur and settlement continued to be sparse. Significant permanent economic activity in Siberia begins with the establishment of the iron industry in the Urals by Peter the Great at the beginning of the eighteenth century. Nevertheless Bashkiria in the southern Urals was only fully subjugated in the 1730s. Movement south-east across the steppe into Turkestan was possible only in the nineteenth century.

The movement of the frontier to the south was the most difficult to achieve because of the existence of the open steppe. The Belgorod line was established and fortified between the 1630s and 1650s. Slowly but surely the fortified lines were pushed to the south and south-east. Cossack settlement had already preceded military control. From the middle of the seventeenth century increasing numbers of settlers moved into the wooded steppe and in the eighteenth century into the steppe proper. In the second half of the eighteenth century settlement penetrated the area of New Russia, a broad band of new provinces running along the north coast of the Black Sea to the river Don. The steppe frontier did not reach into the North Caucasus, between the Black and Caspian Seas, until the nineteenth century and into western Siberia in the twentieth. The frontier was still open as late as Krushchev's Virgin Lands Campaign of the late 1950s and early 1960s, when an area of cropland as large as Canada's was cultivated for the first time in western Siberia and northern Kazakhstan.

The opening up of America had certain broad characteristics in common, the movement from forest and woodlands to grasslands, the movement from moist to semi-arid lands. However the differences are striking, particularly in the early period. Initially, although continuing as late as 1700, settlement hugged the coast with primary settlements, such as Virginia, Massachusetts, New York, Maryland, and later South Carolina and Pennsylvania, slowly expanding to fill the areas with good transport access. The primary settlements were supplemented by a handful of secondary settlements settled from the former; New Hampshire, Connecticut and Rhode Island from Massachusetts, and North Carolina from Virginia. Early on British settlement was accompanied by the foundation of Dutch and Swedish colonies. Although these separate colonies were taken over by the British quite quickly, foreign competition for the colonies was not finally excluded until 1763.

During the eighteenth century the coastal regions were mostly filled in, with pockets of sparse population still existing in the far north, in Maine, in the far south in Georgia and on the Carolina and New Jersey coasts, relatively poor natural environments. Settlement had moved into the interior beyond the Tidewater, particularly up the river valleys. Fingers of settlement pushed into northern and western New York to Lake Champlain and along the Mohawk River, and along the Tennessee River into the South-western Territory. Important enclaves existed in isolation near Pittsburgh on the upper Ohio River and in the lush lands of Kentucky south of the Ohio.

The major trans-continental drive took the Americans across the continent in the nineteenth century, with some leap frogging to the Pacific coast ahead of the main line of settlement. Significant characteristics of the whole movement were the ease of acquisition and the short timelag of settlement behind acquisition. Conventionally, according to the census of that year, the American frontier was deemed to have been closed by 1890.

In the early 1800s the two sets of pioneers met. The Russians controlled Alaska until 1867 and more to the point, at the end of the eighteenth century, even established a settlement at Fort Ross only 100 kilometres north of the future San Francisco. The Russians

Table 2.2: Founding of the 13 American colonies

Colony	Date of first permanent settlement	Remarks
Virginia	1607	Jamestown founded by trading company (London Company) that later failed.
Massachusetts	1620	Settled by Pilgrims, Puritans, Nonconformists; massive immigration after 1630, when Massachusetts Bay Colony was formed.
New Hampshire	1630	Founding settlement was a trading post; under Massachusetts from 1641 to 1679; frequent disputes with Massachusetts, NY after 1679.
New York	1634	Settled by Dutch trading interests; New Amsterdam (NY City) founded in 1626; English captured NY in 1664.
Maryland	1634	Intended by Lord Baltimore, proprietor, as refuge for persecuted Catholics.
Connecticut	1634	Dutch initially settled; English migrants from Massachusetts seeking better land drove out small Dutch element.
Rhode Island	1635	Migrants from Massachusetts who wanted more political, religious freedom; led by Roger Williams.
New Jersey	1638	Settled first by Swedes and Finns; granted to Duke of York in 1664; English settlement followed.
Delaware	1638	First settled by Swedes; Dutch and English fought for control; part of NY, then part of Pennsylvania; separate legislature after 1704.
North Carolina	ca. 1660	Founded by migrants from Virginia seeking good land; an early settlement on Roanoke Island (1587) failed.
South Carolina	1670	Charleston settled in 1680; heavy infusion of Scots and French Huguenots (after revocation of Edict of Nantes).
Pennsylvania	1681	Grew rapidly; proprietor, William Penn, was Quaker.
Georgia	1733	Founded by James Oglethorpe as haven for debtors facing imprisonment.

Source: Vedder 1976: 37

therefore played an important and fairly protracted role as colonisers of North America.

The ultimate failure of Russian settlement in America, vividly highlighted by the extinction of the California colony of Fort Ross in 1839–41 and the sale of Alaska to the USA in 1867, illustrates the fact that a frontier of acquisition does not automatically become a frontier of permanent settlement.

In microcosm Russian America illustrates both the initial problems of an area of new settlement and the particular difficulties of Russian colonisation in distant areas under unpropitious circumstances. The harsh environment and remoteness of the settlements led to a serious supply problem with food shortages becoming particularly acute, despite the miniscule size of the Russian population (at a maximum size of 1,823 in 1839) in three different periods: at the very beginning of the nineteenth century, during the 1820s and again in the mid-1850s.

Initially the returns from the fur trade offset the risk of food deficiencies. The furs of the sea otter and the fur seal provided the revenue to finance necessary purchases of supplies. These furs were immensely valuable, the pelt of the sea otter being worth approximately six times that of the fur seal and 40 times that of the sable, hitherto the most valuable pelt available to the fur market. Progressive depletion of the fur-bearing animals weakened the trade. Moreover the closure of the Chinese ports to Russian ships until the mid-nineteenth century meant that trade in furs had to go through Kyakhta south of Lake Baykal, with an attendant increase in distribution costs. Traders of other nationalities, particularly Americans, could therefore outcompete the Russians. As a consequence of these two difficulties, fur exports from Russian America began to decline in the nineteenth century.

The decline led to a search for new staples, unsuccessfully in the case of whaling and coaling, more successfully but still on an insignificant scale in the case of ice, fish and timber. Import substitution was tried in shipbuilding and food production. The settlement at Fort Ross and the attempted settlement of Hawaii, in 1815–17, represented attempts to solve the food problem directly. Even manufactured commodities were traded with the Californians until British and American competition halted this exchange. The overland supply route through Irkutsk and Baikalia or circumnavigation supply routes from Kronstadt were so expensive that purchase from American traders off the coast from the early 1800s, from Alta California about a decade later, and then from the Hudson Bay Company, particularly between 1839 and 1849, proved a better proposition. Sources of supply changed continually in an effort to increase reliability and reduce cost.

Foreign competition in the fur trade and trade in manufactures; unaccustomedly strong native resistance from the Kolashes who destroyed New Archangel in 1802; labour shortage aggravated by constraints on migration, by disease and privation among both the Russians and the natives; the unfamiliar maritime mould of the colony; the restrictive monopolistic charter of the Russo-American Company, which controlled the colony; and the traditional administrative and technological backwardness of the Russians, all contributed to the financial difficulties of the colonies and the decision to withdraw before being thrown out by force. Vulnerability to fluctuations in food supply was the key to failure (Gibson 1976; Kushner 1975). A high level of risk in a poor resource environment prevented permanent settlement.

Elsewhere settlement was successfully completed, albeit at different speed in the two continents. The extreme rapidity of settlement in the USA reflected both the absence of significant negative elements, as indicated above, but more positively a liberal policy of land distribution and a very rapid increase in population. The latter in its turn reflected a much more benign natural environment stimulating significant immigration and supporting a very high rate of natural increase of population. At its peak, shortly after the end of the formative period, American population grew at a rate of over three per cent a year. Even at its maximum after the acceleration of the nineteenth century, the Russian population grew at scarcely more than half this rate, at 1.75 per cent. In the eighteenth century it probably grew at one per cent a year. In both societies crude birth rates reached as high as 50/1,000; the differences lay in mortality rates, both in their level in a typical year and the frequency and severity of demographic crises.

In Russia settlement lagged seriously behind acquisition. James E. Davis points the contrast neatly by asserting that the combined population of just three states hurriedly carved from the wilderness (Ohio, Illinois and Indiana) today exceeds the total population of all of Soviet Siberia, a frontier for centuries. Often the population figures for America west of the Appalachians and Russia east of the Urals are quoted as evidence of the superior achievement of the Americans in converting acquisition into settlement (Parker 1972).

Within a century of the end of the formative period, peripheral population had overtaken core population within the USA. The implied movement of people and change in economic balance make it scarcely surprising that the frontier has loomed large in American life and mythology.

By contrast in Russia even as late as 1914, more than 300 years after the formative period ended, there existed a rough equality between core and peripheral populations. The more sedate rate of change reflected both the difficult environment of much of the periphery, particularly Siberia, and the institutional constraints on the rate of 'internal' colonisation exercised by the core. In its turn this slow shift reduced the economic significance of the periphery and its potential for changing the nature of core institutions.

From the time of Frederick Jackson Turner, many American historians have stressed the influence of the frontier on the political, social and economic organisation of the United States. Billington has argued that the impulse of the frontier was unique to the USA because of the combination of 'a physical environment conducive to exploitation by the relative propertyless individuals and the invading pioneers equipped by tradition to capitalise fully on that environment' (Billington 1968: 77). Similarities were recognised between the physical environment of the USA and Russian Siberia, a parallel which could be extended quite easily to include other areas of Russia in the earlier frontier zones. While recognising, in the Russian case, institutional modifications resembling those on the American frontier, Billington argues that 'the newcomers were so restrained by absolute rules and tyrannical traditions that they were incapable of developing the go-ahead spirit that thrived on the American frontier' (1968: 79).

The frontier thesis is a classic case of the tail wagging the dog since it underplays the influence of core institution on the pace and pattern of pioneering. The distinct differences in the way the two societies evolved, even during the pioneer phase, reflected the nature of the core areas.

In America frontier areas were largely opened up by free settlers operating within an economic system rapidly becoming more market oriented. Land was cheap and freely available. A substantial group of specialist pioneers emerged, smoothing the way for the more cautious.

In Russia steadily increasing government regulation of society — effective by the end of the sixteenth century — allowed control over internal colonisation. At least until the end of the eighteenth century, the serf system was used as a means of government-controlled colonisation of the new aras of settlement in the southern steppe. There was a little supplementation by government-encouraged foreign immigration at the end of the eighteenth and beginning of the nineteenth centuries.

In Russia there might exist a contradiction between the demands

29

of the service-and-serf state and local frontier requirements. There might even be a contradiction in laws that tied peasants to the village but allowed them to settle if they reached new lands (Yaney 1972: 148–9). However, fugitives were rapidly reabsorbed into the serf system. The existence of the frontier did not 'free up' institutions.

ENTRY INTO THE COMMERCIAL AND INDUSTRIAL PHASES

The entries into the commercial and industrial phases are the key transitions of modern economic development. The present book treats with the former rather than the latter, partly on the supposition that the latter grew out of the former. The dating of both transitions is a subject of much controversy in both America and Russia.

In theory it might be possible to define a threshold level of marketed produce adequate to represent entry into the commercial phase. However there is no one moment of entry, rather a transitional period during which the characteristics of the new phase are established. There is no one-to-one relationship between such a proportion and the significance of commerce. Neumark has rather neatly indicated the irrelevance of mere numbers: 'with regard to frontier expansion, what has to be stressed is not so much the extent of self-sufficiency as the significance of exchange with the outside world'; and 'even if the frontiersmen were 99 per cent self-sufficient, it was the one per cent that tipped the scale, for it constituted the minimum factor in the frontiersmen's economy.' The one per cent might be represented by firearms or salt essential to survival.

Even armed with a threshold figure, properly defined, we are confronted with a serious empirical problem; the lack of statistical data which would allow us to compare the proportion of output marketed in colonial America or early Russia and to note changes in the proportion over time. Similar problems arise if we try to define a simple threshold for the industrial phase, as say the share of the labour force engaged in manufacturing.

It must also be noted that there may be a significant overlap between the different phases. Regions may be opened up deliberately to exploit the market potential of their products, or even to allow the processing of raw materials. The spread of cotton culture across the American south is an example of the former; the establishment of the Urals iron industry by Peter the Great at the beginning of the eighteenth century a nice illustration of the latter.

Very often the story of market growth is told in terms of the production of a growing surplus, or in other words in terms of supply side influences. It may be much more helpful to tell the story in terms of demand factors. Supply decisions may be made deliberately in an endeavour to satisfy a particular level and pattern of demand. The demand may be inherited from the Old World by immigrants who consciously break their pre-existing accommodation to modest levels of consumption. Or the demand may be imposed directly from above, as in Peter's attempt, at the beginning of the eighteenth century, to westernise the tastes of the Russian nobility.

In both cases there was a persistent tendency for expenditures associated with consumption to outrun the capacity to raise revenue. In the Americas this showed itself in a likelihood that the value of imports ran ahead of exports and that the balance of trade was in the red. In Russia the problem was much more limited as it involved the balance of payments of the gentry with other groups in Russian society rather than with the balance of trade at the national level. The national balance of trade appears to have been persistently in the black (Attman 1981a, 1981b).

There were a number of ways in which the shortfall in revenue could be met. The import of capital is necessarily a temporary expedient. In the case where the problem was limited to one group of the population, the government could affect a redistribution of income in favour of the relevant group. Increasingly in Russia it did just that by establishing credit institutions which lent to the nobility on the security of the serfs they owned.

The other two possibilities involve the search for an export staple and the process of import substitution, often considered mutually exclusive options. Typically the former has been associated with movement into the commercial phase and the latter with movement into the industrial phase since attention has been concentrated on the substitution for imported manufactured and capital goods. Because of the constraints of market size and factor supply, imported substitution in these areas was initially less successful than the search for a staple. Allegedly the former depended on an external market orientation, the latter on the development of a domestic market. However there are spread effects from the development of an export staple to import substitution. Moreover import substitution in foodstuffs and agricultural raw materials began very early but has been largely neglected.

Because of the relative unavailability of quantitative data on domestic production and exchange, a focus on external trade is probably inevitable. However the role of external trade must be placed in a proper perspective. First, there is little doubt that the share of output trade externally declines in both economies during the period when statistics allow some quantitative assessment. More important, the decline in external trade is more than compensated by a rise in domestic trade.

Table 2.3: US exports as a percentage of GNP (current dollars), 1710–1848

Rough estimates for early years	%
1710–20	20–30
1775	15–20
1790–1800	10–12
Gallman GNP data	
1834 43	6.2
1839–47	5.9

Source: R. Lipsey, in Davis *et al*: 554

For Russia the statistics are very limited. It is clear that several abortive periods of rapid external trade growth occurred, in particular those following the opening of Archangel in the late sixteenth century, the creation of St Petersburg in the early eighteenth century and the advent of the railways in the second third of the nineteenth. The value of exports per head seems never to have reached anything like the American levels.

Moreover after the initial stimulus given by the railways to the export trade during the 1880s domestic trade began to rise faster than exports, at least according to railway statistics. Later a decisive and permanent downturn in the proportion of GNP exported occurred as a result of the events associated with the Revolution of 1917.

A second reason for playing down the role of external trade is that the growth of domestic trade is more important to the transition from the commercial to the industrial phase. The triumph of a 'pure' cash crop such as tobacco might be represented as the intrusion of foreign commercial institutions into a dependent economy and an obstacle to the industrial transition. Russian external trade was clearly dominated by foreigners.

We need therefore to coincide the main outlines of growth of the domestic market in America and Russia. Existing evidence suggests that frontier societies are characterised by a much higher level of market involvement than is usually assumed. Settlers in both societies desired to enter the market as early as was feasible, consistent with the objective of making secure their own subsistence. Such an objective was more easily achieved in a diversified economy based on subsistence crops. The security of subsistence rested most significantly on the level of yields and on transport access. Initial accessibility is highly correlated with the level of market involvement; as improvement in access occurs, there is an increase in that involvement. Since colonial America was favoured by a benign resource endowment and a good transport system, its involvement in trade began early and was much greater than in Russia.

In the past much has been made of the importance of inter-regional trade. Douglass North has emphasised inter-regional links in the USA between the north-east producing and selling to other regions manufactured goods and commercial services; the south exporting cash crops and selling raw materials to the north-east; and the west selling foodstuffs to both. Jerome Blum has described a less complex two-region model for Russia, with its origins in the eighteenth century, as with the American model. The relative fertility of the south and the greater labour availability in the north and centre allowed a regional exchange of foodstuffs for manufactured goods or commercial services.

However, recent work, while not rejecting out of hand the kind of links indicated, has very much played down these inter-regional links at such early dates, stressing the large degree of self-sufficiency within regions, induced by high transport costs and the importance of intra-regional markets.

In the network of local exchange, three groups stand out as important: urban dwellers; new settlers, soldiers and other transients; and the rural landless or near landless, including professionals, craftsmen, retailers, innkeepers and day labourers. In looking at the level, and growth, of domestic trade, particularly in foodstuffs, we need to consider the importance of these groups. Traditionally the urban population has been the main focus of attention.

The level of urbanisation in eighteenth century Russia and America appears to have been broadly similar. The most frequently quoted statistics include a very low level of Russian urbanisation with a significant decline, not only after the dissolution of the Kievan confederation but also between 1400 and 1600. In 1600 the level of urbanisation appeared as low as two-to-three per cent. In the eighteenth century the level was apparently still low, below four per cent at the beginning, and rising only slowly to about four per cent in 1800. Such figures reflected largely Kizavetter's calculation of *posad* population, the officially designated urban population, of just over three per cent in the early eighteenth century, and Miliukov's of just under four per cent in the late eighteenth. However other groups, principally nobles and peasants, lived in the towns. On this basis Kabuzan and Rozman have recalculated that as much as eight per cent of the population lived in urban areas in 1780, but the figure is probably exaggerated.

Rozman's interpretation of this relatively high level of urbanisation stresses the highly developed structure of central places for a pre-industrial economy and the resulting efficiency of movement of resources from the lowest to the highest level. However there is a far more satisfactory explanation. The level of urbanisation was relatively high at an early date because of the military-administrative role of the towns and the stress on service and revenue functions for town dwellers. Even in the eighteenth century most towns in the south, east and west were primarily centres of administrative and military control. Only in the centre and north did the commercial role of the towns become significant. De Vries has pointed out that Rozman's urban network reflects the administrative needs of a well-ordered military state in which cities stand in a well-defined position of subordination or domination *vis-à-vis* one another. The urban hierarchy did not imply economic integration.

It is interesting to note that Moscow and St Petersburg stand out very markedly from an expected linear rank-size distribution of cities, being much bigger than predicted (de Vries 1984: 262), although elsewhere in Europe during the early modern era of urbanisation the largest cities tend to fall below the predicted size (de Vries 1984: 256). The reason for this is clearly not the linking of these cities with a wider European urban network but the concentration of administrative functions in a highly centralised state.

In 1800 the level of urbanisation in American was similar, if not a little lower, at six per cent. However the Middle Colonies and New England were more urban. The main difference however lay in the potential for future growth. The urban hierarchy in America was already well integrated economically. Russia was to see a slow and steady increase in urbanisation up to 1913, rapid deurbanisation and an urban explosion only after 1929. America's urban population rapidly overhauled Russia's, first in relative and then in absolute size. By 1850 the urban share of America's population was up to 15 per cent and reached 40 per cent by 1900, whereas the Russian share was ten per cent in 1863 and 12.9 per cent in 1897 (Rashin 1956: 98). The rate of urbanisation in America exceeded W.A. Lewis' threshold rate of three per cent by a very significant amount, reflecting both

34

the abundance of resources and the high potential for urbanisation in the American population.

However the significance of urbanisation during the early period of economic development has been much exaggerated. Brady has argued that in the America of the 1830s, even the assumption of a disposable income in the towns triple and in the village double that in the farms would generate consumer expenditure in the countryside accounting for over three quarters of the total, since at the time 89 per cent of households were situated in the countryside. She concludes, 'Rural households in a real sense, were dominant in the market for consumer goods until the twentieth century.'

We need to focus more closely on the new settlers and rural landless. Clearly the more rapid the rate of opening up, the greater the demand for supplies to tide the new settlers over the initial years. New settlers could not produce enough to feed their families for at least two years. The relatively very rapid settlement of America both promoted, and was based on, market development.

Both demand and supply considerations worked to increase the landless proportion of the rural population, but again more rapidly in America than Russia. In Russia the whole social and economic organisation of rural life, with its partible inheritance and repartition, with its passport control and communal organisations, tightened the bond to the land. The payment of *obrok* also imposed a tax on wage employment. A more abundant resource endowment and better transport access in America encouraged diversification of economic activity. The landless group constituted a potential urban population, reckoned to be as great as one third in the northern and middle colonies and one fifth in the south, but probably much smaller in Russia.

Closely associated with entry into the commercial phase and the appearance of a landless rural population was the spread of proto-industrialisation. In the pre-industrial era there was significant proto-industrialisation in both Russia and America, that is, in Perlin's words the appearance of 'pre-factory industrialisation of all kinds in town and country, workshop and home, oriented to a commercial market, be it regional, national or overseas' (Perlin 1983: 43). Perlin refers to proto-industrialisation as 'commercial manufacture', which puts the emphasis on the key element in proto-industrialisation, the conversion of normal household production of goods and handicraft materials of various types for own consumption to market production. However we shall deal with the whole issue of industrialisation later in this section.

Can we generalise about the extent of market involvement in the two economies? The literature on the level of market involvement is lopsided — substantial for colonial America and exiguous for early Russia, reflecting undoubtedly the relative significance of that involvement.

On America the overwhelming weight of opinion has shifted from the frontier tradition of largely self-sufficient and independent pioneering farming to an early and significant market involvement. For late colonial America, limiting the calculation to the sum of items with good statistical bases — commodity exports, invisibles and coastal exports — we have a figure of $2.1 per head, which represents a proportion to average income per head of about 20 per cent. Making a conservative allowance for coastal invisibles and demand from the three domestic groups indicated above, we could increase the figure to $3.9, which represents about 30 per cent of total income per head. A division between external and domestic marketings gives values of $1.7 and $2.2 respectively, indicating the greater importance of the latter.

Since the three groups referred to were highly concentrated in New England (urban and rural landless) and the Middle Colonies (urban, rural landless and new settlers), the level of domestic and total marketings was much greater for the north than for the south, despite the latter's advantage in exports. The relative decline in external trade compared with domestic markets disadvantaged the south and favoured the north.

Particular studies tend to confirm the picture presented above, which suggests a likely proportion of output marketed at the end of the colonial period of at least 30 per cent. Robert Mitchell suggests an idealised progress of a frontier area from less than ten per cent of total produce marketed during the short pioneer period to over a third, or one half or more, after a short interval; in the case of the Shenandoah valley, about 40 years. James Lemon indicated a level of grain marketings in south-east Pennsylvania of at least 40 per cent, for a period clearly beyond the pioneer phase. Both areas were favoured by good natural environment but not by strikingly good accessibility.

Very little is known in quantitative terms about the internal trade of Russia, although in absolute volume it was quite large. The early stress on such essential articles as salt tends to suggest its limitations (Smith, R.E.F. and Christian 1984). Most early exchange was through local markets. However, much of the Soviet literature is concerned with the evolution of a national market which, following a remark of Lenin's, was traditionally dated to the seventeenth century.

Recently the inadmissability of such an early dating has been recognised and the appearance of a national market postponed until at least the 1760s, still a rather premature dating.

Until recently such assertions were based on qualitative rather than quantitative evidence. However qualitative factors suggest that genuine market involvement must have been limited by significant restricting factors; the small size of the surplus, poor transport and by the extra-market supply of key groups in the population. A number of more rigorous studies of inter-regional trade made recently have shown that national markets for a number of commodities, most notably grain, are largely a nineteenth century creation, as is the linking of these regions with international trade.

The only hard statistics we have apply to grain marketings, grain being the principal export in the nineteenth century and until shortly before the revolution the major commodity carried on the Russian railways. These statistics refer to the second half of the nineteenth century, and suggest a significant increase in the proportion of output marketed after the construction of the railways and a period of stability thereafter. The share rises from about 20 per cent to just under 30 per cent between the 1880s and 1913, by which time domestic marketings were rising faster than exports (White 1975; Gregory 1980). Clearly the figure is relatively low and is unlikely to have been higher in a period when transport difficulties were greater and grain production more concentrated in low yielding areas. Broadly speaking, it corresponds with the level of marketings in colonial America, suggesting a much slower penetration of the market.

Entry into the commercial phase, reflecting internal rather than external marketings, occurs in America probably by the end of the colonial period, significantly earlier in some parts of New England and the Middle Colonies and very much later in broad areas of the South. In Russia such an entry comes only at the end of the nineteenth century after major transport improvement. Such an entry was part of a process by which the two continents were economically developed largely on the basis of their own resources.

Entry into the industrial phase came very much later than is often thought. First it is necessary to be precise as to what is meant by entry into the industrial phase. Such entry is achieved when mechanised factories have become the typical locus of industrial production in a significant number of industrial sectors. The key criterion is the nature of the power source. When power can only be delivered in large discrete amounts, as is the case with water or steam power, the emphasis on large factories becomes inevitable. However industrial

37

activity does not begin with factory production, nor does a marked acceleration of industrial production begin with the introduction of the factory system.

Broadly speaking industrial production occurs in three stages which can be associated with our three phases of opening up, commerce and industry; first, the largely self-sufficient family factory involving production for home consumption; secondly, 'commercial manufacture', either cottage industry working on the domestic or putting out system, or artisan workshop and 'nonmechanised' factories; and thirdly, mechanised factories. Stage two includes what is commonly called 'proto-industrialisation'. However, this is usually conceived of as a particular kind of transitional industrial activity located in the countryside in competition with more long-established urban industry. Clearly proto-industrialisation requires some prior market development but gives a very significant stimulus to that development, particularly in rural areas where the vast majority of the population live. Typically proto-industrial activity involves small-scale production in units with few workers, fewer than 15 say, working sometimes only part-time and equipped with little capital, particularly since the main source of power is either animate or if inanimate, organic. However, commercial manufacture is not incompatible with productivity gains arising from increasing specialisation and increased intensity of labour input.

The amount of proto-industry is hard to measure. There is general agreement that the high costs and risks of urban concentration checked the level of urban industrial activity and population before the nineteenth century, encouraging a massive growth in the share of rural non-agricultural population, that is, the population dependent on proto-industrial employment. According to de Vries, the proportion in Europe rises from 20 per cent during the early sixteenth century to 40 per cent by 1800.

There is little doubt that both Russia and America shared in this process. Both displayed features encouraging proto-industrialisation — rapid population increases, areas of low relative fertility and land hunger, a short growing season or labour regime allowing long slack periods. After a substantial beginning in the eighteenth century Russia became in the nineteenth century a major centre of proto-industrialisation. The spread of industrial activity among the peasants of the central provinces has been well documented. In that region such activity had apparently become general by 1800. In Russia as a whole *kustar* industry (peasant handicraft industry) predominated for most of the nineteenth century, outside the cotton industry and the Urals iron industry. On the eve of Emancipation, at least half of industrial production was derived from kustar industry.

In America industrial by-employment was similarly almost universal, particularly in those colonies which later became the main centres of industrial activity, in Pennsylvania and New York, in Massachusetts and the smaller colonies of Connecticut and Rhode Island.

Such industrial activity was typical before the general introduction of the factory system. Decisive entry into the factory industry phase came from the 1880s in the USA and from the 1930s in Russia, which raises the question of explaining the Russian delay.

We can conclude this review by considering briefly the evidence on the rate and nature of economic growth in early modern America and Russia. From the earliest data considered both economies were experiencing considerable expansion. Much of the early growth resulted from the cultivation of more land and exploitation of new resources combined with an increase in the total labour force, reflecting population growth. However some intensive growth existed from the beginning. An increase in scale raised productivity levels by encouraging specialisation, both regional and occupational, and by reducing transaction costs. Entry into the commercial phase represented a significant shift to intensive growth, entry into the industrial phase a reinforcement of that intensive growth.

Once again the statistics on colonial America are very much better than those on early Russia. The general consensus is that even in the eighteenth century population growth accounted for more than 75 per cent of the increase in aggregate economic output. According to Alice Hanson Jones income and wealth per head seem to have already reached quite high levels within 25 to 30 years of settlement. Thereafter growth was slow and steady, gradually accelerating from 0.3 per cent p.a. between 1650 and 1720, to 0.4 per cent between 1725 and 1750, and 0.5 per cent between 1750 and 1775. New England represents an exception, showing a relatively rapid rate, about one per cent per annum in the seventeenth century but declining in the eighteenth, reflecting perhaps the pressure of population on a poor resource base (T.L. Anderson 1975).

Even in New England income levels seem to have attained the English level by 1700. By the 1770s the typical American family had almost certainly attained the highest material standard of living in the world, prompting Alice Hanson Jones to claim, 'over two hundred years ago, our colonial forefathers enjoyed living standards, however sparse, that are still only the aspirations of a majority of the families inhabiting this globe in the 1980s. On a relative and comparative basis, therefore, America has always been an affluent society' — achieved, it might be added, with a population in 1776 already a third the size of Britain's.

The statistics which exist for Russia suggest an early beginning to the transition. The base income levels were low both absolutely and relatively, reflecting the constraints of a hostile environment. Between 1861 and 1914 Russian agricultural growth was to an equal degree extensive and intensive. Earlier but patchy statistics suggest that intensive growth had been occurring for at least a century. However growth of agricultural output per head still reached only 0.5 per cent p.a. in the period 1861 to 1914.

In both Russia and America there is a long history of economic expansion. Although some intensive growth occurs early, the transition from extensive to intensive growth was a gradual process, with Russia lagging about a century behind America in the attainment of similar growth rates of income or output per head. Again we might ask why. The following chapters offer an explanation.

Part 2
Risk, Resources and the
Natural Environment

3

Of Gardens and Deserts

PHYSICAL POSSIBILISM

There is no one-to-one relationship between a particular resource
endowment and successful economic development. Opinions differ
significantly concerning the role of resources in the process of
economic development. On the one side are those who stress the
impetus given to economic development by the increasing pressure
of population on resources. According to this school a scarcity of
resources leads to increased intensity of exploitation of the natural
environment (Wilkinson 1973: Boserup 1981). The problems of
densely populated developing countries today show that this does not
invariably lead to sustained economic development. On the other side
are those who stress the importance of resources in allowing a rapid
rate of growth and encouraging the particular pattern of development
associated with industrialisation (Rosenberg 1972; Christensen 1976).
Either approach underscores the importance of resources.

The apparently contradictory viewpoints may in any case be reconciled. The problem shifts engendered by population pressure provide
the motive, and the resource abundance, the means, for change. The
level of subsistence is not purely physical but varies both according
to the accustomed level of need and according to the needs associated
with the particular consumption package appropriate to each phase.
Pressure on an accustomed level of consumption is sufficient for such
an 'ecological' disturbance. The regions experiencing the disturbance
and those manifesting the abundance may differ; the incentive may
be realised in one area, the means in another. Successful economic
development is a pattern in which an appropriate balance of incentive and means is recurrently recreated. Domestic trade and factor
movements may mitigate the pressures without wholly removing

them. International trade and factor movements perform the same role on a wider stage. The stress in the early modern period tended to be on factor movements because of high distribution costs and extreme labour scarcity in the areas of new settlement. Migration from Europe helped to keep the ecological pressures in Europe within manageable bounds, while promoting the utilisation of a vastly enhanced surplus. Europe increased its resource base by acquiring an enormous 'ghost' acreage; settler societies received a significant stimulus to economic development by being closely associated with Europe.

According to Landes' Faustian mastery of nature, the industrial revolution progressively freed the economy from the limitations on productivity imposed by the natural environment. The further back in time we proceed, however, the greater is the obvious influence of the environment upon economic life. In the pre-industrial world few economic activities involved more than a basic processing of agricultural products whose supply varied significantly with soil fertility and climatic conditions. Technology was pre-eminently site and resource specific. We can argue persuasively two propositions: first, that in the early stages of modern economic growth the natural environment was a significant factor in shaping the pattern of development and that this influence survives into later periods because a pattern once established leaves its legacy for the future; secondly, that the process of counteracting nature's malign influence is not costless; it absorbs resources which could otherwise be used to raise consumption or investment levels.

At any given time the physical environment may be divided into two classes of influence, the benign and the malign, or in W.H. Parker's terminology, resources and anti-resources. Given existing best-practice technology appropriate to a particular resource endowment and a flexible adjustment of institutional arrangements to suit this technology, a corresponding maximum potential level of income or output per head could be calculated. Since resources can only be evaluated in terms of the existing technology of production or transportation this magnitude is variable. Contradictions inherent in the evaluation of Russia's resources, based in one case on repeated denigration of her agricultural potential and in the other on magnification of her mineral riches suggest that dramatic changes in the relevant resource endowment may occur from phase to phase (compare Parker 1972 with Field 1968). A simple inventory of resources grossly oversimplifies such an evaluation. It is true that technical change cannot turn an anti-resource into a resource; it can only reduce the resource cost of counteracting it. We can protect ourselves against the cold or substitute artificial inputs for poor soil but we cannot make the cold or the poor soil an actual advantage. Clothes, heating systems, chemical fertilisers all have a cost.

The clearest distinction which can be made involves an evaluation of the resource environment in terms of its direct relevance to movement through our three phases. In this way we take the first step in making dynamic the static inventory approach to resource evaluation. The first requires an assessment of the environment's ability to meet the subsistence requirements of the pioneer. In the pre-railway period transport difficulties ensure a high degree of self-sufficiency. Attention is focussed on food requirements although clothing, housing and heating needs are also important. The commercial phase reflects the existence of a surplus, perhaps of the basic commodities referred to as subsistence needs, or of pure cash crops, such as tobacco, or even subsistence substitutes, such as cotton. The industrial phase has as its main requirements a source of power, water or coal, a constructional material, usually iron, in addition to other raw materials such as the textile fibres already mentioned.

The following analysis will make clear a distinct advantage in resource endowment for America, an advantage which would make likely both a higher income per head and a faster movement into each phase, other things being equal. Of course other things are not equal, otherwise the Red Indians would have been the first to undertake 'an industrial revolution' (Lebergott 1984).

PHYSICAL MATRIX

A giant closed up in a cave with only a pinhole for light and air.

Massie, on the core of Russia

The little roadsteads, safe havens nestling in bays and river mouths, from Piscataqua around the Cape and Rhode Island, through the Sound to Milford Haven, were the true abiding places of that strong commercial current which tided in and out of New England, and gave force and direction to the domestic development on shore.

Weeden

The colony (Virginia) could boast of what amounted to the largest harbour in the world, with its great rivers that allowed ocean-going vessels to sail deep into the interior.

Morgan

45

Two characteristics of the physical setting of Russia's core stand out as having a strong economic influence — uniformity and continentality; by contrast the core of the USA is heterogeneous and maritime.

The major characteristics of uniformity reflects the topography of core Russia, a wide flat plain with few hills above 300 metres in which even the Urals, the boundary of European Russia and of the core, rarely rise to 600 metres. European Russia is part of the vast tableland, the Great Central Plain, which stretches from northern France across Europe into Asia. Even to the eye the most striking features are sameness and size. However, core Russia did embrace different horizontal belts of vegetation. First, in the far north, above the Arctic Circle, lay the tundra, a region, frigid, barren and lacking precipitation, particularly a snow cover. Very little, even of natural vegetation, grows there. Further south is the largest horizontal belt, the taiga or area of coniferous forest, and the deciduous woodlands, which stretch beyond Moscow as far south as Kiev, Riazan or Kazan. Finally beyond the forest proper lies a narrow strip of mixed forest and steppe. Core Russia encroached little on this transitional zone, and not at all on the flat steppe further to the south.

Core America consisted largely of a coastal plain which stretched some 600 miles along the Atlantic coast, gradually widening to the south. Beyond this plain, the Appalachians represented a more significant barrier to settlement than the Urals, so that in the colonial era settlement was very largely confined to the plain, particularly the Tidewater area. Along that coast, it is possible to identify a series of separate economic niches (defined by separate waterway systems), distinguished by climatic and geographical characteristics, by differing risk environments and consequently by different economic systems and eventually even by distinctive speech patterns (Berthoff 1971). Six main economic niches existed in colonial America — eastern and western New England, taken together for most purposes; the Hudson Region and Greater Pennsylvania, sometimes grouped as the Middle Colonies but the former often more logically joined with New England; the Chesapeake and the Lower South.

The continentality of Russia is its major characteristic. Continentality comprises three main features: an orientation to land-based activities, localism of attitude and activity, and a particular kind of climate characterised by long cold winters and brief hot summers, in a word by extremes.

Kerner has interpreted Russian history as 'a quest for the sea'. Such an interpretation is an oversimplification but Russia has managed to open 'windows' on the world at only a comparatively late date. An outlet was found through the Arctic Ocean in the sixteenth century, the Pacific in the seventeenth — the usefulness of the former being limited by dangerous weather conditions and its remoteness from main trade routes, the latter by inaccessibility to the main centres of population. Eventually control was established over ports in the more useful Baltic in the eighteenth and ultimately the Black Sea only fully in the nineteenth century. Taking account of closure by ice, the proportion of usable coastline in Russia is even today very limited. Hooson claims, 'No country on earth is as crippled by its coastlines or shut in by its own seas as is the Soviet Union' (Hooson 1970: 7). Muscovy was even more circumscribed.

By contrast the American colonies were strung along a highly indented coastline largely free of ice. Many of the rivers flowing into the Atlantic were navigable for long distances. Until the American Revolution population was concentrated within 20 miles of the coast or these navigable rivers.

Because of its size, more than twice the contiguous land area of core America and because of its position, both in latitude and in relation to the Eurasian landmass, core Russia is very much colder than core America. Kiev, for example, is on the same latitude as Montreal. Moscow is at roughly 55°N, Leningrad 60°N. No part of core America is so far north. Philadelphia is at roughly 40°N and the other major colonial ports within a few degrees.

However in both cases the weather is largely governed by air masses approaching over land, in contrast to the maritime influence on western Europe. The initial expectations of settlers, based on the notion that climate varied with latitude, were quickly disappointed by the extremes of north America with its 'genuine winters' and 'authentic summers' and its wide annual fluctuations (Kupperman 1982). The early difficulties of the settlers were at least partly an adjustment problem.

The impact of an extreme continental climate is very significant. Frost limits the length of the growing season and the lack of degree days over 20°C restricts the range of crops. For example, the growing season, essentially the period free from killing frosts, was only five and a half to six months long in Tambov province, a rich agricultural province of Russia located in the southern part of the central agricultural region. Other areas in the south were similar to Tambov. Elsewhere the growing season ranged down to 120 days in the Archangel district. More typical of the agricultural centre was Moscow district at 130 days. Russia was also vulnerable to great variability in the first and last onsets of frost.

In America the growing season ranged much more widely from over 200 days in the south to little more than 100 days in Maine. South of New England the typical growing season was 150 days or more. However initial settlement occurred during the so-called 'little ice age', when the growing season may have been as much as three or four weeks shorter, compounding the problem of initial settlement.

Such a constriction of the Russia growing season results in the concentration of much labour activity into a short six week period from mid-July to the end of August, the so-called *stradnaya pora*, or time of suffering, when winter and spring cereals had to be harvested and the winter grain field ploughed and sown (Hoch 1982b).

The short growing season also created a predisposition to a 'summertime dearth of labour and wintertime excess' (Rudolph 1985). Von Haxthausen calculated that an estate of equal land quality and size in Yaroslavl required almost twice the human and animal power and an additional 40 per cent more hired labour at peak seasons as an estate in Mainz. Moreover the Russian land-owner was confronted by eight months of non-agricultural production time compared with five in Mainz and twice the number of labourers to carry through the winter. To compound the problem winter conditions in Russia prevented a variety of productive activities possible in Germany (Von Haxthausen 1847). The same argument applies with equal force to a Russian-American comparison.

The long cold winter also increased fodder requirements for livestock. Traditionally in Muscovy animals were stalled from the feast of the Protecting Veil of the Mother of God (14th October) to St George's Day (6th May), 204 days (R.E.F. Smith 1977: 43). Even in the Ukraine cattle had to be kept indoors as long as six months. By contrast, in Virginia for example, neither cattle nor horses had to be stalled at all, and although further north this was not the case, the period was still not as long as in Russia. The additional investment in buildings and fodder required in Russia was a significant burden. The logical consequence was to reduce the relative size of livestock herds and hence the scale of an important buffer against food crop fluctuations (R.E.F. Smith 1959). However a a minimum livestock herd was required for traction and transport. It is difficult to classify climatic types in a useful manner. W.H. Parker has attempted to compare the USSR and the USA according to the Köppen classification. On this basis the most typical climatic type in the USA is the 'humid temperate', characterised by rain all the year round with hot summers and mild winters. The type accounts for 34 per cent of the contiguous land area in the USA, but only 0.5 per cent in the USSR, comprising an area outside the core along the Black Sea. In the USSR the 'humid continental' type is the most typical, marked by at least some precipitation all the year round but with cool summers and cold winters. This area occupies 31 per cent of the USSR, but only small parts of Alaska in the USA. All of the American core area falls within the humid temperate type, excepting a large chunk of New England which falls within the humid continental type, but with rather warmer summers than is usual for that type. Most of the Russian core falls within the humid continental. On average therefore the USA is much warmer and wetter than the USSR, particularly in its core area. Unfortunately most of Russia's precipitation falls in thermally-crippled areas, where excess moisture could pose a significant problem.

The almost complete absence of the climatic type most conducive to dense human settlement has left Russia extremely vulnerable to ecological pressure as population increases. Furthermore the combination of low yields and poor transportation has led to a continuing concentration of population within the so-called Fertile Triangle, where over 80 per cent of the population still lives.

SUSTAINING SUBSISTENCE

Self-sufficiency

In that New World they found no silver but the soil itself.

Farnie

. . . a comfortable subsistence.

McMahon of the colonial New England diet

The country is inherently so poor that it affords at best a precarious existence.

Pipes, on Russia

49

According to N.C. Field, in the recent past the productivity of Soviet cropland has been less than 60 per cent of that of the USA. Allegedly the agricultural environment was responsible for most of the difference in yields, operating both through spatial variation in individual crop yields and through the overall crop composition. In this context the agricultural environment is principally climatic, defined by thermal conditions, the number of degree months or mean monthly temperatures above freezing point, and moisture conditions, the percentage of actual to potential evapo-transpiration. The most favourable combination involves adequate moisture (80 per cent) and adequate thermal condition (200 degree-months); 56 per cent of American cropland is in this sense both moist and warm, whereas only 1.4 per cent of Russian cropland is so blessed. 80 per cent of Russian cropland suffers from thermal deficiencies and 59 per cent lies in areas where irrigation is necessary; the relevant figures for the USA are much lower at 19 per cent and 34 per cent.

Table 3.1: Cropland classified by thermal and moisture zones (% distributions)

AE/PE[a]	USA Degree-months				USSR			
	100-99	200-99	300 +	Total	100-99	200-99	300 +	Total
90-100	8	30	19	57	26	0.1	0.3	26
80-89	2	5	2	9	14	1		15
65-79	5	7	3	15	18	6		24
0-64	4	7	8	19	22	9	4	35
TOTAL:	19	49	32	100	80	16	4	100

Note a: Actual evapo-transpiration/potential evapo-transpiration
Source: Field 1968: 10.

Reference to the core areas shows even more startling discrepancies. In the American core only the northern part of New England is below the 200 degree-months level and all of the core has above 90 per cent on the moisture rating. None of the Russian core is above 200 degree-months but nearly all of it comes above the 90 per cent moisture level, less rain sufficing because of the cold.

Such consideration led Field to conclude that the arable land base of North America as a whole, and that of the United States in particular, was much more favourably endowed from the standpoint of environmental quality that that of the Soviet Union (Field 1968: 9).

Such a conclusion applies with equal force to the core areas.

The impact of poor environmental conditions on crop production comprises two elements; first, lower yields for a given crop, and secondly, an emphasis on less valuable crops. The former impact can best be illustrated by the case of wheat. There is a broad tendency for wheat to occupy a relatively small fraction of the arable land in countries where the climate permits the growth of a wide range of competing crops, and a relatively large fraction in countries where climate restricts the range of competing crops. Wheat has tended to lose out competitively against other, often more valuable, crops. It has been pushed into poorer areas, usually semi-arid, but areas similar in climatic conditions. By contrast in the past high transport costs and highly variable harvests caused the more widespread distribution of grain growing, although in Russia climatic conditions were such that in the core area rye was preferred.

Sufficient data exist for the period 1901–35 to engage in a simple counterfactual exercise to show how much higher the average yield of wheat would have been if Russia had been characterised by the same climate zones as the USA (see Timoshenko). The exercise is deliberately organised to give a lower bound estimate. By the twentieth century wheat production had already been limited to similar climatic zones. Moreover the exercise is carried out using either the yields of the relevant climatic zones in Russia or the yields of the same zone-types in America and varying only the relative weights of each climatic type according to their actual distribution in the two countries. Such a procedure effectively excludes the impact of either fertility differences or different inputs. Nevertheless the average difference in yields for the core areas comes out at over 10 per cent (calculations based on Timoshenko 1937).

The impact of climatic conditions is obvious in other ways. Winter wheat was limited to the western Ukraine. The climatic regime of the south east, Siberia and Central Asia - with late but hot summers, dry autumns, and frequently a light snow cover in a cold winter - ruled out winter wheat. Climate also favoured the hard red grain as against the soft wheat, the former characterised by a shorter growing season and a lower yield. Russian wheats were as a consequence usually small-grained with a comparatively low natural weight (Timoshenko 1937). Such considerations further reinforce the degree of underestimation of yield differences.

However the impact of climate has increasingly shown up in the distribution of crops rather than in the different yields for a given crop. Again the limitations of Russia's physical environment are shown by the preference for rye in the central areas of Muscovy. Rye can withstand colder temperatures than wheat and requires less precipitation, particularly during the growing season. Rye also tended to do better in the gray podzolic soils of the core's agricultural zone. The hardier root system of rye penetrated the compacted soils more easily and therefore required less deep ploughing, which suited Russia's lack of horses and use of the primitive wooden scratch plough, the *sokha*. Rye also compared better with weeds. In other words rye suited an inferior environment and agricultural regime (Confino 1969; Vinogradoff 1975).

The most dramatic manifestation of the climatic limitations of Russia is the absence of anything comparable to the Corn or Cotton Belts of the USA. A short growing season and insufficient precipitation rule these out. A brief consideration of corn or maize reinforces the argument. Maize was by origin an American plant and of great significance in cultivation from early colonial days. Its optimum growing season is 150 to 180 days. In normal times it even grew well in New England. Although a flexible crop maize requires for full maturation a thermal level of 200–99 degree-months and a moisture level of 80 per cent, a combination found only in a small part of the western Ukraine but in 35 per cent of American cropland, including most of core America. Consequently its significance in the Soviet Union has increased belatedly. Even in favourable areas corn yields are very responsive to warmth and moisture; in marginal areas the crop is susceptible to frost or cold. As a result average yields in the Ukraine were 35 bushels per acre during the 1960s, those in the USA 55 to 60 bushels, reaching as high as 70 bushels in Iowa. Where climatic conditions were similar to Russian conditions, as in South Dakota, yields were about the same (Field 1968).

As a subsistence crop maize has a number of advantages. Its most valuable characteristic is its high yield per unit of land, which is on average roughly double that of wheat, also providing not much less than double in terms of calories per hectare. Moreover it produces food quickly within a relatively short growing season and good crops in a wide variety of climates. It prospers in areas too dry for rice and too wet for wheat. Geographically it fits neatly between the two. Core America produced all three of these crops in significant amounts; core Russia only one and with great difficulty.

The influence of the climate on crop variety was reinforced by Russian isolation. Colonial America combined the rich variety of high-yielding New World crops and the low-yielding Old World staples. Reputedly the introduction of New World crops explains the significant expansion in the agricultural output of Old World Europe before the Industrial Revolution (W.L. Langer 1975). At the very least the introduction of new crops provided a better cushion against harvest fluctuations (Flinn 1974). There was a crop for each environmental niche. However, even those crops with a favourable environmental niche in Russia arrived there late. The potato became important only in the nineteenth century although its expansion after the middle of that century was dramatic (Blum 1961). By the 1890s the volume of potatoes harvested was 29 per cent that of grain (Christian 1980). The very significance of the potato, as that of rye earlier, hinted at climatic and soil deficiencies.

Since it is easier to improve soil than climate, climate sets the ultimate potential of the land. However soils constituted a significant part of the environment. In this respect the differences between Russia and America were not as pronounced, but the advantage still lay decisively on the American side. Obvious similarities existed between the dark humus-rich soils of the steppe and prairies and between the drylands. A parallel can also be drawn between the soils of the Russian core from St Petersburg right through to Tula, and New England. Both areas contained *podzol* soils, sandy, arid, easily leached of most of their plant minerals and containing only moderate amounts of humus. Such soils can be kept productive only by proper usage and heavy application of fertilisers and require a heavy lime input to grow legumes. Unhappily this area was much more extensive in Russia than in America. Moreover the lack of livestock reduced the potential input of manure. In extensive parts of core Russia poor drainage also retarded agriculture and boulders were strewn in large areas, a legacy of the last ice age. Rocky glacial debris similarly affected parts of New England.

An authority on American agriculture has noted the high percentage of land in the humid areas of the United States (largely the area east of the 96th meridian) which combines three characteristics favourable to crop production - good moisture conditions, deep, moisture-retentive soil and a gentle slope (Cochrane 1979). The largest area so favoured stretched from the middle of Ohio to eastern Nebraska, an area on the eve of opening up at the end of America's formative period. As Cochrane argues, 'This is one of the largest areas of highly favoured, highly fertile farmland on the earth'.

Within the core, Pennsylvania was also said to contain some of the best wheat land in the world (Lemon 1972). In the Southern Tidewater, stretching from New Jersey to Georgia and extending between 50 and 150 miles inland, the soil was for the most part good:

53

rich, deep and enduring in the river valleys but rather thinner on the ridges. As with the rich alluvial lands of the Mississippi, drainage of some excess moisture was required to make full use of the good land. Only the southern land of the wooden steppe within core Russia could compare. In Russia humidity and fertility rarely coincided. The central agricultural region was moist but infertile, the southern steppe, the *chernozem*, fertile but arid. Where soils were comparable in fertility, climate favoured America.

Most of humid America was cultivable and lent itself well to an efficient mixture of crops and livestock activities. The major exception was the Lower South. Heavy rain leached the soil, and excessive heat forced plant growth to an early maturity of high fibre and low combined protein and carbohydrate content, and also tended to parch the shallow-rooted plants. Consequently yields of the main grains, potatoes and fodder crops were low. Heat also reduced milk yields and encouraged animal parasites such as worms in hogs and the cattle tick. But the Lower South was exceptional. By contrast in most of Russia the climate limited the establishment of an efficient crop and livestock mixture by limiting the supply of and increasing the demand for fodder. The harsh and morbid environment rendered the keeping of livestock particularly hazardous.

The existence of a large agricultural surplus in America is attested to by the importance of livestock to the diet of Americans. H.S. Russell has even argued that livestock enabled the Massachusetts Bay Colony to avoid long 'starving' times at the inception of the colony. Livestock were exceptionally important in the early years of other colonies to the south (Wood 1974).

Consumption of meat in early America was very high. An eighteenth century Pennsylvania widow seems to have consumed about 150 lbs of meat annually (Lemon 1967a). Widows in Middlesex County, Massachusetts steadily increased their consumption from between 120 to 165 lbs in the early to mid-eighteenth century, to 180 lbs at the end of the eighteenth century and 200 lbs in the early nineteenth (McMahon 1981). Even a Philadelphia labourer seems to have consumed about 175 lbs (B.G. Smith 1981).

Tueteberg suggests that in medieval Germany meat consumption may have been as high as 220 lbs per person. Thereafter a steady process of 'depecoration' brought consumption down to about 30 lbs between 1815 and 1825. Certainly new areas of settlement with low population density appear to have had a high level of consumption. The highest level found by the author related to Australia in the early nineteenth century, allegedly at 500 lbs per annum (Davidson 1981).

Despite the significance of new settlement such levels of meat consumption were probably never achieved in Russia. The Russian environment did not favour a major build-up of livestock levels except on the steppe in the south before the plough turned the virgin soil. The existence of significant exports of hides, tallow and bristles suggests large absolute numbers but all the evidence confirms a small number of livestock per head of population. It is significant that R.E.F. Smith in his reconstruction of a typical peasant farm in sixteenth century Muscovy makes no allowance specifically for meat consumption. Harder data for the nineteenth century suggest an annual per capita consumption of as little as 40 lbs, and probably very much less in areas outside the main agricultural producing region (Smith and Christian: 263). Even an individual study of a serf estate in the black earth belt during good years gives on a generous interpretation only 60 lbs-plus as the annual consumption (Hoch 1982).

Blum quoted the work of F. Le Play to show that a Urals ironsmith household and a Urals carpenter's household consumed annually per capita about 90 lbs and 85 lbs respectively, which compared reasonably well with other Europeans (Blum 1961: 317). Such a level of consumption is probably untypical and still far below American levels, despite the fact that industrial serfs, particularly in the Urals region, were able to supplement their wages by exploiting the produce of the surrounding land and forest and the labour of their female dependents.

Such a comparison led Crosby to conclude: 'the European in America only rarely experienced famine, and taking plant and animal foods together, have possibly been the best-fed people in the world, a fact that has motivated more people to migrate to the New World than all the religious and ideological forces combined.' The ease with which subsistence requirements were met in America helps explain the relatively high rate of opening up.

The situation in Russia was more complex. Because yields differed greatly both regionally and over time, consumption levels were by no means as stable as in America. The surplus over subsistence in the northern part of the central region and in the north-west was small. Elsewhere the average surplus was greater; with a relatively sparse population and poor transport food could often be locally abundant. This explains the relatively low price of food in 'normal' times. Intermittent harvest failure was still a real problem. However, at least initially opening up was possible at a good rate. Difficulties might appear as soon as population density began to rise.

First-generation staples

The history of the Russian fur trade in Siberia is the history of the conquest and occupation of the northern half of Asia by the Russian people.

R.H. Fisher

The New England colonies were truly maritime colonies. The "ripple effects" of their fishing industries were well understood and appreciated. Pork and salted-meat packing, the manufacture of biscuits, the production of newly-made clothing, the brass crafts serving ship chandlery, the making of barrels, hoops and kettles, all of these trades had been born out of a need to supply the fishing industries. In addition, the entire colonial trade and shipbuilding network depended ultimately on the fisheries.

J.M. Morris

No pioneer community was completely self-sufficient nor successful as a purely commercial proposition. Initial opening up was dependent upon some commercial development, although this might be short-lived. Pioneer communities in their early years usually required some outside assistance, either in the form of a subsidy or trading contacts. It was in the nature of first-generation staples to give only a transitory impulse to trade, but to be a necessary element in successful opening up. A more lasting commercial orientation came later.

The last remarks help us to define different generation staples. A staple is a resource-intensive commodity whose export value accounts for a significant proportion of the total value of exports. First-generation staples can be defined as commodities suitable for trade by virtue of their high value to bulk ratio, but possessing a number of essential characteristics which limited their period of economic significance. They required very limited processing, at least at the point of collection, and as the products of nature no cultivation or care. The assertion of private ownership rights was difficult. Whereas in theory such staples were renewable, that is, could be farmed at a rate which guaranteed a continuing supply, in practice, because of open accessibility, they tended to become exhausted in a series of new source areas. Particular reference is made here to furs, fishes and forestry. In the once-and-for-all boost given to settlement such staples were akin to mining booms.

By contrast second-generation staples are produced rather than gathered, demand an increasing amount of processing, are of a greater bulk to value ratio. They are produced from land subject to full property rights and are renewable. Second-generation staples are associated with the commercial phase in the same way as first-generation staples are associated with opening up.

The generation of a commodity is not inherent in that commodity, it is defined by context. Alluvial gold is a classical use of a first-generation staple, reef gold a second generation staple. Reef gold required full property rights and much processing. Timber in its many guises straddled the different generations.

Fur is a very good example of a first-generation staple. The close identification of the early opening up with the history of the fur trade applies with equal force to America and Russia. R.H. Fisher has noted a similarity of the process by which fur and its exploitation opened up large parts of the USA and a significant proportion of Russia, particularly Siberia. 'Exhaustion of hunting grounds, discovery of new ones, and their subjection to Russian authority - that is the process by which Siberia came under Muscovite control' (Fisher 1975: 34). Since the demand for furs was enormous the exhaustion of hunting grounds proceeded quickly. As Fisher argued, it was this rapid exhaustion, more than any other factor, which explained the rapidity of the conquest of Siberia. It was also the basic factor in the eastward advance of the Russians across Siberia (Fisher 1975: 34).

The lure of the sable in Siberia was matched by that of the beaver for the Russians and Americans in North America. During the seventeenth century it was the fur trade more than anything else which had lured both the French and English deep into the wilderness. Only slightly less fast than disease and the horse, the ripples of trade extended the impact of white settlement from tribe to tribe. Unhappily the fertility of the fur-bearing animals did not match the rapaciousness of the hunters. Relations between Americans or Russians and natives centred on that trade and its ramifications. The skill of the native hunters was used either directly or indirectly through trade and tribute. In America white hunters became dominant only in the late eighteenth century. Russian hunters appeared earlier but the native hunter was still of paramount importance.

The role of fishing was much greater in the establishment of the New England colonies than in Russia, although, according to one calculation fish protein accounted for around 43 per cent of the meat protein consumed in Russia as late as the end of the nineteenth century. This fact indicates as much the insignificance of meat consumption in the diet as the extent of fishing, and the existence of a highly localised activity for own or local consumption, except in the south at the mouth of the Volga.

In New England the submergence of the continental shelf contributed to the dearth of good agricultural land by leaving the shoreline at the very face of the mountain but compensated by providing a submarine plateau characterised by rich fishing grounds such as the Grand and Georges Banks. Fishing conditions were almost ideal, with plenty of food for plankton and therefore for fish, appropriate temperatures and an even bottom for nets. The fish available were large and well adapted for drying and salting. The New England cod in the Gulf of Maine averaged 36 lbs although the size declined rapidly the further north the fishing ground. Proximity of fishermen to sources of supply allowed all-year fishing. Morris concludes that the New England, Nova Scotia and Newfoundland fishing grounds were among the very best in the world throughout pre-colonial and colonial times.

Fishing could leave transitory settlements along the coast as in Newfoundland or Labrador, but in New England the fishing industry, supplemented by whaling, found a permanent base. Weeden stresses the importance of fishing in New England as a stimulus to commerce both directly in sales to the West Indies and southern Europe and indirectly in the use of fishing vessels for off-season trade, in the provisioning of fishing expeditions and in promoting shipbuilding. 'In this industrial evolution, fish from the seas was the chief motor in starting the round of exchanges.' Fishing moved in America from first to second generation status.

A marked difference in attitude existed towards the great forests which covered most of core America and Russia. New England was fairly typical in that 95 per cent of its surface was originally forested, much of it impassable, except by the way of rivers or Indian tracks (Carroll 1973: chap. 2). Moreover the forest did not stretch continuously between the Atlantic and the Mississippi, as Francis Parkman asserted. On the one hand the Russians had from an early date accommodated themselves to the homogeneous forest environment. On the other there is no doubt that the strangeness of the forest environment produced in the English immigrants an initial fear of the forest (Carroll 1973: chap. 3). The early Massachusetts Bay settlements of the 1620s consequently looked more to the sea than the forest for their means of livelihood.

The comparative poverty of the Russian environment and this early accommodation probably explains the significance of the 'gathering' economy in Russia until a very late date. The forest was a source of significant exports, such as wax and honey, as well as subsistence. The extent of the gathering economy is indicated by the importance of tree beekeeping in Russia. At its peak in the middle of the sixteenth century something like 800 tons of wax were exported each year. According to Galton (1971: 17), this would 'probably represent the activities of some million men on perhaps two and one half million trees, and the production of many thousand tons of honey'. There appears to be little evidence of a subsequent decline in production (Galton 1971: 61).

In America a serious learning process had to be undertaken before the distinctive environmental niches could be fully exploited. Timber itself, of a relatively high bulk-to-value ratio, much higher than for furs or fishes, or even wax and honey, was exploited for commercial purposes only at a much later date, although its multiple uses in pioneering activities should be noted.

In cold climates an abundance of timber was a necessity for survival. Even in New England an average family was said to need 15 cords of wood per winter, the equivalent of 0.6 of an acre of standing timber (Rutman 1967: 41–2). A 'genteel' Philadelphia family needed 25 cords a year (B.G. Smith 1981). Collier has argued that 20 to 40 acres of woodlot were needed for a perpetual supply according to the size of the house (A.H. Jones 1980). In New England the vast virgin forests were hewn down at an incredible rate (Carroll 1971). Collier was convinced that the shortage of woodlot was a significant element in migration out of Connecticut after 1760.

Timber requirements in Russia were greater. Even in the nineteenth century the major item transported to St. Petersburg was firewood (Bater 1976). Deforestation was not solely a problem of the steppe. Around Moscow a scarcity of timber became apparent very early (W.H. Parker 1972). In 1754 it was forbidden to set up new metallurgical works within a radius of two hundred versts around Moscow, in order to ward off the depletion of the forests (Madariaga 1981: 466).

While agricultural production might take most of a family's time the labour cost of cutting, sawing or hauling a year's fuel supply for a household in Connecticut was calculated by Collier at about one third of one man's time, quite an investment of effort for a nuclear household. In Russia the demands are likely to have been very much greater.

The forest yielded a whole series of timber products apart from cordwood for heating, from the most processed, highest value to bulk commodities; from naval stores, pitch, turpentine or tar, or potash, through masts, staves, shingles, clapboards to charcoal for smelting. The more heavily processed products could not be regarded as genuine first-generation staples except in so far as the act of clearing the land in itself created the product. Potash, for example, was a boon to early settlers who could sell it to cover their cash requirements.

The natural environment was there to be exploited with the minimum of effort, particularly as the supply of effort was limited by scarcity of labour. If possible that effort was contributed by the natives. The frontier of exploitation was not equivalent to a frontier of settlement. Fishermen, fur hunters or traders and lumberjacks as often as not moved on very quickly. But the staples were significant as sources of both private and government income and established the earliest commercial links.

The speed of acquisition, and indeed exploitation, in both Russia and America is explained by the existence of such first-generation staples. However the step from exploitation to settlement rested on the ease with which subsistence needs could be met and with which first generation staples could mature into second generation staples.

FUTURE POTENTIAL

Cash crops

The following argument applies to the development of both external and internal commerce. Although the latter was ultimately much more important than the former the growth of the former tended to precede the growth of the latter. The data on local trade are sparse, which should not be allowed to lead to an underestimate of its importance.

The transition to the commercial phase depended upon the realisation of three sets of conditions. To a varying degree a high level of demand, by raising the price of a potential cash crop, could offset the disadvantages of the natural environment as reflected in high transport or production costs (Shepherd and Walton 1972). However given adequate demand the other two factors, that is, appropriate conditions of production or transportation, largely determined the level of trade, particularly for areas competitive with each other as sources of supply.

First, the natural environment had to be sufficiently productive to allow most of the food and other subsistence requirements of a particular area to be more than satisfied. In the era of high transport costs trade could meet only a small proportion of subsistence requirements since basic subsistence foods such as grain had a high bulk to value ratio. In the past economic historians have rather overplayed the significance of early trade inter-connections, particularly at the inter-regional level. In America well into the nineteenth century areas such as the cotton belt were largely self-sufficient in basic subsistence commodities (Hilliard 1972; Hutchinson and Williamson 1971; Fishlow 1964). Only very small areas, particularly badly equipped by nature for subsistence production but well suited for trade by transport accessibility, became significantly dependent on trade. Some parts of New England qualified for this role in colonial America (Klingaman 1971).

Outside the major cities of Moscow and St. Petersburg, Russia was characterised by the same tendency to self-sufficiency. Even the capital Moscow, until a very late date, was notable for its garden plots and large numbers of livestock. Petitions from town populations to Catherine's Legislative Commission in 1766–7 repeatedly requested better provision of land, indicating the importance attached to direct control over the supply of food.

Except in unusual circumstances an area was unlikely to enter the commercial phase if it could not comfortably meet most of its subsistence requirements. Either an area could concentrate on the export of a cash crop because a wide variety and abundance of subsistence goods was available, or commerce could develop on the basis of local specialisation within a context of broad regional self-sufficiency. Sometimes the sales consisted of a variety of surplus subsistence commodities, the proportion traded fluctuating with supply conditions.

A second important feature of production involved the particular soil and climatic conditions appropriate to a given cash crop. As early American settlers quickly discovered, particular crops demanded a specific ecological niche. These economic niches were by no means limited to the actual areas of production since production could occur outside these areas with varying degrees of efficiency. Market demand and transport access determined the extent of utilisation of the potential niche. For example, the growing of tobacco in America need not have been confined to the band 35° N–40° N. The latitudinal location of tobacco cultivation on the eastern seaboard of America was largely an historical accident. The variety of climate and soil types in America, the high moisture and warmth in certain areas, created many such ecological niches — the Chesapeake for tobacco, Louisiana for sugar, South Carolina for rice or indigo, most of the south, particularly the south-west, for cotton. Trans-Appalachia provided similar niches for corn and wheat. The searches for appropriate niches for other commodities such as silk, or vines or even hemp, were failures in colonial America. In Russia such niches were limited to flax and hemp in the northwest, and later wheat in the south and south-east.

The second set of supply conditions involved transport egress. The value to bulk ratio of traded goods had to be sufficiently high to offset the transport costs implicit in the natural transport infrastructure. The indented estuarine coastline of the Chesapeake, the Mississippi waterways or the Great Lakes, were as much resources as good soil or adequate warmth and moisture. The close relationship between waterways and settlement points to the major significance of transport in the opening up of new areas.

Two salient characteristics of transportation in the pre-railway era stand out. Water transport was very much cheaper than overland movement; therefore the area with a better water transport system was favoured. Secondly where overland movement was important sheer distance represented a major problem.

The difficulties of Russia in the latter respect can easily be illustrated. In the sixteenth century Herberstein praised the Muscovite state postal service because one of his servants travelled between Novgorod and Moscow in just 72 hours, a rate of 150 km a day. Such a speed suggests the journey between Moscow and Kazan would take five days, that between Moscow and Archangel seven days, both rather faster than was probably the case.

By contrast in 1800 the journey between the two biggest cities of America, New York and Philadelphia, 80 miles apart as the crow flies, took less than a day, although it must be admitted that by this time a level-surfaced road connected them.

America possessed economic advantages in its water transport system. Core America benefited greatly from its Atlantic coastline, Middleton has argued that the significance of tobacco to the American economy reflected not so much the fertility of the soil as the unusually extensive transport facilities provided by Chesapeake Bay and its tributaries. The navigable distance within the Virginian Capes is 1,750 miles. The unsurpassed network of natural waterways opened up 10,000 square miles of hinterland to immediate settlement. The drainage area of the Chesapeake was equal to approximately the combined area of the six New England states. Well might the Chesapeake be called the Mediterranean of America.

Later expansion also gained from the existence of two major water systems which link up considerable parts of the USA, the Great Lake System joined to the Hudson River by the Erie Canal in the 1820s and the Mississippi River system including the Ohio and the Missouri, whose basin occupies more than a third of the total land area of contiguous USA. Both these systems were free of ice for much longer periods than the Volga river system, by far Russia's most important waterway. By the second quarter of the nineteenth century the Volga system included a set of three canals — the Vishnevolotskaya, the Tikhvinskii and Mariinskii, which linked the Volga with the Neva River, St Petersburg and the Baltic (Haywood 1969; White 1975). This system could be closed by ice for more than six months and passage through it limited to short periods in the spring by great variations in the water level. Moreover the Volga flows into the land-locked and economically insignificant Caspian Sea whereas the Mississippi flows into the open Gulf of Mexico and was quickly linked by canals with the other water systems based on the Great Lakes.

Both the Mississippi and the Volga waterways became very much more significant with the introduction of the steamship. It is interesting to note the relatively low speed of steamship development on the Volga. The more difficult conditions in Russia might lead us to expect a more rapid development. However natural factors could still explain this lag. Possibly American rivers lacked suitability for horsedrawn or mandrawn barges; perhaps they were too wide, the boats too big, the banks too untamed or the rivers of inadequate depth; possibly a shortage of labour or horsepower was relevant.

The resource-intensiveness of early exports is quite clear. Such exports demanded little processing, the minimum required to reduce bulk or perishability to a level appropriate for transport. The pattern of exports therefore closely reflected the resource endowment. The roll call of particular exports ran from fur, fish and forest products, through wheat or flour, corn or barrelled pork, rice or rye, to cotton, wool, flax and hemp and tobacco, and even iron or gold. Very often single export staples dominated not just single regions but a whole nation's exports, as tobacco in colonial America and cotton in the new republic, or wheat in post-Emancipation Russia.

Grains stood on their own as a subsistence good in that significant price fluctuation occurred which brought them in and out of the trading network. Much higher value products were required for a permanent trade flow. From an early date prices intermittently covered transport costs but the slow speed of transport prevented a speedy exploitation of temporary markets. Except where the proximity of the market ensured low transport costs, as in colonial America's trade with the West Indies, the grain trade was a sporadic affair. A risk-reducing response to fluctuations in the grain market was the establishment of

63

deposit ports storing grain close to the main markets of Western Europe (Herlihy 1978a).

It is a curious paradox that whereas America's resource endowment promoted trade more than Russia's and Americans dominated American trade and foreigners dominated Russia's trade, the wherewithal of trade, many of the materials required for shipping — iron, hemp, cordage, sailcoth, naval stores — were imported into America from Russia. In particular the dew-retted flax and hemp of Russia proved superior to the water-retted varieties produced in America, despite many efforts to produce these efficiently in America, a nice illustration of resource specificity of technology (Crosby 1965).

Whereas resources alone cannot ultimately be the cause of economic development since other inputs are necessary for their effective exploitation the main argument remains unaffected. American resources evaluated in terms of access were mostly superior to Russian resources.

Raw materials of industrialisation

For all practical purposes, there are no minerals in the homeland of the Great Russian people, the area from Novgorod-Smolensk to Kazan, from Lake Beloozero to the Oka.

Hellie

The relative endowment of Russia and America with raw materials relevant to industrialisation has had an important influence on both the pace and pattern of industrialisation.

At the heart of the traditional industrial revolution was the process of smelting iron with coke, perfected at the beginning of the eighteenth century by Abraham Darby and applied on an extensive scale in Britain during the second half of that century, when economic conditions, principally the size of the market, first made the technology profitable (Hyde 1977). This technology required the availability of iron and coal free of such impurities as phosphorous or sulphur, and limestone, and led to the increased use of iron in a wide range of forms, particularly as a constructional material. Coal and iron, both directly and indirectly through the agency of steam power, present the most graphic image of the industrial revolution.

America and Russia share two major characteristics in this respect; unlike Britain, they were wood economies but shared in developing an important iron trade before the industrial revolution. Indeed in the USA the lumber industry was second by value among manufacturing sectors added in both 1860 and 1890, and at the latter date the largest employer. Comparable statistics are lacking for Russia but a similar picture would undoubtedly hold.

The significance of wood was two-fold. First, it served as the main constructional material and in a whole series of uses from fencing to furniture. Secondly, wood or charcoal, served as the principal non-animate fuel, particularly in the smelting of iron, until a relatively late date. The new technology of the industrial revolution came late to both America and Russia, but very much later to Russia than to America and very largely because of different resource endowments influencing technology either directly through the costs of basic inputs or indirectly through the size of markets.

In the eighteenth century Russia was the world's leading exporter of iron (Portal 1950). The main source of Russia's iron in the Ural Mountains was remote from both population centres and external points of consumption, although a long water route made egress feasible. The initial abundance of timber in the area supported a charcoal-burning technology. However this was the very technology superseded by coke smelting in eighteenth century Britain. No suitable deposits of coking coal were discovered in the area until the twentieth century. A change in technology therefore removed a significant element of environmental benignity in this sector.

An alternative source of iron ore, a rich source at that, existed at Krivoy Rog in the Ukraine and of coking coal about 500 kilometres to the east in the Donbas. Until the construction of the Catherine railway in the 1880s there existed no economic way of transporting either the iron ore or the coal across this gap. Completion of the appropriate railway link was quickly followed by the development of a second metallurgical base using coke rather than the charcoal smelting process (Portal 1965).

The American industry was not untroubled by resource deficiencies. Coal deposits in the eastern part of Pennsylvania and elsewhere had a high sulphur content. With the introduction of the hot blast from the 1820s onwards, anthracite could be used as a substitute. Suitable coking coal deposits were discovered in Pennsylvania at Connelsville during the 1840s. Good iron ore deposits were widely distributed within the core area but the rich deposits on Lake Superior contained a high phospherous content which limited their use until the Thomas-Gilchrist process was introduced in the 1880s (Temin 1964b).

Undoubtedly both iron and coal were more accessible in the USA than in Russia. As a consequence the iron and steel industry grew at a rapid pace from a relatively much earlier date. Alexander Baykov in an important but neglected article has gone as far as to argue that the geographical separation of iron and coal in Russia postponed the onset of the industrial revolution. There is no analogous argument in the case of the USA and with good reason.

There has been a tendency in the past to exaggerate the importance of coal in the early industrialisation of America and even more so in the overall development of that economy in the first half of the nineteenth century, certainly before. This amounts to a significant misdescription of the American 'Industrial Revolution'. The case of America is particularly illuminating, since very quickly the American economy attained the so-called technical frontier, that is, pioneered significant new industrial technology. It did this without any significant transition to inanimate power sources despite the development of the American System of Manufacturing with its graduated introduction of interchangeable parts, its assembly lines, its integration of production processes, its machine bias and creation of a machine tool industry. The internal diffusion of steam technology was delayed until the 1860s, at least outside the transport sector.

In 1800 less than 10 per cent of the energy used in the American economy came from inanimate sources, in 1855 still only just under half. Until the third quarter of the nineteenth century work obtained from animals exceeded the amount derived from all inanimate sources; this was reversed only in 1880. Steam took from the 1780s to the 1870s to move from accounting for one per cent of industrial motive power to 50 per cent. Yet American manufacturing allegedly grew at a rate of 59 per cent per decade between 1809 and 1840. Mechanisation did not require new power sources, it re-emphasised the importance of animate power. As Greenberg writes, 'Neither coal nor oil but rather food for humans and feed for animals constituted the basic fuel.' The increased intensity of work demanded healthy well-fed workers and large numbers of horses. The food-producing capacity and plentiful supply of land were the most relevant resources for energy supply.

The level of *per capita* energy consumption in America was very high. Moreover the actual efficiency of the American energy system declined throughout the nineteenth century. The availability of soft energy sources allowed acceleration in the growth of productivity while removing the need for a parallel acceleration in the efficiency of energy use.

Moreover timber was not the only alternative to coal as an inanimate source of power. In New England water proved to be a very much cheaper source. Coal was not required until all feasible sites on the rivers were used. The abundance of waterpower postponed the use of steam power in New England factories; this was not a symptom of innovational inertia but a reflection of a benign resource environment.

America was greatly favoured by the abundance of 'soft energy' sources, whether they were wood, water or even pasture to support animal power. Russia was not completely bereft of these power sources — note the availability of timber and water power in the Urals Mountains — but enough has been said to indicate their limitations.

America's natural resource endowment, particularly its abundant and cheap energy, has been put forward to resolve the so-called labour scarcity paradox, that is, the advanced state of mechanisation in American manufacturing relative to Britain in the first half of the nineteenth century despite higher interest rates and a lower aggregate capital stock in manufacturing (James and Skinner 1985). The complementarity of natural resources, particularly cheap energy, and capital has been stressed and offered to explain the rapid labour-saving pattern of technical change in key sectors of industry, and later in industry in general. In the words of James and Skinner, 'Technological compatibility between capital and natural resources in the skilled-manufacturing sector provided sufficient incentives to substitute capital and inexpensive natural resources for skilled labour' (James and Skinner 1985: 514), although this was not true in the low-skill sector.

Tardiness in the introduction of steam power combined with slow change in the iron industry emphasised the importance of textile industrialisation, both in New England and in Russia.

Some element of textile industrialisation is possible at an early date on the basis of local supplies of flax and hemp or wool. The process of proto-industrialisation was largely based on textile production. Rapid modernisation of the cotton industry within the factory system began during the 1820s in New England and the 1840s in Russia. Once more the pace of advance was very much greater in America, directly and indirectly reflecting the advantages of the resource environment. Russia's climate and soils had led to an emphasis on the processing of flax and hemp and the export of linen. The availability of flax, hemp or wool was at least the equal of the American availability, whereas America had a clear advantage in cotton. Since the new methods of spinning, weaving and finishing were more appropriate to cotton fibre an advantage was given to America. Russia, until the end of the nineteenth century and the spread of cotton culture in Russian Central Asia, had to rely on imports, increasingly American imports. Russian industrialisation became very much dependent on foreign sources of raw material.

67

Despite the repeated assertion that Russia enjoys a wide variety and abundance of mineral resources, including coal and iron ore, the exploitation of a significant part of these resources was to be heavily dependent upon a major increase in their value and an improvement in transport technology. The core area of Russia which contains today important urban-industrial regions centred on Moscow and Leningrad has almost no local natural resource base.

4

Economic Impact of Shocks and Disasters

INCIDENCE AND IMPACT OF SHOCKS

Shocks as a class of phenomena are virtually ignored; they are treated as individual, transient events of no general significance.

Jones

The village annals contained no important events, except bad harvest, cattle plagues and destructive fires, with which the inhabitants seem to have been periodically visited from time immemorial.

Wallace,
of Ivanofka in the northern forest of European Russia

They (the American colonists) were more likely to be concerned, day in and day out, with the weather than with continental politics, with crop yields and commodity prices than with the prerogatives of the king. What lawyer James Madison might say at Congress about the powers of parliament and the rights of man was doubtless important to those who could understand it. But would the Shenandoah flood this spring? For many colonists that kind of question was equally important. After the way essayist John Dickinson of Philadephia viewed his state's unicameral legislation with alarm, what many other Pennsylvanians viewed with even greater alarm was the Hessian fly moving westward toward their wheat. John Adams' scholarly pronouncements from Boston about the nature of the British constitution were important, all might agree. But so were the questions of how large the poll and land taxes would be this year and whether the collectors would take grain in payment.

Becker

The second stage in making dynamic the evaluation of resources is to consider directly the instability of the natural environment. The catalogue of natural shocks is enormous — earthquake or volcano; storm or hurricane; flood, fire or drought; epidemic or epizootic; frost, hail, excessive snow or rain; animal attacks; pest infestations and plant diseases. Such shocks can be purely local in scope or widespread in their effects. Alongside the natural shocks there occur social shocks, acts of arbitrary violence or even war. Jones has suggested a possible classification of shocks as geophysical, climatic, biological or social. More useful in terms of economic impact is his classification by 'factor-intensity' of effect. Some disasters are capital destructive, others labour destructive (E.L. Jones 1977, 1978, 1981a, chap. 2).

On the whole the 'capital-intensive' shock has been of marginal importance to Russia and America, occurring only on the periphery at comparatively late dates. The core areas are outside zones of major volcanic or seismic disturbance. Floods were of intermittent and usually local significance since both lacked the vast river control system of the hydraulic societies. The one great exception to this generalisation involved fire, the 'red rooster' (Billington), representing a major scourge in the forest environment of the core and the wood civilisations of America and Russia. There is strong evidence to suggest fire was a frequent devastating visitor in the forest-fire frontier of America and Russia but more often to the cities, particularly the Russian cities, which were extremely vulnerable as they were constructed largely of inflammable materials.

A totally unexpected shock, unrepeated and once-and-for-all, has a direct economic cost, sometimes very high, but little influence on the organisation of an economy. The direct costs comprise a series of losses: a short-run loss of production and working capital caused by dislocation arising from the shock; a longer-run effect on the size, and the rate of growth, of population, occasioned by changes in mortality or birth rates; a particular impact on groups relevant to economic activities — entrepreneurs, merchants or skilled workers; finally the destruction of fixed capital. The direct economic cost of such shocks could be calculated as an annual stream of lost output, although in practice the relevant data are usually unavailable. Most shocks are repeated, however irregularly. They therefore have both direct and indirect effects.

The speed at which recovery has been achieved from 'modern' shocks has often been noted, although the powers of recovery of an economy increase with economic development. The impact of war or earthquake is short-lived provided the basic human capital is not destroyed and provided, in a pre-industrial economy, the underlying productivity of the land is unaffected. Often too a significant shock leads to compensating changes in birth and death rates which quickly restore population.

Attention is concentrated on the role of famine, disease and war, essentially labour-destructive shocks. However, one characteristic of a high risk environment is a tendency to short time horizons. Such short horizons have a powerful shaping influence on the level and kind of capital investment. Such shocks may not be directly capital destructive, therefore, but capital may nevertheless accumulate slowly because of their indirect impact.

It is difficult to measure incidence independently of impact. In a context of labour-intensive shocks mortality rates can be taken as an indicator of the crisis level since for an individual survival is a basic objective. However it cannot be claimed that mortality rates correspond exactly with levels of economic cost; they act only as a crude proxy, indicating rough orders of magnitude.

Average mortality rates conceal fluctuations of varying degree. An economy experiencing mortality rates equal to that of another economy is in a very different position if that average conceals large fluctuations in the one case and stability in the other.

For analytical purposes we distinguish three levels of mortality; the background or 'plateau' level, representing the average or some carefully-defined typical level; secondly, the shock or 'peak' level representing a sharp, upward movement of mortality, let us say, a doubling of typical mortality, or ten per cent mortality over a two-year period — that is, a crude rate of 50/1,000 sustained for two years (Schofield 1972): and thirdly, the catastrophe or 'range' level when population fails to recover a pre-shock maximum within a decade. It is also necessary to note the geographical coverage of a shock. Shocks which are genuinely national rarely occur — and for that reason are of particular interest. Most shocks are regional or even local.

This chapter deals with the incidence and direct impact of shocks and the next the indirect impact in establishing a risk environment. The argument advanced is quite clear in its main outlines. Shocks were often frequent enough in Russia to constitute catastrophe; in America shocks were less frequent and less severe. Such shocks had both a high direct and indirect cost.

The most disturbing shock to an economy threatens its means of subsistence through a failure of food supply, often arising from harvest failure. Famines are, as Jones asserts, not 'pure' disasters in themselves but the economic summation of other disorders. However,

71

the state of the harvest was integral to the economic life of a society. Supply difficulties were inherent in pioneering and explain the frequent concern with self-sufficiency. Violence constitutes another shock which is likely to be present in the pioneer period when political or administrative control is precarious. Disease on the other hand often awaits an appropriate density of population to become a significant threat, at least in so far as epidemics of infectious disease are concerned, except in some cases where new disease pools are being confronted. The absolute scale of shocks may increase in the course of settlement undermining the potential for urban areas to grow but the vulnerability to shocks is likely to be at its greatest in the early stages, during opening up.

FAMINE

Weather conditions . . . were of overwhelming significance: it is no accident that personal diaries from this period are about 50% meteorology.

Demos, in speaking of the Plymouth colony
in the seventeenth century

In each century of recorded history Russia had to cope with problems of national calamities which caused famines.

Kahan

Even a brief survey of the relevant literature indicates that famine was a much more frequent and threatening visitor to Russia than to America. The chief problem is to establish, in the absence of reliable statistics, that the incidence of famine was really greater and that the historical references do not simply reflect an inadequate response.

Harvest failure in itself did not inevitably lead to famine. Moreover famine was likely to occur in combination with other shocks. We need first to establish the conditions under which the harvest is likely to fail and then to suggest in what context that failure might result in famine.

There is a modern school of thought which argues that all famines are man-made (Sen 1977; Dando 1976; 1980). Such an argument is based on the truism that, given the political will and a disregard for cost, any shortfall of a harvest can be countered by the import of grain from surplus areas. However the cost of such policy directly reflects both the extent of the supply disruption and the ease of transport for grain imports. Clearly a major disruption affecting a wide area in the pre-railway era could not be countered at any feasible cost. Such a comment does not deny that harvest disruption could occur as a result of epidemic or war but that the most likely cause in the pre-railway world was climatic, as even the summaries of causation made by the proponents of human causation show (Dando 1980).

The weather was the most important influence on the harvest. Sometimes climatic variations are dramatically manifested in flood, hurricane or blizzard, but just as important are the subtle changes in rainfall, temperature, wind strength, date of first or last frost, or depth of snow cover. Alternatively the weather affects the supply of foodstuffs indirectly through transport problems. It regulates the ease, reliability and cost of transport through such factors as the supply of feed to oxen and horses, the restrictions on water transport imposed by ice and water depth and on overland movement by snow, mud and dust.

Since grain is the staple foodstuff, attention is focussed on the grain harvest. A number of background elements are relevant. First a very much greater diversity of crops characterised colonial America compared with early Russia. The more diversified an economy, the less likely is an unhappy combination which severely reduces all crop production and livestock rearing. Rain which ruins the harvest can increase the supply of fodder. Climatic and soil conditions in core Russia encouraged a stress on rye, oats and later potatoes, essentially poor man's foods, whereas in colonial America wheat, rice and maize were produced in significant quantities.

Secondly, Russia's output to seed yields were as low as 3 to 1 in the late sixteenth and early seventeenth centuries and rose above 3.5 only in the 1870s when yields began a significant increase. Yields in the American colonies were very much higher.

Low yields meant that during the annual cycle of production and consumption a poor family might in spring or early summer find itself in difficulties, even in a normal year. The threat and impact of the *soudure* — the critical period between the exhaustion of the previous year's supply of grain and the harvest of the current crop — was critical in peasant Russia, and not entirely absent from colonial America. The annual shortages in the springtime acted as a kind of famine drill for most families and a constant reminder of the threat of famine. Consequently harvest fluctuations did not alter the normal dietary regime; they merely distorted the seasonal variation. Such fluctuations might mean that even rich households had at least occasional experiences of temporary malnutrition (Christian 1980). Such difficulties lead first to the elimination of less essential foods and finally to the elimination of bread.

It is also true that bad harvests tended to come in series. Even when the harvest was good, poor transport reduced the marketed proportion. Low yields allowed little beyond the immediate producer's own consumption. At such low levels of average yield, any sharp decrease meant a higher share of the current crop to be used as seed in the next crop year, or even a continuing adverse effect on the harvest through the scarcity of seed.

Low yields, greater feed and building requirements, the ravages of animal disease kept the starvation buffer of livestock herds to a minimum (Bairoch 1969). The impact of low yields was therefore cumulative. Russia was deprived of a cushion against harvest failure.

In Russia the variability of grain yields was much greater than in colonial America. Hard data are difficult to come by. Timoshenko has produced evidence for wheat yields in the late nineteenth and early twentieth centuries. According to Timoshenko's data (1942 and 1943) the average coefficient of variability of wheat yield, measured over a 50 to 70 year period, was in most of Russia almost double that of the USA. In the Ukraine, which includes wooded prairies similar to some core area conditions, the coefficient of variation was above 24. In core America the coefficient was nearer ten. The core area difference was undoubtedly very much greater, since core Russia was unsuitable for wheat production, and winter killing more than made up for lower aridity. The choice of rye as a main consumption crop compensated for lower yields by lesser variability, and is itself indirect evidence of the problem. Equally interesting is the Timoshenko conclusion that regional variations are more likely to be mutually offsetting in the USA than in Russia. The area of uniform climatic conditions is much larger in Russia.

The main cause of the variability was undoubtedly climatic. When wheat production came to be concentrated in semi-arid, drought-vulnerable areas, variations in rainfall were a major factor, if not the major factor, determining fluctuations in yield. However where the producing areas were relatively moist as in core America or Russia, variations in temperature became of greater significance. On both counts Russia was disadvantaged. Before 1830 an approximately equal number of famines resulted from excess or insufficient precipitation and from temperatures too high or too low.

In addition to the direct impact of the climate on the state of the harvest there is the indirect link through plant disease. A potent but largely invisible destroyer of the harvest is at work, year in year out, steadily devouring a significant proportion of the crop and only becoming clearly visible when climatic conditions help in its destructive task — plant disease, the 'famine on the wind' as Carefoot and Sprott so aptly name it. For each seed type there is a fungal parasite; rusts, smuts, mildew, blights, ergots all take their toll (Large 1940). It is said that in bad years fungus devours as much as a quarter or even a half of the world's wheat crop. A bad year tends to occur when warm rain, fogs and heavy dew encourage the germination of the fungus spores, particularly after a cold winter. The lack of adequate statistics prevents the identification of either normal losses from fungi or peak periods, although occasionally dramatic events focus attention on these losses — the potato blight in Ireland in the mid-1840s or the worst outbreaks of ergotism.

There is little doubt that both America and Russia suffered from the onslaught of fungus. A dramatic outbreak of ergotism is said to have killed 20,000, mainly soldiers, in and around Astrakhan in 1722 although the assertion that this marked the first appearance of the purple cockspur in the area is dubious, since rye originated in the area near the Caspian. The 'Holy, or St Anthony's, Fire' continued to reappear through to the twentieth century. The New World also had its problems. In New England rust made the growing of wheat practically impossible after the 1660s (Russell 1976).

An impressionistic view inclines the writer to the greater vulnerability of Russian agriculture partly because of its monocultural tendency and partly because of greater exposure to such disease. Like human disease, plant diseases could be devastating when introduced into a disease-free environment but America's isolation again helped it. Quarantine authorities in present-day America are apparently heartened by the fact that many of the diseases which affect the world's crops are entirely absent from that nation. Particular reference is made to potato and rice diseases. Such a relative freedom from plant disease is unlikely to have been less characteristic of the past. By contrast Carefoot and Sprott have graphically suggested the seriousness of rust infestation in Russia. 'In some of the bad rust years in Eastern Europe, the dews were yellow with spores, and the fogs and rains were as red as blood.'

Because of the low yields the situation is one in which an equal proportional variation in yield could take Russia below the subsistence margin while still allowing a significant surplus in America. Yet variations were unlikely to be similar, Russia being much more prone to large fluctuations. Poor transport access and wider drought coverage increased the dangers of harvest failure. The occurrence of famine conditions could result from the repetition of adverse weather within a large territory or from major reductions in grain yields, say, exceeding 20 per cent. From Kahan's catalogue of disasters such a repetition appears not unusual. A major local harvest failure at least once every four years has been noted by many commentators as a regular phenomenon of Russian history.

Good quantitative evidence of famine is hard to come by since both mortality rates and harvest figures are lacking even for large stretches of the nineteenth century. Two nineteenth century tendencies confuse the Russian picture. First, there appears to have been an increasing incidence of potential famine conditions. The movement to the south and east, by reducing the significance of winter grains and exposing grain production to a lower and more variable rainfall, increased the danger of harvest failure, although average yields might actually be significantly higher than in the core. Deforestation in already lightly wooded areas further increased vulnerability to harvest failure.

Secondly, in the years for which quantitative evidence exists the appearance of the railway and of vastly improved transport and communications makes the absence of famine, except in periods of political breakdown, scarcely surprising. The alleged Russian famine of 1891 does not qualify as a national shock on mortality rates alone. Indeed the period from 1860 to 1916 does not give a single case of such a shock. Even the famines of 1921-2 and 1933-4 led to only a brief and small reduction in population and do not qualify as a national shock on our definition.

However in the period 1811-1911 downward deviation of more than 20 per cent in yield occurred six times with another five years registering a reduction little short of this. The potential for a famine existed and in the pre-railway period it was likely to have been translated into reality. The standard deviation of the gross harvest was 10 per cent between 1801 and 1861, and 12.1 per cent between 1850 and 1900. Some decades saw the average top 15 per cent. In individual years the harvest might diverge by little short of a third, a variation which would imply a harvest in a good year double that in a bad.

Local variations, particularly in the net harvest, that is, the gross harvest minus the seed needs of the following year, could be much more dramatic. The statistics of the net harvest for Penza province in the central agricultural region show that during the decade 1848-57, the 'famine' year 1848 had a harvest only about one twentieth of the net harvest of the best year 1851, or one fifth of the next best year (Smith and Christian 1964: 341, 343).

It is worth while considering the situation in New England where soil and climatic conditions were the most disadvantageous in colonial America. There has been a tendency to assume that diet was plentiful from the beginning. Susan Norton reflects this attitude best; she generalised the remarks concerning Ipswich, Massachusetts, as valid for all New England: 'the most striking difference between Ipswich and Europe in this realm must be the New World prosperity and/or natural plenty that led to a low level of mortality from starvation and related diseases.'

However Sarah McMahon has pointed out that a 'starving' time, the 'six weeks want' in the early spring remained a problem on the frontier throughout the eighteenth century. More particularly she has argued that the crops harvested in the late summer and autumn in the seventeenth century were often insufficient, and stores reached low levels by the late spring and summer. On the smallest homesteads, she asserts, the grain chests and meal bags might be empty a month or two before the mid-summer crop of wheat and rye was harvested. However, by the middle of the eighteenth century, the autumn harvest on most New England homesteads provided sufficient bread corn for the whole year. McMahon talks of a potential Malthusian subsistence crisis in the eighteenth century which never eventuated.

During the early years, therefore, there was a sharp seasonal demarcation between the stored provisions of winter and the fresh foods of summer. Later the supply and variety of food expanded sufficiently to deseasonalise the diet.

In marked contrast to the Russian experience is the absence of a comparable famine potential in America after the initial 'starving' years. Infrequent local harvest failure, more differentiated climatic conditions, better transport links, a more diversified agriculture — all these factors helped America avoid the plight of Russia.

There were certainly local shocks particularly in the south. Middleton describes the ravages of a rogue hurricane, with its accompanying rain and floods, in the Chesapeake in 1667 which on one calculation, probably inflated, destroyed 10,000 homes and between two-thirds and four-fifths of the crops. Such a shock was never repeated. Middleton himself notes that hurricanes, storms and exceptional freshets were uncommon occurrences, rarely as destructive as the exceptional example described. In general life was serene and uneventful.

However the humid continental climate of the Chesapeake, usually predictable and favourable to tobacco culture, was occasionally punctuated by uncertain extremes of drought, frost, hail, wind or rain. The high rate of evapo-transpiration in summer could reinforce drought. For example, in the 1760s the cattle and pig herds, which had been steadily built up over the eighteenth century, were decimated as a result of exceedingly scanty grass and fodder, caused by cold winters and prolonged drought, a nice illustration of their buffer role in unusual conditions. The number of cattle and pigs per inventoried estate was almost halved, and sheep numbers came down by a third. The very unexpectedness of such shocks reduced their long-run impact. Moreover, the odd paradox prevailed at times, of natural shocks actually acting to decrease the degree of market instability, since weather conditions could reduce the glut of tobacco.

After the early years famine was not generally regarded as a serious possibility, even in the most disadvantaged area of colonial America. The generally high level of nutrition accounts for the only occasional reports of scurvy and ricketts and helped reduce the incidence of disease in general. The most cogent evidence is the lack of reference to famine in the relevant literature — newspapers, diaries, letters, reports.

PESTILENCE

The story is told that Dean Donham of the Harvard Business School once asked Professor Schumpeter, after a lecture on the entrepreneur — Schumpeter's plumed knight of economic development — what was the most important single factor in accounting for the success of the businessman. Quick as a shot came the answer, 'Good health'.

Diamond

The predominance of infectious disease in pre- and early industrial societies was closely associated with low levels of nutrition, and an improvement in nutrition was a necessary condition for a substantial and prolonged reduction of mortality and growth of population (McKeown 1976). However in Europe this was a long drawn-out process, with frequent temporary reversals and with some tendency for the increasing density of population in urban areas to offset locally the effects of better nutrition, and indeed on occasion even to reverse that movement towards better nutrition. The recent tendency to note the gradual beginnings of economic development and by implication the early rise in living standards, implies a similarly early and long drawn-out reduction in mortality.

The best empirical evidence for such an argument has been the fall in death rates from a number of important infectious diseases well before any particular campaigns began or any significant medical breakthroughs were made. For example, the fall in the death rates from tuberculosis and pneumonia had begun in the most advanced societies by 1800. Even earlier a number of other infectious diseases had receded in importance, notably plague, ague or malaria, even measles, without any obvious cause. Some of this decreased virulence may, however, simply reflect the mutual adjustment of host and parasite.

At levels of income close to subsistence therefore disease is not an autonomous influence on mortality, as it operates in tandem with malnutrition. In view of the poor resource position in Russia it is not surprising to find tendency for epidemics and famine to coincide (Kahan 1968). At levels of income well above subsistence, however, disease can become, and often is, an autonomous influence. Since American income levels were already by the end of the colonial period among the highest in the world, we might expect this situation to prevail.

Recently it has been argued that fertility change was mainly responsible for the great upturn in the population of Western Europe beginning in the eighteenth century (Wrigley and Schofield 1981). To some extent the movement of population to the higher mortality towns concealed a significant secular improvement in life expectation, particularly in the nineteenth century. The argument advanced here is that fertility change could be more important than mortality change only in already comparatively rich areas; mortality change was more important at an earlier date. The contrasting examples of Russia and America appear to support the main contention. In 'rich' America fertility change was more important than mortality change in determining the rate of natural increase in population. Moreover fertility was undoubtedly adjusted to suit economic circumstances. In 'poor' Russia mortality change was more significant and fertility rates less flexible.

The long drawn-out fall in European mortality was due as much to the decrease in severity and frequency of epidemic shocks as to

79

a reduction in the mortality of an average year. Often it is difficult to disentangle epidemics from endemic disease. Societies prone to endemic disease also tend to be subject to epidemic disease through similar causes. The following pages seek first to distinguish a largely disease-free environment in New England from more morbid environments in the early Chesapeake and Russia, particularly the latter. Secondly, they seek to show the much more limited frequency and geographical coverage of epidemics in America.

A whole series of recent studies have emphasised the healthiness of early New England. Demos argues, 'The Plymouth Colony records suggest a standard of life and health that would compare favourably with that of any pre-industrial society today' (Demos 1970). To support this Demos points out that men reaching adulthood could expect to live to about 70, women to about 63. Greven comments that 'the initial period following the settlement of Andover seems to have been one of exceptional healthiness' (Greven 1970). Andover continued to be 'a surprisingly healthy place' in which to live and raise families. 'Stability and health' were the basic characteristics of life in the seventeenth century. This showed itself in a remarkably low death rate. Average life spans were long and few marriages were broken by premature death.

By contrast in the first half of the eighteenth century Greven noted striking changes in overall mortality levels, an increased incidence and severity of epidemics and the appearance of dramatic peaks in mortality, as in 1735 when, because of diphtheria, deaths actually exceeded births. Clearly this phenomenon was associated with increased population density, with 41 people per square mile by 1764. Greven talks of Andover being 'relatively crowded by the mid-eighteenth century'.

Lockridge and Norton confirm this general picture for Dedham and Ipswich (Lockridge 1970; S. Norton 1971). The death rate in Dedham was as low as 27/1,000, explicable, according to Lockridge, by such long-term factors as good diet or housing. In addition there was a significant absence of short-run demographic 'crises'. For well over half a century Dedham failed to experience a single crisis which removed as much as ten per cent of its population within a two year period. The average man in Dedham knew 'little of plague and less of famine'. Lockridge also notes a deterioration in mortality rates as overcrowding occurred, broadening the scope of his analysis into a general crisis in New England by the time of the Revolutionary War.

In a review of demographic studies on Massachusetts, Vinovskis concludes, 'In general, seventeenth-century Massachusetts was relatively more healthy than Europe' (Vinovskis 1972). She notes the very high life expectancies in small agricultural communities such as Dedham, Andover, Plymouth, or even Ipswich, while admitting the much higher death rates in larger coastal towns such as Boston and Salem, although these are still low by Western European standards. Vinovskis suggests that the most surprising finding is the relative continuity of death rates throughout the entire period, including the nineteenth century, especially for the smaller agricultural towns. There is an absence of similar studies for the Middle Colonies but no reason to doubt a similar picture.

By contrast Duffy described Virginia as 'a pest-ridden place' afflicted by an 'unending epidemic of dysentery and malaria' (Duffy 1953). In the early years of settlement there was something like an 80 per cent mortality rate among newcomers. By the end of the seventeenth century 100,000 settlers had arrived in Virginia. Despite an extraordinarily high birth rate the total population in 1700 was still only about 75,000. Without sustained immigration the Chesapeake colonies would have failed (see Horn in Tate and Ammerman 1979: 51).

There is considerable disagreement about the causes of the early difficulties in the Chesapeake colonies. Kupperman (1979) has laid stress on the problem of food supply and the impact of nutritional problems combined with the vulnerability of a starving population to disease. The label, the Starving Times, neatly summarises this argument.

Carville Earle (Tate and Ammerman 1979) has rejected the existence of food deficiencies during the first years of settlement. The actual causes of death, according to Earle, were typhoid, dysentery and possibly salt poisoning. The main cause of the trouble was a contaminated water supply and the exact location of Jamestown on the James River. The problem was seasonal; during the summer, the salt plug located around Jamestown trapped sediments and organic wastes. Fevers, fluxes, sickness and death were recurrent from 1607 to 1624.

Increased healthiness after 1624 was achieved by dispersal of population and by dietary change, which included the consumption of liquids other than water and a reduction in the consumption of sea fish.

However the decline in mortality was only relative. The Rutmans' explanation of high mortality based on malaria offers an alternative, with a particular stress on higher mortality in the second half of the seventeenth century after the more lethal strain, the *Falciparum Plasmodium*, was introduced. Throughout the malarial area sickness was almost universal among newcomers and 'seasoning' was a crucial aspect of immigration. Only when a native-born generation appeared did mortality begin to fall. South Carolina was for example much troubled by malaria as well as dysentery and its reputation as a place of devastating ill-health clearly slowed its development (Clowse 1971).

In the moist part of America malaria eventually afflicted every colony or territory at one time or another. It represented a serious hazard to backwood's pioneering, being directly associated with half-cleared forests and newly opened land (Lillard 1973; Harstad 1959–60; 1960a; 1960b; 1963). Poor diet, close proximity to the watery breeding places of the mosquito, dark and damp dwelling places, the absence of livestock all promoted the disease.

The situation in the seventeenth century was, as D.B. Smith concluded, rather tentatively, one in which mortality probably decreased as one travelled northward along the Anglo-American coast from the West Indies to New England, but was rather checkered. Malaria was not a problem in New York nor in Charleston, although in the eighteenth century it became a serious problem in the interior of New York and New Jersey and of South Carolina. D.B. Smith has shown the full impact of malaria in a 'severe malarial environment' of low, marshy soil, mosquitoes, high temperatures and poor drinking water, through his study of Charles Parish, York County, Virginia (D.B. Smith 1978). Because of persistently high death rates, natural reproductive population increase was rare in colonial Charles Parish.

Other important killers endemic in America, as elsewhere, included tuberculosis, or respiratory diseases such as pneumonia or influenza, although the last named often had epidemic characteristics. During the nineteenth century tuberculosis was probably the most significant endemic killer in both Russia and America. Nor were its ravages new. The disease appeared to have a particular relationship with urbanisation and industrialisation but such a relationship may follow simply from the vulnerability of a dense population to a highly infectious disease. More to the point the death rate from TB has historically risen with any major shock, for example war. There is every indication that TB responds very sensitively to environment, in particular good nutrition.

The notoriously poor housing of the frontier provided inadequate protection against the cold, a factor which encouraged the onset of influenza, pneumonia and even tuberculosis. Adequate nutrition, cheap and abundant heating materials, masonry, brick or tile-building materials, good personal hygiene reflecting in particular the availability of soap and cotton clothing — all these factors helped to reduce the incidence and virulence of disease, and were closely associated with a good resource environment and high income levels.

Superimposed on the background diseases were the epidemic peaks. Plague was happily absent from the Americas, largely because of their isolation from the main Eurasian land mass, except perhaps for an outbreak among the Indians before permanent white settlement (Cook 1973). Smallpox and measles, endemic in Europe were only epidemic in America, although the latter became endemic in the late colonial period. Diphtheria, apparently erupting on the scene in the epidemic of 1735, spread slowly in practice to become endemic in successive regions. Yellow fever, endemic in hotter climates, was introduced only in the ports.

The concentrated mortality of certain epidemic diseases, principally smallpox and yellow fever in the eighteenth and cholera in the nine-teenth centuries, make them stand out, in practice far beyond their real significance, although their psychological impact was immense. As hindrances to colonial development their importance has been overrated. The greater threat of epidemic disease among the dense population of the eighteenth century was counteracted to some degree by the development of a more permanent society with a higher standard of living.

The key role of trade and immigration in introducing epidemics into Ameria is shown by the very high death rates in the main immigrant port and fastest growing commercial centre, Philadelphia (B.G. Smith 1977). There the death rate rose as high as 50/1,000 at the end of the 1740s and during the 1750s. A peak as high as 71.3/1,000 was recorded in 1759, and numerous cases occurred where ten per cent of the population died in a two year period.

In the early eighteenth century the death rate in smallpox epidemics reached as high as 14 per cent in 1721 and 12.5 per cent in 1731 of Boston's population, New York losing seven per cent in 1731 and Charleston nine per cent in 1760 (Duffy 1953). Smallpox was also the greatest killer in Philadelphia. On the whole the south was less prone to the disease.

Yellow fever was well established in the West Indies, which explains the outbreaks in the main ports trading with that area, Charleston, New York and Philadelphia. The first outbreak occurred in Boston in 1693. Yellow fever also could kill a high proportion of the population in a major outbreak, as in Charleston in 1699 — seven

83

per cent, five per cent in Philadelphia in 1701, ten per cent in New York in 1702. Again the disease, a mosquito-born tropical disease, was highly localised in its incidence. In this case, the south, particularly Charleston, was the hardest hit.

With minor exceptions epidemic diseases tended to hit the towns and cities much harder than the countryside, although transport improvement, the gold rushes and the movement of settlers, later spread cholera throughout America in the epidemics of 1832, 1849 and 1866 (Rosenberg 1962). The diphtheria epidemic, which hit the New England countryside from 1735 and spread throughout the colonies, is an exception.

Russia was quite clearly a much less healthy place, both in terms of endemic and epidemic disease. Crude mortality rates give a reasonably accurate reflection of the disease environment. The typical crude death rate in pre-industrial England seems to have been about 30/1,000. The most likely crude mortality rate in colonial America during the eighteenth century was significantly below this at 20 to 25/1,000 (Potter 1965). Data for a comparable period in Russia are sparse. On the Petrovskoe estate in Tambov the mortality between 1750 and 1820 seems to have been stable at about 38/1,000. For the late pre-industrial period, that is the 1860s, the rate was as high as 35 to 40; it could hardly have been much higher at an earlier date (Heer 1968). Moreover Russia was subject to recurring mortality peaks comparable to those characteristic of pre-modern England. Except as localised phenomena, such crises were absent from colonial America. Many diseases totally absent from, or infrequent visitors to, America were significant killers for long periods of Russia's history; bubonic plague, smallpox and cholera are prominent.

A number of factors made Russia more vulnerable to disease. The poor natural environment made chronic malnutrition a persistent problem. Famine conditions weakened resistance to infection, particularly to tuberculosis, dysentery and typhus. Fungal poisoning in rye bread may have dictated the pattern of epidemics (Matossian 1984). Proximity to significant disease pools also increased the possibility of devastating epidemics. This contrasts significantly with the isolation of America, protected by the natural quarantine of its oceanic surrounds. The high population densities of the major cities and of long-settled rural areas, particularly in the Russian centre, increased the vulnerability of the population. Colonial America lacked such congested areas.

As in medieval and early modern Europe, plague had a particularly important role to play in Russia (Langer 1975; 1976; Kahan 1979;

McNeill 1964; 1977). McNeill has even argued that plague was endemic among the burrowing rodents of the steppe, thereby at least partly explaining its emptiness until the eighteenth century. Certainly the countries to the south were characterised by endemic plague. After the violent eruption of the fourteenth century, plague regularly afflicted particular regions, initially tending to enter from the west but increasingly from the south. All areas were regularly affected after the Black Death, even the centre — frequently until the epidemic of 1654–6 and again in 1770. Biraben has isolated a significantly different pattern of damping down in a number of occurrences in the north and west of Europe as compared with the east, essentially Russia and the Balkans, and the south, the non-European Mediterranean. In the former a significant reduction occurred as early as the middle of the sixteenth century with some resurgence at the beginning of the eighteenth. In the latter the quietening occurred only in the second half of the nineteenth century. Kahan refers to nine epidemics in the eighteenth century, most of which are limited to the south, except a serious outbreak in the Baltic Provinces and the Northwest in 1709–12 and the dramatic outbreak of 1770–1. Other serious outbreaks occurred in 1727–8 and 1738–9. All these were marked by the coincidence of plague, warfare and internal disarray. Clearly too the coincidence of famine often made the population more susceptible. As Alexander asserted of plague, 'Its periodic recurrence compounded the pervasive insecurity of Russian life and sapped demographic growth, especially in urban areas.'

The death rate from epidemics is mainly conjectural. For example the 1654–5 pestilence is said to have killed nearly 80 per cent of the taxpaying population of Moscow and ten per cent of the total Russian population (Miller 1976: 42). The most serious outbreak in the eighteenth century occurred in 1770–1 probably killing as many as 120,000 people in the Empire as a whole and 50,000 or 20 per cent of the population, in Moscow (Alexander 1980). Nothing on this scale, absolutely or proportionately, occurred in America after the 'starving' years.

Epidemic outbreaks continued to be catastrophic into the nineteenth century, with the main actors changing as in America, where cholera replaced smallpox and yellow fever. In Russia too cholera appeared, as plague receded in importance. Cholera is reported to have carried off as many as one quarter of a million in 1830–1 and well over one million in 1847–51 (McGrew 1965).

The cast of endemic killers in Russia was long, including cholera and typhus, particularly in the cities. Measles, smallpox, syphilis, tuberculosis, pneumonia, dysentery — all were major killers. The very high mortality rates in city and country reflected this malevolent background of endemic disease.

VIOLENCE

The pirates on the coast have been completely exterminated, and vessels came and went, unarmed and unguarded.

American report 1742

These invasions were the ransom of the geography of the region.

Anderson, on early Russia

A man who undertook to be a pioneer had to accept as an occupation hazard the risk of being scalped.

Leach

Violence of various kinds constitutes another element of the risk environment which poses a threat to economic activity. These include individual acts of arbitrary violence or personal crimes often involving theft; secondly, organised acts by those operating beyond formal jurisdictions, brigandage and piracy being the best examples; finally, acts of war when violence is institutionalised against rival powers, aboriginal inhabitants or even fellow citizens in a civil war. There is little doubt that the economically successful were vulnerable to acts of violence; they had more to lose.

Unhappily it is next to impossible to quantify the incidence of violence in the two societies. Any attempt to calculate the financial losses in either society is doomed to failure. We are left with a number of generalisations reflecting the general drift of the literary evidence.

There is some evidence that the level of violent crime decreases with economic development (Gurr 1981, Stone 1983). Such an argument is based on the great secular decline in homicide in England. By this criterion medieval English society was twice as violence-prone as early modern society, and as much as five times as violence-prone as contemporary English society. During the early periods most violence occurred outside rather than inside the family as today. Moreover already during the early acceleration in economic development, English society appeared to be significantly less violence-prone than other societies.

Translating this into our terminology the level of violent crime declined from phase to phase. If this really is the case we are once more confronted with the problem of cause and effect. The logic of our argument is that a reduction in violence is a precondition for inter-phase movement.

Frontier societies are notoriously characterised by a high level of violence. However, despite the graphic pictures of lawlessness on the American frontier presented by the media, it is striking how quickly law and order prevailed in these areas (Friedman 1973). It is highly likely that America was much more ordered than is generally thought. American society has accorded great respect to both the law and lawyers.

On the other hand the Russian countryside was particularly lawless both by repute and according to the evidence. This comparative situation reflects partly the relative density of the law enforcement apparatus. Moreover individual violence was linked with two other factors, the nature of native/settler relations and the time lag between acquisition and settlement. On both counts Russian society was more vulnerable to violence.

Piracy and brigandage reflected again the effectiveness of government. Both were significant in the early years of American and Russian history.

Brigandage was endemic in both the towns and the countryside of Russia and sometimes reached astonishing dimensions (Madariaga 1981: 49). Some of the most spectacular incidents occurred as a result of the violent competition between landlords for land and serfs. Peasant unrest also took three principal forms: brigandage itself, flight and open revolt against the landlords. Brigandage was at its worst in the Volga region and in the south where there were large numbers of fugitives and Cossacks nearby and the absence of large numbers of administrative and military personnel. There was a constant hunting down of 'free wanderers', who sought to escape the burden of poll-tax, military service and serfdom. An old tradition of the resentful *muzhik* was 'losing the red cock', that is burning down the local manor house (Hingley 1978: 142). Murder of the landlords was common. An incomplete listing for Moscow *guberniya* alone covering the period 1764–9 yields the murder of 21 landowners, nine noblemen and five other attempted murders. In the period 1835–54 there were 144 murders of landowners and 29 of government officials (Madariaga 1981: 127). Troops had to be called in regularly to deal with peasant revolts and brigandage.

In America piracy, the seafaring version of brigandage, was a serious problem right through to the 1720s in an area stretching as far north as Chesapeake Bay (Lebergott 1984). In wartime piracy was supplemented by privateering, a semi-official form of piracy. However, piracy was never a serious problem on the coast of New England and the Middle Colonies and rapidly receded in significance in the south from the 1720s.

In both cases, brigandage and piracy, the main threat was less against life than property.

There are three main kinds of war relevant here — the resistance by native peoples to new settlement; internal rebellion or civil war; and confrontation with major powers. Each of these sources of shock could be important during the period of opening up.

New settlement itself depended upon the subjugation or ejection of the technically backward native populations of America and Russia, both numerically large enough to present a significant concerted opposition. Opening up depended on the protection of lines of forts and blockhouses. In America the Red Indian was the incumbent, in Russia Finnic peoples and the remnants of the Mongol horde. In both cases the native peoples were scattered, divided and weakened by disease and internal strife. The long-term impact of the Tartar yoke is a controversial issue, but there is little doubt that even after the fragmentation of the Golden Horde, relatively strong outposts existed in Kazan, Astrakhan and the Crimea. Settlement in the steppe was long delayed by Tartar bands and Moscow was at risk as late as the seventeenth century.

Both Tartars and Red Indians presented potential obstacles to opening up, the former much more formidable both in terms of magnitude and duration. The greater threat in Russia was associated with two characteristic features of Russian society.

First, the militarisation of Russian life, particularly on the frontier, was much more marked than that of America. In a sense the southern frontier had to be pushed further in the interests of security. Concerted military campaigns demanded the investment of considerable resources in Russia on a scale beyond the minor skirmishes in America. The relative size of the armed forces illustrates the argument. Prucha described the American army as 'pathetically small'; before 1855 it seldom reached 11,000 dropping as low as 6,000 in 1821 (Prucha 1967: 29). During the first half of the nineteenth century the army's size relative to the male population dropped from just over 0.2 per cent to below 0.1 per cent. By contrast the number under arms in Russia at times reached 100,000 even in the eighteenth century, although Duffy discounts the frequent talk of what he calls 'vast phantom armies'. In the 1760s 3.3 per cent of the Russian male population was under arms, in the 1790s 3.1 per cent (Duffy 1981: 125).

Secondly, the Russians assimilated the native peoples, adopting a deliberate policy of divide and rule and by necessity using the native soldiers to fight the frontier wars. Such a policy provided a low-level accommodation to the new environment and helps explain the frequent link between native resistance and internal rebellion.

Although native resistance was weaker in America, King Philip's war (1675-7) illustrates the economic impact of a major Indian war. Under King Philip almost all the Indian tribes of New England rose against the white settlers, killing, destroying and all but sweeping the whites into the sea. Few areas of New England were unaffected by the rising.

There is disagreement on the extent of deaths and destruction in King Philip's war. Billington argues that as many as 600 men were killed, or one sixth of the contemporary male population of New England; £90,000 was expended on military operations, 25 towns were destroyed. In Maine all but six villages were destroyed. Others have broadly agreed, Leach offering 1,000 as the death toll excluding indirect deaths. Demos argues that mortality in the Plymouth colony was higher than in any subsequent war, a five-to-eight per cent loss of adult men.

It could be argued that Indian resistance merely altered the direction, not the size of migration. The war halted settlement along the Maine coast and in the valleys of the Connecticut and Hudson River until at least 1720, thereby indirectly encouraging the opening up of Pennsylvania. However, the cost of any new settlement was increased by the resources devoted to the militia and to fortifications and guards. Indian guerrilla tactics must also have strongly influenced attitudes through the risk of attack.

The war also illustrates the ability of some societies to adapt their demographic history to economic circumstances. Interestingly demographers are agreed that there was in New England at the turn of the eighteenth century an interlude of slow growth between two eras of very rapid growth in population. D.S. Smith has argued that a perceived disequilibrium between population and resources, arising from the relative closure of the frontier for a 40 to 50 year period after King Philip's war, produced an adjustive response, which was of the kind helping America to avoid the famine problem of Russia. The initially low age of first marriage among women converges on the higher, more European age of marriage among men. There was also a very significant fall in completed fertility, less than half of which can be explained by a rise in the age of marriage. Our analysis highlights the potential significance of such shocks and the flexibility of American behaviour in meeting potential risk.

Such a war was not exceptional. In a rising of the mid-eighteenth century Pontiac's braves reached as close as 30 miles to Philadelphia (Lemon 1972). Certainly potentially rich land was left underdeveloped because of the Indian threat. This was also true in the cotton south (Whartenby 1977). For more than a century the success of the English colonies was predicated on the friendship of the powerful Iroquois Confederacy. The absorption of the Indians into the market system was an important element in this process, with the English ability to undersell the French in the brightly coloured cloths called Strouds, gunpowder and West Indian rum crucial.

The negative contributions of the Tartars to Russian settlement far outweighed the positive. For something like four centuries slave raiding, particularly from the Crimea, was a major threat to the factor of production scarcest on the frontier, labour (Hellie 1979, McNeill 1964). The losses were enormous. The data are fragmentary but suggest that Muscovy may have been losing as many as 2,000 a year, a rate which almost certainly increased from 1475 when the Ottomans took over the Black Sea slave trade from the Genoese and slave trading became the major economic activity of the Crimeans. In the 1570s close to 20,000 a year were sold in Kaffa, and in 1589 taxes were paid on the sale of 4,000 imported slaves in Istanbul alone. Some have calculated that Muscovy lost on average 4,000 people a year in the first half of the seventeenth century, the Poles even more throughout the century. Catherine the Great referred to a gross seizure rate of 20,000. Even at a conservative annual rate of 2,000 losses, the total sustained on four centuries would reach 0.8 million. Clearly losses were greatest in years of weakness, compounding the impact of other shocks.

Moreover, as McNeill argued, a long series of annual raids, directed against the bordering agricultural population far to the north and west, had pushed the fringes of agricultural settlement back within the tree lines and, perhaps helped by pestilence, had produced something approaching a desert across the entire Pontic steppe.

The barrier presented by the Indians, in combination with the Appalachians and the Great Forest, may indirectly and perversely have had a beneficial effect on the economic development of America, by limiting the core area to coastal settlements and thereby reinforcing the maritime, trading orientation of the American colonies in their formative period. Through trade the desire for a high level of consumption imported with the immigrants could be realised. Accessibility was an early goal of American settlers, in early Muscovy inaccessibility an unfortunate necessity. In the Russian forest self-sufficiency was a much more acceptable situation.

A desultory glance at Russia's history will confirm the prevalence of internal disarray, with combined serf, Cossack and native rebellions such as those of Stenka Razin and Pugachev, major civil wars as during the *Oprichnina* or Times of Trouble. Famine and epidemic were often the occasion for major unrest. America's Civil War, immensely destructive as it was, occurred at a time when the powerful forces of economic development had already become prominent and represented the triumph of an economic system more closely associated with economic development.

Again the role of foreign powers is much more significant in the opening up of Russia than in the American case. In the colonial period the umbrella of British naval power did much to protect the Americans from rival colonial powers. The removal of serious French or Spanish opposition was a major factor allowing the assertion of independence. After the War of Independence British and American resistance to American territorial expansion was muted, the whole process resembling the Russian movement across Siberia. The Louisiana Purchase shows the ease of acquisition of much of the area between the Appalachians and the semi-arid lands to the west. By contrast Russia on its western and southern frontiers had to confront the power of Sweden, Poland-Lithuania and Turkey in order to safeguard its own existence. The Great Northern War (1699–1721) against the Swedes, which established Russia's control over part of the Baltic coastline, dominated Peter the Great's attempts to modernise or westernise Russia. Ever since the assertion of autonomy from the Mongols, Russia has been involved in defensive wars, so that a terror of encirclement has become engrained in the Russian mentality.

CATASTROPHES AND CONSEQUENCES

Our analysis of shocks can be concluded by a discussion of their direct impact, particularly in combination, and by a comparison of the incidence of catastrophes.

The direct impact of shocks reflects both the cushion of resources available per head and the associated ability of a society to manage disasters. A crude measure of resource availability is the amount of land available per head. The relative vulnerability of Russia during

91

the formative period is shown by the following figures for population density per square mile of acquired territory.

Table 4.1: Population density per square mile

	1500	1600	1724	1796	1913
Russia	9	6	2.3	5.3	118
	1700	1790	1820	1850	1900
America	1	4.5	5.6	7.9	25.6

Sources: Cole 1967; Blum 1961; historical statistics.

In Russia it follows that land availability in the formative period was relatively very poor, even if lower population figures than the nine-to-ten million in 1500 and twelve million in 1600 used here are assumed. Even a halving of the sixteenth century population would not alter the substance of the argument. Indeed the argument is reinforced if account is taken of the inferior quality of Russia's land. A marked increase in land availability after 1500 reinforced the impact of declining or stable population. Only in the eighteenth century did population increase begin to reduce the *per capita* land availability.

America started off with a very large land endowment, with a decline occurring only in the eighteenth century as population pressed, if weakly, on the area east of the Appalachians. Thereafter land availability almost kept pace with population from the time of Independence through to the 1830s when a slow decline began which accelerated after 1850.

The ability to manage disasters is discussed in the next chapter but there is little doubt that the problem of manageability increased with the frequency and severity of shocks. There is a vicious circle element in the response to shocks, which becomes more evident the further back in time the analysis goes.

War, famine and epidemic all caused massive short-run economic dislocation. The short-run economic dislocation caused by disease can be generalised from McGrew's specific comments: 'the cholera's influence, if not its immediate effect, permeated the Russian system; recruiting for the army stopped, interior commerce came to a standstill, and quarantine regulations strait-jacketed the nation.' In both America and Russia the prospect of an epidemic struck such fear in those threatened that a mass exodus of officials, merchants, landowners and even workers, commonly occurred. Economic activity came to a standstill. The breakdown in supply often caused a subsistence crisis. The flight of the producers extended the crisis beyond distribution to production. Very often there was also a conflict between the short-term disruptive consequences to the economy of anti-epidemic measures and the long-term beneficial effects of reducing the incidence of disease. Quarantines and the isolation of those infected were often reduced in their efficiency by deliberately late recognition of the presence of an epidemic. Ignorance compounded the terror and disruption.

Similarly harvest failure, by raising the price of food, reduced the demand for other commodities and ultimately by causing a breakdown in the whole supply system brought economic activity to a halt as consumers sought a supply of food. A major civil disturbance could have exactly the same effect. External wars, unless fought over home soil, tended to divert economic activities rather than disrupt them. Both epidemic and war could cause a breakdown in food supply.

The impact of famine, epidemic or war on the rate of growth of population can be exaggerated. However, Kahan has shown that in Russia as late as the nineteenth century natural calamities could significantly slow the rate of advance (Kahan 1968). The great demographic crisis of the late sixteenth and early seventeenth centuries was the consequence of combined war, disease and famine. However, since shocks such as disease and famine very often culled the weak, that is the very young or the old, they did not always, at least alone, cause a prolonged setback to population growth. Moreover they lowered the dependency ratio. Some epidemics, such as that of 'throat distemper' in the late 1730s in the American colonies, were almost solely limited to children. War usually affected men much more than women, thereby leaving fertility rates largely untouched. In aggregate, moreover, death rates from disease greatly exceeded those directly experienced in war.

There is good evidence that birth rates could adjust to fill the population gaps caused. Within a short period, say a decade, even the losses from such a major epidemic as the Moscow plague of 1770–1 could be replaced. Even in the cities, where normal mortality was high and conditions of overcrowding and poor hygiene prevalent, immigration could regularly offset an annual net decrease in population. In the case of St Petersburg and Odessa immigration accounted for even more than the prodigious increase in population right up to the 1880s (Bater 1978; Herlihy 1978b). However, since labour was scarce in the areas of new settlement in both countries, the difference in the rate of population growth, reflecting much more differing levels of mortality than of fertility, had a direct impact on the rate at which opening up occurred.

Certain diseases hit key economic groups in the population very hard. The urban population was particularly vulnerable. Before the nineteenth century the penalties of size seemed to have placed limits on the expansion of cities, with notable exceptions such as London and Edo (Tokyo). Vulnerability to infectious disease often combined with difficulty of food supply to put restrictions on size and growth. The harsh disease environment arising from the ease of communication of infectious disease, crowded housing, problems of pure water and sewerage disposal acted to raise the death rate to a very high level. Such an environment continued to contribute to the impermanence of the city population, even in nineteenth century Russia. Moreover it has been argued that a general breakdown of urban modernisation was an important factor contributing to the final demise of the imperial regime (Hamm 1976).

The commercial nature of, and the concentration of the military in, Russian cities increased the possibility of infectious disease. Merchants, notably the petit bourgeoisie, were particularly vulnerable to disease. The plague of 1770-1 in Moscow illustrates the selective nature of epidemics (Alexander 1980). Textile raw materials such as wool and silk, imported into Russia from the south, carried plague, and came to be known as 'plague goods'. Alexander noted that, 'Paradoxically, the plague caused more damage in the more modern, urbanised, and industrialised sector of the Russian economy and society.' It decimated the city's industry by killing the labour force, by closing most enterprises for at least six months, if not for good, and by depleting working and fixed capital. Economically important groups such as lesser merchants, artisans, manufacturing workers, drovers, peddlers, were particularly hard hit. Such effects caused Alexander to assess the plague of 1770-1 as one of the worst urban disasters of the pre-industrial era. Again the bourgeois were particularly hard hit by the cholera epidemic of 1829 when they accounted for 16 per cent of Moscow's population and 22 per cent of the deaths (McGrew 1965). There is no reason to doubt that this was a general rule. Some groups — the richest merchants, large landowners, even unskilled 'peasant' workers — could escape the cities, but the loss of human capital invested in the permanent urban population was clearly vital to the health of the economy. One commentator considered the death of a few thousand textile workers in the Moscow manufacturing enterprises as one of the more serious setacks of the 1770-1 plague. Such outbreaks encouraged industry to leave its urban setting. It is not accidental that disease tended to follow the trade routes, these being the main chains of human contact. In both the cases of plague and cholera, the rivers were major channels of disease movement.

War also tended to follow the trade routes and to hit particularly hard producing areas. Any stocks of commodities were extremely vulnerable to official requisitioning or looting.

The links between epidemic, famine and war were particularly strong in Russia. Empirically such shocks often occurred simultaneously. The interactions are not difficult to analyse. War often spread disease with the movement of large numbers of military personnel and the establishment of regular movement along supply lines. It disrupted food production by direct destruction or by indirectly removing the fruits of production. On the other hand both famine and disease were powerful inducements to civil unrest and rebellion. A series of such shocks created the precondition for major uprisings. Finally disease removed the producer and malnourished producers easily fell victim to disease — yet another vicious circle. Each shock increased both the probability and severity of other shocks.

Russia and America differed significantly in their exposure to catastrophe. A catastrophe involved one of three situations; exceptionally severe shocks with mortality rates well above even peak levels, repeated shocks of a similar kind or the simultaneous occurrence of shocks of a different kind. The last was by far the most likely to occur. Such catastrophes were absent from all but the earliest years of American settlement, except in so far as the native Americans were themselves decimated by disease, famine and war. The catastrophic decline in native population cleared the way for the white settler. The demographic history of the white settlers in America was one of continuous upward movement. Setbacks were rare even for small areas and immigration assisted in the replacement of scarce human capital.

Russia on the other hand experienced a medieval or pre-modern demographic pattern. Catalogues of shocks show the repeated onset of famine, epidemic or war. Very pronounced bunching of such peaks occurred in particular from the Black Death through to the first decades of the fifteenth century and again from 1550 through to about 1620. It seems evident that population in the first case only reached its precatastrophe peak after 150 to 200 years and in the second after 150 years. Shorter periods of catastrophe occurred at the time of the Mongol invasion in the middle of the thirteenth century and at the end of the seventeenth century.

It is interesting to speculate that despite the low density of Russian population ecological pressures built up in the period preceding the two main catastrophes. Because of the poor resource environment such pressures appeared at a low level of the man-to-land ratio. The dramatic increase in the price of foodstuffs relative to other prices in the sixteenth century is clear evidence of such a pressure (Blum 1961). Pressure of this kind does not cause a catastrophe but makes a population much more vulnerable to shocks, particularly in an extremely unstable environment.

On the basis of the remarks about the degree of ecological pressure and the onset of catastrophe, two speculative propositions are worth making. Firstly the ending of the Russian pattern of catastrophe — excepting some reassertions temporarily in the nineteenth century as a result of political breakdown and war — is associated with the opening up of the fertile steppe area, which began to be cleared for agricultural purposes only in the eighteenth century. A phenomenal increase in population of the steppe began, matched by a growing emphasis on the steppe as a source of agricultural output. However, it is easy to exaggerate the importance of inter-regional trade in Russia as well as in America (Munting 1979). The expansion of food supplies allowed a massive increase in population, although the movement into semi-arid lands did not reduce the size of harvest fluctuations. The turning over of the steppe eradicated the burrows of the allegedly plague-carrying rodents. The eighteenth century therefore sees the reduction to insignificance of two major sources of shock, the plague and the Tartars, and some easing of the ecological pressures arising from the growth of population in the poor environment of the centre.

In a phased sequence catastrophes cease in the early eighteenth century; national shocks disappear with the construction of the railways in the second third of the nineteenth century. Regional shocks, however, continue right into the twentieth century. By contrast America never experiences more than local shocks.

Secondly the timing of catastrophe increased its impact on institutions and attitudes in Muscovy. The early catastrophes increased the cutthroat competition between principalities, particularly for labour. The period of expansion from 1450 to 1550 occurred simultaneously with the rise of Muscovy to dominance, thereby assisting in the achievement and retention of that dominance. The second long catastrophe acted as a background to Muscovy's consolidation of power. Muscovy's formative period was thereby strongly influenced by shock and risk. In particular control over the increasingly scarce factor of production, labour, became critical. Not for the last time significant deurbanisation also occurred.

There can be little doubt that Russian society was more 'shocked' than American — more frequently, more severely, more extensively and more inopportunely.

5

Pioneer Risk

ITS NATURE

The Americans had no desire to be neighbours to the Indians; the war whoop and the tomahawk were realistic enough in grandfathers' tales. The fevers and agues that visited pioneer clearings were also well known. Moreover, the journey was long and costly, at least in time and supplies. The planting of one season was lost and a year of hand-to-mouth living was inevitable.
Hansen, in arguing that the western advance was not inevitable.

In present societies in general, the variability of the harvest is probably a better index of living standards than the absolute size of the harvest. For those living near the subsistence level, it is far more important to be reasonably sure of getting by, than to aim for a high average standard of living.

Smith and Christian

This was not a regulated, systematic agriculture, but a sort of agricultural roulette.

Sergei Tolstoy (son of Leo)

Risk arises from the existence of shocks whose general incidence is expected but whose exact timing is unpredictable. Such risk brings long-term economic costs over and above losses arising directly from the shocks themselves. It seemed appropriate to label the short-run costs arising as part of the immediate impact of a shock, the direct costs. The indirect impact of shocks relates to the risk environment which they constitute; it may be far more significant than the direct costs. The indirect costs arise from adjustments in attitudes and institutions which cause both to be less efficient in promoting growth. Institution and attitudes are adjusted either to help modify the impact of the shock or redistribute the cost. Considerable, if recent, evidence suggests that irregular shocks are often ignored unless repeated reminders of potential threat are made. In this context the plateau level of mortality is highly relevant since it conditions the attitude to shocks. Similarly low harvest yields remind the vulnerable of famine since repeated spring shortages act as a dress rehearsal for the real thing. There may very well be a frequency of shock below which the perception of risk falls abruptly.

In chapter four we have already established the following background information. The 'average' Russian was severely disadvantaged by the greater incidence of shocks and their concentration as catastrophes. In both cases, however, the pioneer was faced with an especially high risk environment, uncertainty being compounded by ignorance. Pioneer risk is defined as a particular mix of risk elements inherent in the natural environment subject to opening up and its associated social setting, risk elements which involve the possibility of economic loss but in the ultimate case threaten life itself. Pioneer risk is significant in setting a maximum to density of settlement; in the extreme case settlement is impossible and that maximum is zero. Clearly some element of natural risk exists at all times but it has been one of the achievements of economic development to reduce the incidence and impact of the underlying shocks.

The potential of pioneer risk for shaping a society, or more particularly an economy, is greatest during the formative period. Since the nature of each shock and the exact combination of shocks in the historical experience of a particular area differ so significantly, the long-term impact can be evaluated only by examining the unique historical experience of individual societies.

Since by the end of its formative period America was well into the transition to the commercial phase, implying thereby a marked reduction in pioneer risk, except as a local problem on the frontier, and even some reduction in commercial risk, its institutions and attitudes reflected the problems of a market economy. Russia on the other hand failed to contain the impact of pioneer shocks before the end of the formative period and its attitudes and institutions have continued to show their influence through to the present.

Risk is of its nature unmeasurable. Even as a crude proxy for risk the measurement of the incidence of particular shocks lacks both theoretical validity and empirical precision. The evaluation of impact is only a little better. In principle the calculation of direct costs is possible but the lack of historical data largely rules this out for any period prior to the twentieth century. A problem more significant yet arises; mortality rates, indeed any alternative index, reflect to some degree the success of an economy in mitigating the sources of risk. Two economies subject to the same risk environment could show very different levels of economic cost or mortality according to their success in mitigating such risk.

In the absence of a detailed record of incidence we have had to lean heavily on crude comparisons. The descriptive comparison of shocks, as outlined in chapter four, serves as a specification, albeit vague, of the relevant risk environments.

Government is as vulnerable as the individual economic agent to the vagaries of shocks. In a poor resource environment a government may have little choice but to adopt institutional mechanisms to transfer the cost of risk to others. In a better environment the role of government may be more positive in reducing the incidence of shocks or providing some kind of insurance against such shocks. The government's ability to contain shocks or spread their costs depends on the technology of communications and transport and on its organisational structure.

On the whole both governments and historians with a particular interest in the formers' activities, have tended to direct their attention to the risk peaks. The concurrent outbreak of war, disease and famine might threaten the very survival of a particular government. Even the existence of a high background level of risk in a poor resource environment can weaken the government's administrative structure. In these circumstances the onset of a peak inevitably imposes on a government with limited control and financial resources, crisis measures which in turn impose the government on the populace as a fresh source of risk. Individual economic agents may have to learn to adjust institutions, attitudes and behaviour to such unpredictable government actions as grain confiscation, land seizures, forced loans, abrupt tax changes, recruitment levies. Indeed even normally rational responses to disease, such as quarantine, can appear as an attack by the government on the people. For the Russian peasants, as R.E.F. Smith has noted, 'Their struggle with nature was hard, at times brutal, but they often evidently felt it was not as hard as the exactions and injustices imposed on them by the state' (Smith 1977: 221). A poor resource environment, a high level of background risk, frequent and pronounced peaks, all these factors, made the Russian government unable to deal with particular risk elements at the appropriate level of administration and made it likely that inconsistency of government administration and policy would be perceived by the peasants as an additional element of risk.

Epidemic disease neatly highlights the danger of secondary risk and thereby in particular the relationship between government and governed. In both Russia and America it might be expected that the merchant, out of self interest, and the poor, out of ignorance, would oppose measures taken to contain epidemics. In Russia epidemics revealed the deep-seated deficiencies of provincial administration, making plain the rudimentary mechanism of government authority at the local level. More serious there was, as Alexander notes, a popular identification of public servants with exploitation and persecution, in the context of which any government measures were likely to be counter-productive. This led Alexander to conclude that, although no medical assistance was given in the plague outbreak of 1654, 'Paradoxically such neglect may have been no more damaging to Moscow than was the anti-plague campaign of 1771' (Alexander 1980: 254). In the 1829 cholera outbreak the measures taken made, in McGrew's words, 'the anti-cholera campaign appear to be a full-scale attack on the people' (McGrew 1965: 69). McGrew went on to say that Kursk and the neighbouring provinces suffered as much from the anti-cholera campaign as they did from the epidemic itself and that areas actually hit by cholera ceased to be functioning parts of the empire. Violent and strong animosity was felt towards the doctors. Nothing quite so dramatic was found in America, although tensions did arise over inoculation and quarantine (Duffy 1953, 1968; Blake 1959). In Russia the government was not only ineffective, it was itself conceived as a threat, which made its economic policies doubly difficult to implement.

Jones has stressed the positive role of government in Europe in disaster management. Clearly this role was an important one. However, our comparison between America and Russia illustrates both the positive role assumed by American governments, on the western European pattern, and the negative role forced on Russian government by a less favourable resource endowment.

That the Russian government could act in a positive way to mitigate the impact of shocks is illustrated by the famine of 1891–2, successfully managed by the government with the aid of the railways and improved communications (Robbins 1975; Simms 1976: 77). The lasting legacy of the image of government as threat is shown by the distortion of the government's role in this famine. Even the positive elements of government policy could be interpreted in a negative way. As suggested above any shock highlights the nature of the relations between the governors and the governed, either strengthening these relations in a positive way, or making a successful cooperation unlikely.

The same argument might be extended to other groups in Russian society. The government did not have a complete monopoly of coercive power. Others also wished to pass on the costs of shocks and the associated risk. In particular serf owners or landlords, in so far as they could dictate the terms of their economic relations with the serfs, shaped them so as to minimise their own risk.

The same argument applies to slave owners and slaves in America. Even after emancipation the blacks in the south largely continued to produce cotton despite the terrible risks of natural shock, particularly the attacks of the bollweevil, or market fluctuations. They cultivated a cash crop rather than a subsistence crop, because their creditors minimised their own risk by forcing the sharecroppers to continue with cotton. The market is not the location of contract-making between equal partners, it is not a neutral venue; it is often simply another occasion for the concealed exercise of coercive power.

Although a high risk environment may not discourage gambling with the prospect of a high immediate pay-off, it will almost certainly discourage activities whose pay-off is spread over a long period. The closer to a minimum subsistence the greater the discouragement.

Economic development is the result of decisions which demand the incurring of costs now and the reaping of benefits later; any investment, whether in fixed, working or even human capital, is of this kind. The problem of decision-making can be conceptualised as the application of an implicit rate of time discount or time horizon to these future streams of costs and benefits. Uncertainty or risk clearly influences the evaluation of benefits but it impinges most dramatically on the choice of time discount or time horizon. Despite an interest in promoting the wellbeing of children, a short average life expectancy must be associated with a short implicit time horizon for decisions involving such economic activities. The next section looks at the question of life expectancy, implicit time horizons and ill health.

LIFE EXPECTANCY, TIME HORIZONS AND ILL HEALTH

Part of the American population was the most future-oriented of any in the world.

Cochran

Toute nouveauté les effraye.

Scherer of the Russians

Clearly the risk environment influenced economic decision-making. The problem is to conceptualise the relationship between the two. Average life expectancy might act as an index of the degree of threat to human life represented by the risk environment. Considerable variability is usually associated with a low level of life expectancy. Plainly individuals could not ignore the risk of early demise; uncertainty itself would also tend to focus attention on the present and away from the future.

Differences in the timing of costs or benefits can be reconciled by using a rate of time discount or more simply a time horizon, equivalent to a target pay-off period. The relationship between average life expectancy and the time horizon of economic decision-making would seem on *a priori* grounds to be a positive one but one in which, at low expectancies, an increase would have a more than proportionate impact on time horizon. Clearly whether the same relationship holds in comparing different societies depends on the structure of attitudes, in the current jargon, the *mentalités* of the two societies.

Figure 5.1: Relationship between life expectancy and economic time horizon

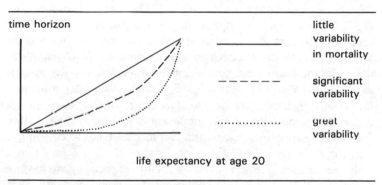

time horizon

———— little variability in mortality

— — — — significant variability

················ great variability

life expectancy at age 20

In conditions of certainty that each individual will live the average life span and in the absence of short-term variations in the life span, the time horizon should coincide with the average life expectancy, that is, lie on the 45° line (Figure 5.1). As uncertainty and variability increase the line bulges outwards. For simplicity we ignore the possiblity that the time horizon might change over time.

Given the crude data available for most societies before the twentieth century, demographers have found it difficult to calculate average life expectations, except in a handful of local family-reconstitution studies. Calculation of average life expectation demands a close knowledge of age-specific death rates, which are commonly lacking. Crude mortality rates are often used as a measure of the incidence of disease, although they reflect both age-specific rates and the age structure of the population.

The age structure of a population, whether at the national or the local level, can be significantly affected by immigration. In the USA, where immigration was at times very considerable (Davis *et al* 1972: 123), its influence on mortality rates is on balance probably upwards. There is considerable evidence that immigrants had a markedly lower life expectancy than natives. The youthful age of immigrants fails to offset the problems of 'seasoning' in a new disease environment and the higher age-specific mortality rates characteristic of the immigrants. The extremely high mortality in eighteenth century Philadelphia, particularly striking by colonial American standards, has been explained by its importance as the main port of immigrant entry (B.G. Smith 1977). Cycles of mortality in the largest cities of late nineteenth century America have been explained by cycles in immigration (Higgs 1979). The death rate of children of foreign-born women has been found in particular case studies to be significantly above that of the children of native-born women (Haines 1977). Such a contrast is easily explicable in terms of the rigours of passage (Duffy 1951), the poor economic standing and location of immigrant communities and the exposure to a new disease environment (McNeill 1977). One implication is that the life expectancy of the native American population must have been even larger than the figures available suggest, particularly for periods when immigration was significant. The risk environment of the native population is more relevant to economic change since economic decision-making, wealth and income tends to be concentrated in their hands.

In the absence of complete tables for life expectancy we have to use the few figures available supplemented by crude mortality rates. Moreover we also have to rely mainly on life expectancy at birth since there are even fewer figures for life expectancy at the age of 20. The latter are more relevant to the formation of attitudes or the establishment of an implicit time horizon for economic decisions. Because of high infant and child mortality significant differences can exist between these expectations. Moreover in recent times the major gains have occurred at birth rather than at age 20. Minor differences between

Russia and America could possibly involve differences in the level of infant or child mortality, although this is unlikely since these are usually a good index of general mortality. Both societies were characterised by high infant or child mortality until very much later. Some significant killers hit in particular the 15 to 30 age group, tuberculosis being a case in point. Moreover for TB, as for pneumonia and bronchitis and for diarrhoea and enteritis, the age from five to 15 has been the golden age for resistance, although for the latter two groups a dramatic rise in mortality occurs rather later than for TB.

Wigglesworth's corrected life tables provide us with a figure of 35.5 years as the average expectation at birth in Massachusetts and New Hampshire in 1790, rising to 39.4 in 1850 (Vinovskis 1971). There is some evidence that the former is an underestimate. The most likely figures for male life expectancy in the USA appear to be 41 in the 1850s and over 53 in 1915 (Meeker 1972), although it has been argued that the expectancy deteriorated in the first half of the nineteenth century. The only figure for Russia is based on the 1896 census and gives an average expectation of 29.3 years for European Russia and 31.4 for the Russian Europe as a whole (Rashin 1956). Very little earlier demographic work has been done on Russia. Hoch's work on the Petrovskoe estate of the Gargarins in Tambov province yielded a mean expectation of life at birth of 27.3 years. Clearly a very large gap existed between Russian and American life expectancies, one which differences in infant and child mortality alone could hardly have closed.

Some information on life expectation at age 20 exists for seventeenth century America, which graphically illustrates the extent of possible difference in time horizon (D.S. Smith 1972; Vinovskis 1972). The data for New England in the seventeenth and eighteenth centuries show that an average person of 20 could expect to live to nearly 60, unless he lived in Salem or Boston, while rural inhabitants could expect to live well beyond 60. In seventeenth century Plymouth, Ipswich and Andover the average expectation reached as high as 68, 66 and almost 65 respectively. There is some evidence that these expectations are exaggerated (Fischer 1978). By contrast in Charles Parish, Virginia, the average 20-year-old could expect to reach only 40, a Maryland immigrant little more and a native Marylander or inhabitant of Middlesex, Virginia, his or her late 40s. Even in the relatively healthy colonial America substantial differences existed. By 1860 the average life expectancy of any American aged 21 was 40 years (Vinovskis 1972); that is, they could expect to live into their 60s.

105

In a stable population average life expectancy is identical to the reciprocal of the crude death rate. For a growing population in which mortality was evenly distributed a calculation of average life expectancy on the basis of existing crude death rates would exaggerate expectancies. On the other hand a high concentration of mortality in the early years of life would reduce the gap. A quick check of the predictions for America and Russia on the basis of the crude death rates for years in which calculated life expectancies exist shows a large and growing gap for America but a very small one for Russia. This is probably explicable by less pronounced infant and childhood mortality in America than Russia, particularly during the nineteenth century, in itself a reasonable index of general mortality, and by the impact of more immigrants.

Table 5.1: Actual and predicted life expectancies

USA	Actual	'Predicted'	CDR
1790	35.5	over 40	20-25/1,000
1850s	41	47	21.3/1,000
1915	over 53	69	14.4/1,000
Russia	Actual	'Predicted'	CDR
1896-7 (European)	29.3	31	32.5/100
(whole Empire)	31.4	32	32/1,000

Sources: Potter (1965); Rashin (1956).

'Predicted' life expectancy could therefore be regarded as an approximation of actual for the early period when high early mortality offset the impact of rapidly growing population. On the basis of mortality rates of 25 and 40/1,000, the respective life expectancies would be 40 and 25. This would appear to be a minimum difference for the early part of the formative period, particularly as the difference at the end of the nineteenth century was 20 years. If the mortality rate were 20/1,000 in colonial America and 45/1,000 in late sixteenth century Muscovy the difference would widen to almost 30 years. The effect of different assumptions on the length of an economically useful life would appear to be similar, since life expectation at age 20 appears in most societies to be similar to expectation at birth. The most likely difference, on average, must approach 20 years.

A number of other considerations reinforce the significance of this gap. First, the more volatile behaviour of mortality rates in Russia increased the degree of risk associated with a given average life expectancy. In other words, the 'average' citizen might behave as if the average life expectancy were significantly lower than it actually was. The Russian case corresponds to line c in Figure 5.1: by contrast, in the American case to line a.

Secondly, the high concentration of urban population in Moscow and St Petersburg within the Russian Empire created a particularly virulent disease environment, whereas the much smaller size of American cities until the nineteenth century reduced these differences. Urban/rural differences were greater in Russia than in America. Certain economically important groups residing in the towns, such as merchants or artisans, were much more vulnerable to death, notably in their early years before success might allow them to quit high-risk environments.

The arguments advanced so far have been that the risk environment was significant in both areas but that the risk of death was far higher in both rural and urban Russia.,

Differences in the level of interest rates provide indirect evidence that greater risk is linked to differences in time horizons. Homer has noted the saucer-like shape of the curve graphing the behaviour of interest rates during the rise and fall of empires, very much in accordance with changes in the risk environment associated with the establishment and extension of a stable environment and its breakdown later. Unhappily other influences impinge on interest rates, particularly short-term interest rates. There is no doubt that official rates were higher in Russia than America although these rates are untypical. The rates applicable to private transactions are the relevant ones. Strictly speaking lending at interest was illegal in Russia until 1754, when a maximum was set as low as six per cent. In the seventeenth century wealthy merchants, landowners and monasteries charged rates anywhere between 30 and 120 per cent p.a. In the eighteenth century private credit still cost 10 to 40 per cent p.a., with short-term rates as high as one per cent per week, a very significant improvement. Does this suggest a marked reduction in risk? Certainly other factors expanding the supply of funds were absent.

Part of the new orthodoxy, however, stresses fertility rather than mortality as mainly responsible for the great upturn in West European populations, and links Europe's primacy in economic development with the ability to adapt fertility to economic circumstances, mainly but not wholly through the age and frequency of marriage.

On this argument the massive and sustained rise in European population reflected improved economic opportunities, but this still leaves the improved economic opportunities unexplained. The current argument would explain these improved opportunities as a consequence of an extended time horizon, resulting from both a longer average life expectation and the removal of periodic epidemic crises. Comparison of Russia and America illustrates the argument by contrasting a context of a long life expectancy with few local demographic crises, with a context of short life expectancy and frequent, severe demographic crises.

There is little doubt that death was a very real threat. Even in New England written evidence displays a great concern with the possibility of death (Vinovskis 1979). In an environment of large families and small dwellings, death was inevitably close. In cultures which accepted the permanent presence of death there can be little doubt that economic decision-making was influenced by this acceptance.

These conclusions are reinforced by the impact of a relatively high rate of illness. Mortality was only the tip of the iceberg. There is little doubt that there was a close correlation between mortality and morbidity. To be old was to be wracked by illness. The ageing process was accelerated in a hostile environment. The agony of old age could bring on, what has aptly been termed a *tedium vitae*, weariness with life. It was not only the aged who were reduced to economic impotence. Disease affected all age groups equally.

Debilitating diseases such as malaria, tuberculosis or scurvy discouraged risk-taking by reducing mental agility and physical energy. Malaria was not simply a killer; indeed its destructive mortality receded over time. it has been described, however, as 'the mother of inertia and poverty' (Lillard 1973: 95), 'the great debilitator' (Rutman and Rutman 1976: 50), lowering the level of general health and the ability to resist other diseases, such as dysentery. As a consequence millions lived enervated, socially unproductive lives. For example, a connection between the incidence of malaria and agricultural decline has been noted in early Italy (Cloudsley-Thompson 1976). Tuberculosis could have the same kind of impact. Often the onset of the disease was protracted.

The nature of the diet even in normal times exposed many Russians, especially pioneers in the forested areas, to deficiency diseases. The heavy stress on the consumption of calories in the forms of cereals (60 per cent) and the lack of fresh meat, or emphasis on salt meat, and the importance of fermented or preserved foods, led to a need to counteract scurvy (Christian 1980). The frequent use of acid drinks like *kvass* or sour dishes (*kislota*) was very important. The lack of kislota was reflected in the amount of work done, in the health and even in the mood of the workers. The diet of Sibiryaks and their predecessors in the northern forests, consisting largely of fish, game, wildfowl, berries and nuts, was deficient in vitamin C and B. Especially in spring, scurvy was a constant companion of the Siberian pioneers, and a frequent visitor throughout Russia after below-average harvests. The greater the scarcity of good agricultural land, the greater the problem; the forested taiga was a particularly dangerous environment in this respect. Berriberri and pellagra also added to the general debilitation and underpinned the reputation of the Sibiryaks for indolence.

The emphasis on the consumption of rye bread created its own problems. Malnutrition is not simply a result of a lack of proper nutrients. It also involves the presence of harmful substances in the food. A notable example is fungi-produced poisoning from so-called mycotoxicoses in grain, particularly rye (Matossian 1984). Mortality from ergotism epidemics can be high: as high as 41.5 per cent of those with symptoms in nineteenth-century Russia (Matossian 1984:673). More relevant were Fusarium toxins associated with the fungal attack which endangered the immune system of the body in a condition described by Soviet researchers as alimentary toxic aleikia.

There is no doubt that malnutrition affects physical capabilities, but in this context even more importantly mental agility. Malnutrition among children can permanently impair the capacity of the brain.

Malaria and scurvy represent particularly debilitating diseases but often death from other disease followed a protracted period of illness. A general lethargy induced by disease reduces the possibility of a positive attitude to risk reduction or management. Apathy and fatalism are common in a severe disease environment.

Death destroyed scarce human capital; sickness reduced the efficiency or productivity of labour. Risk through the length of the relevant time horizon can influence a whole range of economic decisions creating a society that is present-oriented and organised primarily to reduce or manage the main sources of risk. The early death of fathers might give the sons early autonomy, but the juxtaposition of early control over wealth and a high risk environment was likely to encourage a wasteful use of resources. In America where resources were relatively abundant, conditions of high risk produced a perverse combination of high mortality and conspicuous consumption. As Diane Sydenham has written, 'South Carolina was well known for its lavish life style and unhealthy climate' (1980). A contrast based on similar factors has been cogently drawn between Virginia and New England (Dunn 1972). It is interesting to note that in the formative period significant differences existed within the American colonies, differences which might very well be associated with the different pattern of economic development experienced later.

RESPONSES, INDIVIDUAL AND GOVERNMENTAL

The impact of shocks and risk reflects not only the incidence of shocks but also the nature of the response by individual economic agents or governments. A strong and positive response may compensate for a more frequent incidence, or even a greater severity, of shocks and moderate a potentially hostile risk environment. Moreover secular growth may of itself diminish the significance of risk.

There were clearly different levels of response to the risk environment. First, risk impinged on the specific decisions of individual economic agents. Such decisions related to a whole series of areas — to production, consumption or investment, to occupation, to nuptiality or fertility. Secondly there were the responses specific to shock or disaster management which occurred as a result of individual, group or government action. Thirdly, since risk permeated the whole structure of attitudes and institutions, the nature of the risk environment influenced the very principles on which society came to be organised. In particular it affected the locus of decision-making and the nature of the interaction between government and market. The particular combination of resources and risk could lead either to a stress on centralised decision-making through government agencies or to decentralised decision-making through the market.

In this section we deal briefly with the response of individual economic agents. The main part is concerned with the responses specific to shock management and its role in opening up. Part 3 introduces the wider issues.

Pioneer risk discouraged investment through a higher implicit rate of time discount; consumption was encouraged at the expense of investment, whether in fixed plant or equipment, buildings, working or human capital. The extent of this influence must be spelled out.

High risk promoted what we might call the rapid-replacement economy. The use of more durable but more expensive materials was discouraged. For example, housing tended to be constructed of cheap but highly inflammable building materials, wood and thatch, wattle and daub. The absence of brick, stone or tile increased vulnerability to fire. Costs were minimised over a short time horizon but not over a long one. Typically a strong divergence between social and private returns existed since a severe fire would still consume a property of fire-resistant materials built amid inflammable properties. Some collective corrective action was necessary. Furthermore, crude home-constructed furniture, clothing or tools were preferred over long-lived items purchased on the market.

A high risk environment also discouraged investment in human capital. The choice of occupation or economic activity was guided by the considerations that early returns were very much more valuable than late returns. The acquisition of skill or knowledge took time. The long learning process involved in developing techniques of successful market operations, or in developing a profitable skill implied that many of the fruits of success were likely to be reaped towards the end of a career. The loss of ten years or more at the end of a successful career removed a more than proportionate share of benefits. Thereby specialisation was discouraged. Some correlation has also been discovered between life expectancy and expenditure on schooling (Jones 1981b). Significantly at the beginning of the nineteenth century, over 20 per cent of the white population attended school in the USA whereas only two per cent did in Russia. Again public action was often considered necessary.

Risk also encouraged and perpetuated economic polarisation of wealth. Where labour was scarce, identured labour, serfs or slaves were an important form of capital; hence the intervention of owners to encourage universal and early marriage. The severe mortality of a high risk environment threatened the small men for whom the loss of an indentured labourer, a slave or serf was crucial. Possession of a large labour force was itself a protection against risk.

In a high risk society there is also a vicious circle in the relationship between economic opportunity and population. E.L. Jones has suggested a heavily shocked society requires people for recovery; they may be the only useful resourse available. Certainly in Russia there was strong pressures to regulate nuptiality in order to increase the number of births. A deterioration in economic activity often led to an increase in such pressure.

Direct but positive responses to risk can be classified either as shock mitigation or shock management, involving both deliberate and unconscious adjustments. Shock mitigation involves the reduction of the economic impact of a shock. While it is to some degree a by-product of economic development, the crucial contention advanced in this book is that it is also a necessary precondition for that develop ment. In our terminology shock mitigation precedes phase movement. Shock management involves largely short-term efforts to spread the cost of shocks. Over the long run institutional risk-sharing arrangements may evolve imperceptibly to suit particular risk environments. Effective short-term shock management however requires either a low risk environment or significant previous risk mitigation.

The simplest form of risk management involves an informal spreading of risk beyond the affected groups, although this naturally leaves unaffected the aggregate losses incurred. Mutual help has existed in all societies, whether it takes the form of some crude insurance against fire provided by neighbours assisting to rebuild by their own labour or materials, as in colonial America, or more institutionalised mechanisms such as repartition of land to spread the tax burden, as in Russia. High risk levels, low incomes and inadequate statistical data preclude more formal insurance. In a very real sense insurance is a consequence of previous shock mitigation or risk reduction and general economic development. When fire insurance made its entrance into late colonial and early republican America it was of necessity accompanied by government efforts at shock mitigation. Insurance was imported into Russia as a foreign service only in the middle of the nineteenth century. Equally the smoothing out of fluctuations in individual income by the use of credit is precluded by the poor development of the capital market and by extremely high rates of interest, rates which in themselves reflect a high risk environment. In a pre-insurance world of high interest rates where mutual self-help cannot cope with shock management, only self-insurance or government action can be effective, usually the latter.

Government actions tend to precede economic development; the actions of individual economic agents are part of that development. For example governments may reform rural organisations or promote transport improvement in order to expand and redistribute food supplies. At the individual level the latter also results from improved methods of cultivation and the introduction of new foods. The government could take action to contain disease by organising quarantine or vaccination, by providing medical services, municipal water or sewerage works. Improved housing, clothing or food supplies would have the same effect. Again appropriate laws, effective defence, an efficient policing and legal system are the concern of governments, but improved incomes or employment opportunities may also help reduce violence, although increasing the range of temptations. Fire is contained with the help of government regulations on the use of non-combustible materials and the provision of suitable fire-fighting equipment or fire services, or simply by an improvement in building materials.

Also invariably these public goods cannot be supplied by the market because of divergences in social and private benefits or costs, indivisibilities in investment, or differences in the rate of time discount. A virtuous circle results from their provision since the other individual actions follow.

Appropriate here is a brief analysis of shock mitigation and management in the three chosen areas of study: famine, disease and violence.

Individual producers and governments in Russia clearly responded to the difficulties arising from harvest failure. The simplest act of shock management would have been for individuals or goverment bodies to build up carry-over stocks in years of good harvests, stocks sufficient to take the economy through the bad years. Why were attempts by the government to create such stocks, or to persuade other to take the appropriate action, so unsuccessful? Kahan has suggested that the savings implication, a minimum ten per cent savings ratio, to cover a harvest failure once every ten years, represents the very limit of what peasants could manage. Dando agrees that in most regions of grain surplus, a year's stock was the maximum peasant households could afford and that as a consequence, in the majority of regions deficient in grain, stocks were minimal. He continues that serf owners or large landowners did not normally maintain substantial grain stocks specifically for famine relief (Dando 1980: 85). Indeed, while others, landlords or governments, might be better able to bear the cost, in a poor economy the burden was likely to be heavy. In a context of high interest rates the opportunity cost of such a policy was enormous. In the absence of good transport the total stocks held would rise with the variability of the local harvest.

The cost in provision of adequate storage facilities was an additional burden, facilities underutilised most of the time because of the very fluctuations in the harvest. An abundant harvest often rotted in the fields of Russia for want of sufficient harvesters. The greater wetness of the Russian core accelerated spoilage there. In the absence of good storage facilities spoilage was a major problem.

Probably more important, peasant producers were reluctant to accumulate visible surpluses, which could be taken by landlord or governmet. Before 1861 the arbitrariness of serfdom allowed the former much scope to take advantage of the situation. Government policy, allowing tax arrears to accumulate in bad times as a shock management device imposed on them by necessity, regarded surpluses as a means by which such arrears could be reduced. The peasants reacted in two main ways, by deliberately over-producing grain in the hope that production above the requirements of an average year ensured a bare minimum in a bad year, and by storing and consuming any surplus as liquor, often illegally. Alcoholic drinks, such as kvass or vodka, were a means of storing cereals for a relatively long period, though an important source of calories alcohol can worsen the threat of scurvy by destroying vitamin C in the body. However, these drinks were often cleaner than the water available, therefore sometimes a lesser threat to health. Drinking is both an index of a present-oriented and a practice which is unlikely to promote economic activities associated with long time horizons.

The whole organisation of Russian agriculture was permeated by the influence of risk aversion. The tenacious attachment to the strip farming of the three-field system in the core was premissed on the local nature of climatic disaster and fungal attacks (Confino 1969; compare with McCloskey 1976). The main response to a poor resource and risk environment was the dangerous tendency to a monoculture induced by low yields, poor transport and uniform climate. Crop diversification moderates harvest fluctuations since individual crops respond to particular weather conditions in a differing manner. The tendency to a monoculture is scarcely surprising in that Central Russia was characterised by poor transport and adverse natural conditions, the combination most likely to lead to a grain monoculture. Where transport was good and other conditions adverse as, say, in New England, or the northern Chesapeake, diversification of agriculture was a more likely response, since any small surplus could easily be marketed and major harvest failures met by imports. Where transport was poor and other conditions favourable, as in the forest-steppe zone of Russia, or where both sets of conditions were favourable, as in the Middle Colonies, either diversification or a monoculture was possible, depending upon demand conditions.

The Russian grain market, characterised by low price and income elasticity of income and price, by great variability of supply and by market fragmentation arising from high transport costs, often experienced enormous price fluctuations and persistent regional differences (Tegoborskii 1855–6). Even these price differences were often insufficient to generate the saving flow of grain imports. Indeed the target consumption of the 'Chayanov' household implied a reduction in marketings when prices, and therefore incomes, were high and an increase when prices were low. Such aggregate behaviour promoted self-sufficiency even further.

In the context of a grain monoculture, when the harvest was

deficient the government's budgetary situation was apt to deteriorate significantly. Moreover, the weakness of government administration made it very difficult to collect taxes. The institution of collective responsibility and the development of the commune with its repartitional functions were reactions of the government and peasant to this situation. The lack of administrative control helped to direct the government to the use of the landowner and the commune as government surrogates. Such institutional arrangements operated in the long run to slow the rate of economic development, by limiting mobility and breaking the link between an individual and a particular piece of land, including its improvements. It is not accidental that these institutional forms appeared in a country with a relatively malign natural environment vulnerable to severe harvest fluctuations.

The main response to primary risk lay therefore in the tendency to a monoculture, to overproduction of grain, and the late retention of strip farming within the three-field system. Superimposed on the primary risk was secondary risk reflecting the government's attempts to protect its own position. The response to secondary risk took the form of storing grain as alcohol, of widespread repartition of land and of collective responsibility for tax payments.

From the fifteenth century onwards the Russian government, in an attempt to alleviate the short-run problem, took measures to spread the impact or cost of harvest failure. Such measures included accumulation of food and cash reserves in areas particularly vulnerable; the making of grain or money loans; public works to provide employment; the restriction of grain exports and promotion of internal grain movement; the support of accumulation of relief funds abroad and internally (Dando 1980: 85). However the efficiency of such measures was severely limited by transport and administrative difficulties, the more so the earlier the period.

Risk of this kind also acted as a brake on commercialisation of the economy by encouraging self-sufficiency and discouraging either diversification or the emergence of cash crops. The appearance of second-generation staples could only occur after significant transport improvement when either a large potential grain surplus was released with a rush, as in the 1860s and 1970s (White 1975), or when new areas of cultivation could safely move from grain to other forms of production, as with cotton in Russian Central Asia or butter and eggs in western Siberia (Spring, in White 1975).

Disease is much more superficially arbitrary in its incidence, but did stimulate major attempts to mitigate its impact. The vulnerability of the American ports to epidemic disease promoted attempts of

115

varying success to moderate mortality. Even in Philadelphia the death rate fell to the mid-30s per 1,000 at the end of the 1760s and below 30/1,000 by the early 1820s. From 1760 the city joined other major American cities in their experience of a significant rate of natural increase of population. A decline in mortality from smallpox underpins this decline, which may be due to the extension of inoculation. The effectiveness of inoculation in containing smallpox is controversial but its success in Boston seems difficult to refute. The initial tests in 1721 were followed by a steadily increasing number of inoculations. In 1721 only two per cent of smallpox cases were due to inoculation, in 1730 ten per cent, 1752 28 per cent and in 1764 87 per cent, when the poor were inoculated for the first time, but the benefits of inoculation usually outweighed the costs and resulted in a very marked decline in the average death rate. By 1792 97 per cent of cases were a result of inoculation. Vaccination also spread very quickly after Jenner's work and the first general vaccination in the USA in Milton in 1809. Boston saw general vaccination in 1816 and 1824, between which dates not a single death from smallpox is recorded. Fortunately, as Blake asserts, smallpox was among the few common acute infectious diseases transmitted by contact or close proximity to the sick in which the phenomenon of the well-carrier is apparently unknown. In other words direct contacts could easily be traced. This made it possible with efficient organisation to make smallpox an epidemic disease.

Quarantine arrangements, if effective, as in Boston where immigration was slight during the eighteenth century, also helped to stop regular outbreaks of disease. Elsewhere, as in Philadelphia, this was not the case. In Boston temporary quarantines were introduced as early as 1649 and 1665. The first attempt to introduce a general quarantine came in 1700, but was only really successful after a pesthouse was established on Spectacle Island in 1717. An act of 1731–2 made notification of infectious diseases compulsory. A land quarantine was introduced in 1739. The quarantine system helped to exclude yellow fever as well as smallpox. There is no record of yellow fever in Boston from 1693 to the 1790s, and only minor outbreaks in 1798, 1802 and 1819. At the height of the yellow fever epidemic of 1798, the death rate in Boston was no higher than the usual rate in London.

The healthiness of a city was related to size and rate of growth, as much as to the nature of external contacts. Even in the eighteenth century, New York was said by Duffy to be 'still relatively clean and, compared with its European counterparts, quite healthy'. In 1700 New York's population was only 5,000, Boston's 6,700. Philadelphia had less than 5,000 as late as 1720. From the middle of the eighteenth century the population of New York and Philadelphia grew much more rapidly than Boston's. At the time of the Revolution, Philadelphia had over 32,000 inhabitants, New York 20,000 and Boston 15,000 to 16,000. By 1800 New York's population was more than double Boston's, 60,000 compared with 25,000 and another burst again doubled that population in the next 20 years. Partly as a consequence smallpox and yellow fever were much greater problems, smallpox killing five-to-eight per cent of the population in the 1730 outbreak and recurring quite frequently before the Revolutionary War. Yellow fever killed four per cent of the population 1798, though ten-to-twelve per cent in 1702.

It is no accident that mortality rates peaked in Philadelphia and New York during the period of fastest growth. Where immigration was significant and growth fast, quarantine arrangements were less effective. However, smallpox and yellow fever receded in importance, particularly after the last major outbreak of yellow fever between 1795 and 1805. After that date the ports of the South Atlantic and Gulf Coast were the hardest hit. In the nineteenth century the urban environment remained a relatively high risk environment, certainly until sewerage and water supply problems were solved by municipal action late in the nineteenth century.

The low incomes associated with the poor resource endowments of Russia prevented the development of an adequate medical profession and the general use of inoculation against smallpox which, propagandised by Catherine the Great, became a fashion limited to the small upper class elite. Even in America the high cost was an obstacle to the poor undergoing inoculation. Catherine the Great had herself inoculated against smallpox by a Scottish doctor, Dr Dimsdale. She is said to have kept a carriage and post-horses available so that he could flee the country in the event of some medical disaster which, fortunately, for both of them, did not occur (Hingley 1978: 116–7). Such a story is an interesting comment on the novelty of the operation but even more on the attitude of the populace to doctors.

Catherine at least went through the motions of providing the required public goods. As part of a general programme in which she made efforts to improve hygiene and sanitation, to reduce the risk of fire and industrial pollution and to improve drainage, she set up hospitals and apothecaries, centres in which inoculation against smallpox was dispensed. At first parents were even paid to bring in their children. Subsequently the practice was introduced into the national schools. Smallpox houses were set up in Kazan in 1771,

117

Irkutsk in 1772 and dealt with 15,500 in five years. The wealthy were usually inoculated at home. The total numbers by no means compared well with the American figures.

The vast unwieldy size of Russia meant that the frontiers were beyond effective centralised control. Indeed controls were difficult to maintain in the heart of European Russia. Russia's position astride some of the main disease routes from India, those of the plague and cholera for example, made this a matter of great significance.

The high degree of centralisation of government and the importance of military garrisons reinforced the great size of Moscow and St Petersburg and encouraged a significant degree of concentration of population. Moscow had a winter population of between 250,000 and 300,000 in the 1770s, St Petersburg 200,000 in 1788, both far larger than any contemporary American city. Enormous problems of overcrowding and the provision of municipal services were obvious, and a dense population very vulnerable to disease was thereby created.

The question of a response to violence raises the whole issue of the structure of the government. The size of the problem and the efficiency of the protecting institutions determined the level of protection costs and the degree of risk uncovered.

Nothing distinguishes America and Russia more than the attitude to, and the role of, the law and the army. There is an insoluble chicken and egg problem about the relationship between the level of violence and the efficiency of the protecting institutions. However, there is little doubt that Russian society was much more vulnerable to the threat of violence.

In a comprehensive way Russia was a lawless society. Justice was a branch of the administration, and as such its foremost concern was enforcing the government's will and protecting its interests (Pipes 1974: 288). The very concept of crime, as a failure to comply with the law rather than to obey the will of the ruler (governor, director of a factory), was first introduced only under Catherine, although it then took a long time to percolate through the law courts and society (Madariaga 1981: 557). Until then crimes perpetuated by one private person against another, or even by an official against a private person, were often traditionally regarded as matters of no public concern.

Until the 1860s Russian jurisprudence did not even recognise the distinction between laws, decrees and administrative ordinances, all of which, once approved by the sovereign, were treated with equal solemnity and entered in pitiless chronological order in the full collection of laws of 1830. However, between 1649 and 1830 there was no full law code. Each section of government dispensed justice

118

as part of its administrative obligations. Even the owners of large estates frequently legislated for their own private domains by drawing up their own codes which reflected customary law (Madariaga 1981: 94).

Indeed most of the fundamental laws affecting Russia's system of government and the status of its citzens were never promulgated at all in a formal way. Pipes gives an impressive list: the fixing of peasants to the soil and of urban inhabitants to the cities (*i.e.* serfdom); the principle that all secular land had to bear service; the introduction of the Oprichnina; the authority of landlords over the peasants; the rule that civil servants were to be automatically promoted on the basis of seniority (Pipes 1974: 289). Moreover laws did not need to be made public in order to become effective; they were often promulgated in confidential memoranda known only to the officials charged with their execution. There also existed many laws which were never applied in practice.

The attitude of Russian society and bureaucracy to law and justice has been neatly summarised by Madariaga: 'the very idea of legality, of a system of formal rules valid yesterday, today and tomorrow for everyone, was quite alien to Russian society at all levels.'

Even in the eighteenth century law at the governmental level was more like a moral ideal than a system of rules. That is why so many of the statutes of Russian law throughout the period 1711 to 1905 were not enforceable legal rules but exhortations to behave or work according to this or that ideal. Peter the Great in particular used the preambles of his abundant legislation as propaganda for his policy of westernisation and development. Ronald Hingley offers Catherine's Instruction and Nakaz of 1765–7 as an exercise in official *vranyo*, leg-pull or creative fantasy (Hingley 1978: 80). There was no prospect of any practical outcome to the harangues on the desirability of equality or justice.

There was in any event a general problem of law enforcement given the poor level of education of Russian officialdom. Even high officials failed to grasp the meaning of legality. The gentry generally despised the law, which they frquently took into their own hands. The concept of the primacy of law was somewhat alien to Russian political culture. Madariaga quotes an illustrative example in A. Radischev's *Journey from St Petersburg to Moscow* (p91 ff), in which a judge puts away his law books and acquits a serf of murdering a landowner because he was morally justified (Madariaga 1981: 558). The study of native law began only in the late 1780s. Wortman has noted the lack of trained lawyers for the administration of justice

119

and also for the actual drafting of the laws.

At the bottom of society, law was largely ignored and local customs accepted in its place. Corruption undermined the efficacy of what law did exist. Moreover the whole concept of law in Russia was idiosyncratic. Elsewhere law defined the no-go area and outside its boundaries the citizen was free to act as he chose. In Russia, unless a particular course of action was expressly sanctioned by the law, it was dangerous to undertake it. The law prescribed acceptable courses of conduct. All that was not specifically authorised was forbidden, and only that could be done which was specifically authorised.

As Raeff has asserted, Russia did not succeed until well into the nineteenth century in bringing about a modern legal consciousness and culture, with regularity of procedures, security of person and property, and respect for the law and its applications by autonomous institutions (Raeff 1982: 616).

By contrast the Americans inherited the British respect for law and lawyers. Fairly quickly there emerged a semi-independent judiciary and in theory a body of law independent of government and private individuals, quite predictable in its effects. Moreover the law clearly prescribed what was not allowed, in particular protecting persons and property. There might be some argument over which English laws applied in America but in any particular area there were laws regulating relevant behaviour. Increasingly over time a clear distinction was made between statute law, common law and administrative rulings.

There were very obvious differences in response to the threat from outside the relevant society, that is, from native inhabitants or foreign powers. British armies and local militia dealt with the problem in colonial America; it dwindled to insignificance in the nineteenth century. By contrast, war, for example the threat from the nomadic Tartars, moulded the very nature of Russian society. Only a professional military force with firearms and a standing army could counteract nomadic parasitism. In so far as one cost, the loss of slaves, declined, the other, the financial burden of the army, increased. It is unlikely that a barely self-sufficient peasantry, free, equal, and politically unorganised, could have resisted nomad harassment any better in the eighteenth than in the fifteenth or sixteenth centuries. As McNeill argues, 'To maintain a civil administration and a standing army capable of breaking nomad power on the western steppe required all or nearly all of the panoply of the Russian imperial state.' McNeill himself drew a direct parallel with the United States, where 'no such political overhead was needed because no military formidable enemies had to be overcome' and it might be added, because the invention of the repeating rifle made the subjugation of the plains Indians a much easier task when the white settlers began to exploit the prairies. Hellie has argued that a garrison state and near-caste system were both 'second-order consequences of Muscovy's attempt to meet its need for defence against slave raiding'. The acquisition of the potentially productive steppe exacted a price in resources diverted from potentially productive purposes, and , in so far as the protection provided was inadequate, it increased risk.

PIONEER RISK AND OPENING UP

It is in this context that we need to consider the influence of pioneer risk on the rate of opening up. For the pioneer, risk was compounded by ignorance of the new environment. At a distance a bland over-optimism concerning the potential of a new area was always possible; this explains many of the difficulties during the so-called 'starving times' in the early American colonies. America was described as an 'ever-flowing Cornucopia'. It was assumed that the early settlers could largely live off the land; but close-to reality looked a little different. For a new settler his 'baggage' of survival techniques, let alone his immunity to disease, borrowed from the country of origin, may not have been relevant in the new environment, depending upon the degree of consonance in environments at source and at destination. However, a 'low-level' accommodation may occur if the environments were not too dissimilar, in other words the new settlers may get by with only minor adjustment of their survival techniques. From the point of view of long-term economic development the situation may be more promising if the degree of dissonance is large and assimilation problems involve a marked discontinuity of institutional and attitudinal patterns. Such accommodation involves adjustment to a new risk environment, or a complete failure of the new settlements.

The rate of opening up in any area of new settlement depends upon a complex relationship between resources, risk and the institutional organisation of the economy. Our understanding of that relationship reflects a general neglect of failure. The members of the sample available for study are largely successful settlements, a bias which distorts for us the nature of the relationship and tends to underplay the significance of resources and risk. Individual cases where the resource position is poor and the level of risk high are excluded from consideration by the selective nature of the historical evidence.

Such an argument applies at two levels, at the level of the settlement as a whole and at the level of the individual household. Even if the settlement survives there may be many individual failures. Failure may involve death or simply the abrupt curtailment of a household's role as a pioneer. Again history is written by the winners and the failures generally disappear from sight. Losers rarely have the leisure to dwell on their unfortunate experience. The individual's concern with security is again downgraded as a result of the nature of the evidence.

Even in a resource-rich environment with a low level of risk, government action in directly or indirectly mitigating and managing risk is crucial to the rate of opening up. The government may directly promote settlement by a subsidy or indirectly by the provisions of critical public goods. The attitudes, and therefore the actions, of government with respect to phase movement are never neutral. The poorer the resource position and the more hostile the risk environment, the greater the necessity for active government intervention but the less likely successful government action.

During the initial phase of opening up there is a strong tendency for polarisation of decision-making to occur. Such a polarisation follows from the nature of pioneer risk and increases with the severity of that risk. Early colonisations involve adjustment to both natural and human environments. The former involves a whole series of particular adjustments to local conditions of climate, soil or vegetation, the latter mainly the question of defence.

Defence, of its nature a public good vulnerable to the 'free rider' problem, had to be a concern of the highest level of decision-making, if potential enemies were individually powerful and could concentrate their hostility. The degree of effort required reflected both the technology of warfare and the implied organisation of the military. if defence was the paramount concern of government, it was possible, even likely that other areas of concern would be subordinated to the requirements of defence. The distribution of land, the availability of labour and the whole legal system may reflect defence needs. Samuel Huntingdon, noting the close relationship between the European nation state and defence requirements, quotes Clark: 'just as the modern state was needed to create the standing army, so the army created the modern state, for the influence of the two causes are reciprocal.'

The relationship between the state and the military differed markedly in Russia and America. The dual threat to the American colonies, from rival colonial powers and from the Indians, was dealt with at two levels, the first largely by the Imperial government and almost wholly at its costs, and the second at the level of the individual colony or even township. The nature of the Indian threat and the dispersed settlement pattern allowed continued reliance on local militia. There was little incentive to create European-type military forces and a European-type state to support them. A professonal army came relatively late to the United States.

By contrast Russia confronted much more significant enemies without the umbrella of another nation's military protection. The geographical context increased both the potency of the threat and the difficulty of marshalling the resources to meet it. As early as the seventeenth century Russia had to develop a professional army but even before this, attempts to achieve the same purpose had fashioned the society to suit military objectives. The institutional arrangements of a service state reflected largely the early military requirements of defence (Hellie 1971; 1977). In particular agriculture was impossible in the steppe without the protection of a strong standing army supported by the centralised, bureaucratic state.

Other aspects of risk had a similar impact both in encouraging polarisation of decision-making and in having a bigger net impact in Russia. The quarantine arrangements occasioned by plague made much greater demands on administration in Russia than comparable requirements in America, where organisation was focussed on individual ports as the entry point of epidemic disease. Again the more widespread harvest failures of Russia demanded centralised rather than local relief.

Since the Russian government was closely involved in the distribution of virgin land and in regulating labour mobility, it could not help but influence the rate of opening up in a more direct way. The government could use the abundant factor, land, to help in regulating the use of the scarce factor, labour. The deficiencies of any government on the frontier made detailed regulation of land distribution impossible. Surrogate government or market agencies are required to break up holdings into a manageable size.

In America speculative purchase of land began as early as the seventeenth century. After the initial starving years the environment on the frontier was extremely benign, with a low risk level, at least until the crossing of the dry lands in the nineteenth century. The promise of a reasonable standard of living promoted settlement. For immigrants generous land distribution policies resulted from the competitive position of the separate colonies.

In Russia the serfowner largely regulated the detailed land distri-

123

bution. Internal colonisation was much less of an individual affair than in America. Government subsidy or sponsorship was omnipresent whether it involved foreign immigrants under Catherine or native Russians when the government did finally promote free movement at the end of the nineteenth century. The military nature of many settlements reflected both the high level of risk and the crucial importance of the government. Much settlement occurred within the framework of the serf estate system, settlement being realised by government surrogates and subsidised indirectly by massive land grants. Sometimes native landlords were assimilated to the serf estate system.

In its own way each area was characterised by a risk environment hostile to new settlement. Overall the Russian environment was the more hostile. Within colonial America the disease environment of the south constituted the most dramatic obstacle. However, in the south the possibility of good returns offset risk. In the early years pioneer and commercial risk were fused together.

The 'average' American has been not only better endowed with relevant resources but less vulnerable to national or social calamity. His economic life has as a consequence been less shaped by adjustment to external shocks. In the terminology of the anthropologist the American was very responsive, although not obliged to be — a creative response, whereas the Russian was forced to adjust — an avoidance response.

The New England environment was by no means favourable to new settlement. The combination of harsh climate, poor, rocky soil, uneven topography and short rivers created problems for successful pioneering. New England provides a good example of a positive response. In the early years the township acted as the main agent of land distribution and ensured the provision of these services crucial to successful pioneering. In Billington's words, the system of land distribution and stress on communal life ' . . . induced a planned migration that spared the settlers most of the discomfort of pioneer life and assured them spiritual and economic security.' The nice blend of differential status and economic homogeneity limited conflict and violence. Closeness to government made the citizens of Sudbury, as no doubt the citizens of other townships, show, in Powell's words, 'a definite willingness to tax themselves for the good of the town and to make economic regulations in the name of orderly government'. Both formally through local town government and informally the new settlers helped each other, thus mitigating and managing risk. In Bushman's words, 'The economic ambitions of the people were attainable only because, living together in a town, they cooperatively mitigated the difficulties of exploiting the wildnerness.'

By contrast opening up in Russia was by no means as fast, partly because of the resource and risk environment and partly because the government sought to control the process closely. Although there was considerable informal, or even illegal, movement colonisation was organised either directly by the central government, often under military supervision, or indirectly by government surrogates such as the serfholding landowners. In this context colonisation was significantly free of market influences.

On the one hand in Siberia the lucrative fur trade was made a government monopoly, more honoured in the breach it is true but allegedly lucrative enough to pay for the establishment of administrative control in Siberia. On the other hand the serfowners' estates were not organised on a cost-account basis. The serfowner was subsidised by a free grant of land to which he could attach the scarce factor of production, labour, already under his control. Thus the absorption of new areas, at least in European Russia, simply replicated a previously existing pattern of settlement.

There is little doubt that the high risk environment slowed the process of opening up, which would have been impossible without considerable government help. However thinly government personnel, civil or military, were spread, their presence was crucial to the establishment of settled agriculture. The interaction of high risk and poor resources in Russian history has perpetuated low-level accommodation within areas of new settlement, has underpinned institutional and attitudinal structures unconducive to economic growth and highlighted secondary risk. The likelihood of a negative response was made very much more likely by such factors. High risk in the context of poor resources is an unbeatable duo of opponents.

Part 3
Risk, Regimes and the
Human Environment

6

Creation of Government

DENSITY OF GOVERNMENT

Each early town was, in a real sense, a little commonwealth.

Powell

Russian political power was polarised between a highly centralised autocratic state and highly localised (even intra-village) institutions, notably serfdom.

Black

There is a sense in which every decision-maker is part of a little
commonwealth, a separate sphere of limited jurisdiction. The Commonwealth may comprise only the related members of a household
or it may extend to an empire.

During opening up pioneer households interact more or less as
equal. Although initially largely self-sufficient, settler households provide mutual assistance as they spread amoeba-like across virgin territory; they interact horizontally. Over time personal contact declines
in relative importance as the impersonal contacts of the market
multiply. Within markets the little commonwealths — now more frequently partnerships or enterprises — continue to interact horizontally. Such horizontal interaction also occurs at other levels, as for
example between nations or government bodies.

Superimposed upon the economy of horizontal units there exists
a structure of political control, broadly called government; any
organisation has a hierarchical structure of control. In this context
an economy is seen as a hierarchy of decision-makers, each comprised
within an ever-widening, and sometimes weakening, system of linked
economic jurisdictions. An individual economic agent at the bottom

129

is as much part of the whole system as the commanding political institutions.

It is commonplace to distinguish a spontaneous stream of economic development from an induced stream, contrasting the economic decision-making of individual economic agents operating within a relatively free market and that of governments (Crisp 1976). Such a distinction is misleading. It is appropriate to emphasise the differing level of decision-making relevant in particular cases, but each economic decision has both a horizontal and a vertical dimension.

Government and market are inextricably intermeshed. Moreover in the pre-railway and telegraph world of slow communications the effectiveness of government control was inevitably limited. Direct administrative supervision was an inadequate mechanism of control, state involvement in economic production almost invariably a failure. Governments were forced to work through decentralised decision-making, successful implementation of government policy being dependent upon the successful operation of markets. Governments revenue potential reflected the development of such markets.

In its turn the efficient operation of the market depended upon the provision of crucial public goods. The securing of an appropriately stable and secure context was important. The elaboration and implementation of a set of legal rules, relating to property rights, debt or contract, shaped economic decision-making. The provision of cheap and reliable transportation, crucial to market development, was also very much a responsibility of government, as of course was risk mitigation or management. Moreover the various levels of government were in a strong position to concentrate benefits or disperse costs, particularly where social and private diverged, in order to promote the provision of public goods by non-government bodies.

It is no accident that the national state, with its developed bureaucracy, and the market system, with its associated auxiliary institutions, grew together. While individual production decisions were rarely made at the topmost level, such decisions were influenced by a mass of detailed regulations relating to such basic market characteristics as entry into a given industry, the conditions of operation within that industry, the number of operators or the quality of the product or service (Hughes 1977). The particular mix of government and market interaction moulds the emerging institutional systems.

A key concept is the degree of government penetration of the economy defined in terms of the effectiveness with which the government can intervene in the economy to achieve a set of broad objectives (Grew 1978). There are three separate dimensions of penetration: the specification of public objectives, the scope of government intervention and the efficiency of implementation.

Clearly it is impossible to define penetration independently of its purposes. The broad purposes are threefold: to exercise political power and sovereignty — that is, to determine overall policy, to carry on daily administration and to reform the system where appropriate. The specific purposes range from risk mitigation to resource mobilisation, although such purposes are merely instrumental in the achievement of broader objectives such as security, stability or prosperity. Penetration appropriate to one purpose is often inappropriate, indeed even inimical, to other purposes.

Moreover the scope of penetration may be limited geographically, socially or institutionally. The speed of acquisition of new territories, or new peoples, is highly relevant, as is the size of territory and sparseness of population. Problems of effective law and order may inhibit government penetration. The government's writ may not run at all in certain areas, as for example on the frontier, or among a peasant population, or within a black market.

Alternatively, according to the speed of communications and the degree of bureaucratic development, information transfer often leads to distortion of instruction and allows various interest groups to redefine these instruction, the more significantly the more distant from the instructing authority. At the same time the growing bureaucratisation of government creates an institutionalised pattern of self-preservation, instructions being reinterpreted to protect the position of the bureaucrats. The more centralised is authority, the more distant the implementers from the centre of authority, the greater the likelihood of government institutions acquiring a life of their own. Further, it is often argued that government reflects the interests of a ruling class. But, to take a pertinent example, far from the Russian government reflecting the interests of a ruling class, it became, in Gerschenkron's terms, the 'state's state', evaluating policies in terms of whether they advanced its own interests or not (Gerschenkron 1971).

Douglass North has argued that the main constraint on economic development, a lack of incentive resulting from the failure to define property rights appropriately, arises because governments seek to maximise their own income, or the income of interest groups associated with them, rather than provide the proper institutional organisation to equalise social and private returns (North 1981).

Within Europe there were significant models for government penetration, particularly the church. Even in eastern Europe the

131

Byzantine Orthodox Commonwealth represented a structure of universal penetration, a precedent that could be appealed to and imitated (Meyendorff 1981). Religious penetration in America was from the beginning fragmented and pluralistic.

During the period discussed here the central bureaucracy was relatively weak in both countries. Communications problems, lack of finance or trained personnel, and a lack of urban centres made this inevitable.

For long periods of Russian history the army, through military governors and military settlements, acted as a significant tool of penetration. Other government surrogates such as the serfowners, the urban or rural commune, acted as *ad hoc* agents of penetration. In Madariaga's words the Crown delegated to the nobility certain functions it could not hope to fulfil 'by means of a non-existent bureaucracy it could not afford to pay' (Madariaga 1981:585). There was a failure to separate the bureaucracy from the nobility by creating two discrete scales of social worth, a failure which prevented both the formation of a genuine nobility and the formation of a genuine bureaucracy (Madariaga 1981:88). Personalisation of power precluded a genuine official class, based on obligatory or semi-obligatory service within the framework of the Table of Ranks, and weakened the corporate identity of the nobility. In more prosaic terms it is fair to say that the serf owning gentry filled in for the missing bureaucracy.

The choice of tool in America reflected the much greater density of government and small size, and largely amateur nature, of the army. There were some similarities. The slave owner on his plantation represented a close parallel with the serf owner. Town proprietors paralleled the communes of Russia.

The effectiveness of such penetration depended upon the density of the vertical implementation structure and the willingness of economic agents to accept the jurisdiction of the government institutions. Ineffectiveness might result from either a fracture in the vertical structure or a fracture between the vertical structure and the horizontal units at any level.

In areas of new settlement there are two broad influences on the structure of government, the environment and the institutional inheritance from the source countries. The institutional inheritance can be imposed, or simply represent a range of possible options. The former condition often characterises the relationship between core and periphery. During the formative period of the core, however, the institutional inheritance often plays a passive role in that it provides a starting point for choice and adaptation to the local environment.

The Hartz model of newly settled regions as dependent fragments of the mother culture in arrested development rightly stresses the structure of the mother culture at the time of settlement but wrongly ignores its adaptation and later development.

Possible models of organisation were presented to America by the presuppositions of British polity, particularly those inherent in the common law in a decentralised political and economic structure and in strong local government, and for Russia by the Mongol invaders and Byzantine empire, but such models were adopted only if they provided a pattern suitable to the particular environment. Such models were only loosely articulated and allowed considerable flexibility.

The influence of the environment on political structure expressed itself in three ways; in separate geographic and climatic identities, in differing resource endowments and in differing risk environments. The physical separation of North America from Britain, by making probable eventual political separation, allowed a close adjustment of political structure to natural environment. Individual climatic and geographical characteristics marked out a series of separate economic niches along the American coast. Initial independent settlement was thereby reinforced by differing environments. The combined effect of discrete geographical identity and continuing political separation was for the main economic niches of New England, the Chesapeake and the Lower South, and the Middle Colonies to be characterised by different export staples, by differing economic systems and different currencies.

There is a strong parallel between the American colonies and the multi-cell states system of Europe so well described by Jones (1981): 'in many ways these "sections", the separate colonies, resembled the countries of Europe; each had its own history of occupation and development.' (Billington 1974:10). In their encouragement of migrants and land distribution policies, the colonies were competitive, but Colonial America was characterised by both a beneficial complementarity and a healthy competitiveness. Fortunately the states were homogeneous enough to benefit from available economies of scale.

In the homogeneous environment of the Russian plain the cutthroat competitiveness of the principalities was likely to lead eventually to the dominance of one, although not necessarily Moscow. Gregory has pointed the contrast neatly. 'Individualism, independence, nonconformity, variety, competition and inventiveness born in the West European environment, with its numerous small states, were transferred to the North American continent, while the Russians developed a mystique based on the concept of the strength of the nation as a

133

whole, under God and the Tsar, with a destiny of conquest of the whole plain' (Gregory 1968:18). The lack of physical separation of the periphery in Russia from its metropolis bound these areas of new settlement very much to the institutional pattern of the metropolis.

The relevance of resource endowments to the institutional structure of government is through the revenue potential of government. Administration absorbs resources; the supply of administrative services is plainly revenue elastic. A good resource endowment is a necessary, if not sufficient, condition for dense government.

Both the previous factors, geographical in nature, operate on the supply side of government services. On the demand side the nature and level of risk represents an important occasion of their supply. The present study places most emphasis on risk as an influence shaping the hierarchy of economic decision-making. Particular kinds of risk require large inputs of resources marshalled by the government. Basic security against violence demands enormous investment of resources. Famine relief and epidemic control both increase the expenditure of current resources and decrease revenue potential.

The previous chapter has noted the tendency during opening up to a polarisation of decision-making and the particular pressures leading to this result in Russia. The nature and severity of pioneer risk in Russia explains the hypertrophy of central government. In America a relatively dense framework of government existed from the beginning.

The decision-making structures resulting from these influences differed in significant respects. Firstly government in America was dense both in number of vertical tiers and in range of horizontal agencies. At each vertical level, but particularly in the bottom half of the pyramid, self-help groups, both formal and informal, abounded. Moreover the growing specialisation of government, and separation of legislature, judiciary and executive, led to a proliferation of government agencies at different levels. The court system almost exactly paralleled the government's administrative apparatus. The lower the level the more government, staffed in the colonial period by amateurs on a part-time, often unsalaried basis, approximated to the self-help groups already referred to.

The most striking aspect of density relates to the number of significant vertical levels. In colonial America there existed a four-tier system involving at the top the Imperial government and its representatives in America; then the government of individual colonies, governor, councils and assemblies, only weakly representative of the Imperial government; the township or county and alongside them largely independent municipalities; and at the bottom the family farm, the plantation or business partnership.

Even before independence, government penetration by the British was weak, owing to ignorance and the difficulty of implementing policies. Parliamentary ministers were unfamiliar with the financial capabilities of the colonies and acquiring accurate information from overseas was slow and difficult (Becker 1980:131). With the exception of the royal governor and a few highranking military officers, the poorly paid customs officers were the only visible representatives of the British government in the colonies. The War of American Independence was fought to resist an attempt by the Imperial government to increase its penetration of the American economy. Polarisation at the upper end was reduced by the stripping away of the topmost level. The new constitution embodied deliberately a system of limitations on central power.

After independence little changed except that the Federal government replaced its British predecessor. In Russia the legislature and judiciary, in so far as they existed at all, were subservient to the executive. Self-help groups only appeared as semi-official bodies to promote government policy. Major decision-making occurred at three levels: the central autocracy; a thin sprinkling of local government officials assisted by government surrogates, in particular the serf-owning landlords and peasant communes alongside weak and subservient city governments; and at the bottom the family household or small economic enterprise. The middle tier was particularly weak. This weakness prompted two authorities on Russian officialdom to write, 'Prior to the "reforms" of Catherine the Great, provincial government was as close to non-existent as the political and fiscal survival of the empire would tolerate' (Pintner and Rowney 1980:106).

Since the topmost level was integral to the whole hierarchical structure of the Russian service state it could not be stripped away, only substituted, as it was intermittently in palace coups and ultimately after the Revolution of 1917, by the new Soviet government. Paradoxically the large demands made on government in Russia created, in the context of limited resources, a situation both of overdevelopment at the centre and underdevelopment of the decision-making apparatus in the periphery. It is not difficult to accept that in contrast to eighteenth and nineteenth century America, Russia was undergoverned (Starr 1972). Even in the nineteenth century Russia had fewer public servants per head of population than *laissez-faire* Britain. This had continued to be the case despite a dramatic increase in numbers from just over 10,000 officials in 1755 to well over 100,000 in 1855, or one official per 2,000 population in 1755 to one per 500 by the 1850s (Pintner and Rowney 1980: Chap. 8). Russian could only be governed with the help of government surrogates.

The lack of a dense system of government had a number of consequences. Communication problems made government policy insensitive to local needs, economic or otherwise. A serious fracture in the echelons of decision-making reinforced an alienation of the bottom units, the peasant households, from the government at the top. This further increased the difficulty of implementing government policies in the provinces. As a consequence government policies were often out of touch, strongly opposed and ineffectively implemented.

THE 'LITURGICAL' STATE

The primary juridical and organisational principle underlying the Russian state and all forms of Russian social order from the beginning was that a person acquired status and identity by virtue of the service he rendered.

Yaney

The Muscovite service state, or in Weber's words, the liturgical state, was initially a creation of the sixteenth and seventeenth centuries, finding its most complete expression in the Law Code of 1649. According to Richard Hellie the service obligation was renewed by further service revolutions under Peter the Great at the beginning of the eighteenth century and by Stalin after the Great Turn of 1929, and represents therefore a continuing theme in Russian history (Hellie 1977). The service revolutions were revolutions imposed from above, by the government, but made possible only by the interaction of certain characteristics and events.

The most relevant characteristics of Russian society were a poor resource and hostile risk environment associated with remoteness and backwardness; an unpropitious political tradition and institutional inheritance; ethnic diversity and the weakness of such key groups limiting state power as the church and landed oligarchy. The events comprised the sequences of famine and epidemic linked with military threats, civil disorder and dynastic problems.

The service state was characterised by a highly centralised autocracy, a hypertrophic government and a garrison state. The negative features of such a state were absence of civil rights, repression and the use of forced labour, but on the positive side it helped protect national independence, supported considerable territorial expansion and encouraged the successful emulation of enough foreign technology to maintain a 'great power' status.

Service was demanded of all sectors of society. Indeed the top levels of Russian society were the first to suffer subjugation to the service of the state. The Russian landed nobility was not truly a landed nobility so much as it was a hereditary class of state servitors supported in part through the possession of landed estates (Hellie 1971). The replacement of the traditional boyars by the service gentry began as early as the fifteenth century with the assimilation by Muscovy of the important north-western trading city of Novgorod. Ivan IV, the Terrible, carried the process even further by deliberately creating a subservient but disunited and fragmented service class. The dispersion of the old ruling class was also a feature of the *Oprichnina*, the terrorist administration imposed on a large part of the Muscovite heartland by Ivan (1565–72). Deliberate attempts were made to break the association of the landholding class with particular regions. Estates were scattered, control over inheritance by the state asserted. The ruler of Muscovy became the sole source of power, influence, status and income, the local land base fully at his discretion. The general lack of resources limited available rewards but thereby produced much sharper competition, further fragmenting the landholding group. Perversely even the *mestnichestvo* system, by which the position of an individual within the service hierarchy came to be determined by the rank of his ancestors, encouraged an emphasis on service, since a failure to perform the required service would handicap all members of a class or family. This engendered social pressure on potential deviants and an informal system of collective responsibility.

By the middle of the seventeenth century a caste-like, rigidly-stratified urban population had also been created. In 1618, if not earlier, the 'forbidden years', years when those subject were not allowed to move, were extended from serf to townsman. Finally in 1649 the townsmen became a closed caste, migration into and out of the towns being made illegal. In return urban taxpayers were granted a monopoly on 'town' occupations and the ownership of urban property. Unlike the serfs townsmen did not have to be returned to their original towns of residence, provided they were fixed to the current townships of residence. On the government's side this represented an attempt to increase revenue and included both abolition of the free settlements within the towns and a reduction in the number of tax-exempt proprietors. Clearly the towns differed significantly from the towns of western Europe or America. As simply another arm of the state they lacked autonomous municipal government and independence of economic action.

For both groups, state servitors and townsmen, the 1649 Law Code reflected an implicit compact. Each group demanded monopolies or the exclusion of competition. The compact therefore balanced privileges against obligations. The exact extent of the privileges varied over time with the outcome of a struggle between the landed nobility and the merchantry over the right to hold land or serfs. The implicit compact promoted the achievement of security for both parties. To a much lesser degree this was also true for the serfs.

The enserfment of the Russian peasant is a contentious issue (Hellie 1971; Culpepper 1965; R.E.F. Smith 1968; Blum 1957). There is a recent tendency to uphold what has variously been called the decree, legal or statist interpretation. Its two main propositions are: first, that the peasants, as a whole, were not effectively enserfed, either in law or in fact, until the promulgation of the *Ulozhenie*, or Law Code, of 1649; secondly, that the peasants were enserfed only after a series of deliberate actions taken by the state over the course of two centuries. In these conscious actions the state's primary motivation was the need to support the military in the defence and expansion of the Muscovite state.

Such a viewpoint contradicts the oft-repeated assertion by Soviet historians that the Russian peasant had been a serf throughout nearly all recorded Russian history. This view rests on the syllogism: all of recorded Russian history up to the Emancipation of 1861 falls within the 'feudal' period — serfdom is an essential part of feudalism — therefore, the Russian peasant was a serf right up to 1861. The legislation of the period between 1497 and 1649 betokens a tightening of feudal bonds, a 'second enserfment', rather than constitutes the origin of the institution.

The Soviet interpretation rests on a rather loose definition of serfdom. In the usual conception serfdom exists where any form of exploitation exists, be it only the payment of rent to a landlord. Professor Smith has put this point of view clearly: 'serfdom . . . is the legal expression of one of the means by which the ruling groups in a peasant society make sure that they get big a share as they can of the product of peasant labour' (Smith 1968). A more rigorous definition stresses the bond of the serf both to the land he cultivates and to the person of his lord. In Muscovy the establishment of the first bond preceded that of the second.

A genuine alternative interpretation does exist. This second view, once the prevailing orthodoxy, has been described variously as the non-decree, genetic, gradualist or environmental interpretation. As the titles suggest, in this interpretation the juridical process is considered as giving a final legal sanction only to what had already become a fact of life. The state did not act as the main instrument of creation but only participated as one actor among a number. According to this view alternating periods of economic decline and expansion resulted in a growing indebtedness of the peasantry which acted as an important check on its mobility. The peasant lost the right to move by failing to exercise that right.

Despite disclaimers of compatibility, the statist and environmental interpretations can be reconciled. No legislation introduces completely novel institutional arrangements, nor does legislation perform the function of simply validating practices already general. The degree to which legislation can be enforced depends on two preconditions. First, it depends on the elaboration of appropriate juridical language and on the strength of the enforcement apparatus. In this case the registration of the peasants in land cadastres and the establishment of courts to return fugitives were crucial. Secondly, the legislation must accord both with the interests of powerful groups in the society and also build on already recognisable tendencies. In short the state took the initiative but strong 'environmental' pressures, not the least a series of shocks, already pushed in the same direction.

The story of the enserfment is best told by tracing the tightening of the bond to the land. Before the reign of Vasilii (1425–62) the peasant was undoubtedly free to move where he willed. This mobility matched that of the gentry servitors and is scarcely surprising since the fragmented state of 'appanage Russia' ensured that there was little point in limiting the mobility of the peasant within a given principality if mobility between labour-short principalities could not be controlled. The increasing unification of Russian lands under Muscovy established the overall control necessary for such limitation of mobility.

There were four stages in the legal enserfment. During the first stage, from the mid-fifteenth to the mid-sixteenth century, the peasant's right of departure was protected by law but the time and conditions of departure were strictly regulated. The peasant was entitled to move during a period usually one week before and one week after St George's Day, *Iur'ev Den'*, on 26 November. Such a restriction may have been general before embodiment in the *Sudebnik*, or Law Code, of 1497, which was in substance repeated in 1550. The general aim was possibly to prevent destructive competition for scarce labour. The Law Codes also introduced an exit fee, which is interpreted by some as amounting to a virtual prohibition on movement and by others as a reasonable recompense for expenses incurred by the landlord. There may well have been at least some extension of restrictions on mobility in this period.

During the next stage, a period of extreme political and economic dislocation ending with the accession of the Romanovs in 1613, the right of departure was abrogated, apparently on a temporary basis in the 1580s but semi-permanently from 1603. The 'Forbidden Years' legislation represents the most formidable argument in favour of the statist interpretation. However, the door was not completely closed. Quickly a statute of limitations was introduced limiting the period of recovery of fugitive peasants. Hence, *de facto*, if not *de jure*, mobility was still possible with the support of a prospective landlord. Peasants could simply disappear for the relevant period.

During the third stage the middle service class engaged in a concerted campaign to repeal the statute of limitations and to allow recovery without time limit. The so-called allotted years were gradually extended.

Finally the Law Code of 1649, after another series of disruptive events, tied the peasant irrevocably to the land.

Thus each Russian citizen was obligated to provide a particular kind of service. The labour of the peasants freed the service gentry, and later the *dvorianstvo*, or landed nobility, for military and civil service duties. Even the commercial services required in a modern state were provided with the help of at least some compulsion. Peter the Great, in his second service revolution, extended compulsory service to the industrial sector, in attaching whole villages of so-called professional serfs to industrial or mining enterprises, particularly in the new Urals iron industry. Until the abolition of obligatory gentry service in 1762 the whole system rested on a consistent, if distorted, rationale.

In the context of a poor resource and risk environment, this system promoted the achievement of such broad government objectives as survival and expansion. The colonisation of new areas of settlement was largely conducted by the serf economy. Indeed the existing political and social system was simply replicated in new areas of control. The success of the system consisted in its effective utilisation, indeed rigid control, of the only resource available in any quantity, peasant labour.

One element of such a system was the tendency to transform Russia into the ruler's patrimony between 1450 and 1650 (Pipes 1974). In a 'patrimonial' state political authority is conceived and executed as an extension of the rights of ownership; sovereignty and ownership are one and the same. In a patrimonial state there are no formal limits on political authority, no rule of law, no individual liberties. However, authority was centralised at the cost of limiting that authority in terms of actual control: 'the Tsar possessed great power to act arbitrarily according to his whims but very little control over what his subordinates actually did'. The autocracy was also encouraged in its failure to force a functionally professional civil service, particularly in the eighteenth century under Peter and Catherine.

Raeff has talked of the establishment in eighteenth century Europe of the *Polizeistaat*, an organised polity in which productivity was maximised and society disciplined (Raeff 1982). Because of technological and financial limitations on government actions the sovereign sought to coopt various social groups and set up estates and corporations — Montesquieu's famous *corps intermédiaires* — to help in the task. Such a corps did not exist in Russia, or at least only as a pale shadow of its European contemporaries. Moreover the technological and fiscal constraints in Russia were such as to limit the creation of a new bureaucracy to the central institutions only. The members of the service elite were too few, too uneducated, too poor to play the necessary role. Thus the Petrine state was prevented from penetrating into the very fabric of Russian society in the manner of the *Polizeistaat* of Central and Western Europe; the state apparatus seemed often to hang in mid-air. The powerful constraint on the ability of the bureaucracy to penetrate the fabric of society led to a prudent concentration upon the central institutions. Only this concentration made government in Russia possible at all. Service sprang from state weakness rather than from excessive state power; it was a substitute for government proper.

The key features of the government's relations with its citizens were recruitment and revenue-raising, the administrative framework consisting largely of a tribute-collecting hierarchy. The isolation of the village from the government bureaucracy was thereby reinforced. The countryside lacked the institutions capable of interacting coherently with a systematic administration. Yaney has pointed to a recurrent theme in Russian history, the persistence of myths, or capital-city habits of thought, assuming the existence of a rational legal-administrative system in the countryside, or at least the possibility of its 'spontaneous' establishment (Yaney 1972). The reality was otherwise. Government attempts to impose a general pattern of administration, taxation or education on the whole empire were counterproductive. The government was viewed as part of the risk environment, a source of arbitrary enactments and actions.

The emancipation of the gentry in 1762 seems to mark the beginning of the destruction of the service state. Thereafter the history of Tsarist Russia has often been told as a series of belated normalisations, adapting the Russian polity or economy to the western pattern. Nearly all western historians have been guilty of this approach, implicitly if not explicitly. In practice Russian history was marked, not by a steady 'progression' towards the western pattern, but by recurrent cycles of reform and reaction. To a significant degree the service state remained intact.

A brief consideration of the gentry emancipation confirms this. The Manifesto on the Liberty of the Nobility made it clear that abolition of the formal requirement did not imply the cessation of service. It was assumed that the compulsion to serve had been 'internalised'. Social pressure, a desire for esteem, a fear of disgrace all operated to reinforce the service obligation. Moreover no-one in service was to retire until the state agreed. No lesser authority than Klyuchevskiy believed that the manifesto merely abolished the compulsory length of service, not the fact of service. The measure therefore represented a recognition of a lesser need for service at the time and an attempt to improve the quality of service.

The Charter to the Nobility in 1785 confirmed that nobility was a hereditary status conferred as a reward for service to the state. The Petrine Table of Ranks, linking noble status with service rank, still continued as valid. The Charter also confirmed freedom from obligatory service but this was conditional on acceptance of service in times of crisis. Article 20 asserted that 'In every hour of need, whenever the autocracy requires the service of the nobility for the common good, every Russian nobleman is obligated, at the first call from the autocracy, to spare neither his labour nor his very life in the service of the state.' In normal times social sanctions would suffice to generate the service required.

The vulnerability of the system to setbacks or shocks established a cyclical pattern. Initially recovery was achieved by reinforcement of the service state. Recovery was then often followed by reform or decentralisation of the system. The bunching of reforms in the 1860s — emancipation of the serfs, the introduction of municipal self-government or the *zemstvos*, judicial reforms — or, after 1905, the introduction of the Duma and the abolition of the commune — illustrate the pattern. All of these reforms were severely circumscribed in their scope and often later reversed. The legacy of service was there to be revived when needed.

PLURALISM IN PRACTICE

In the eighteenth century strong institutions of local government were the basis of political power and at the heart of political culture in England and in most of the American colonies.

Waterhouse

Their concentration of judicial and executive power gave the justices far more control over individuals than any single agency of government has today.

Carr, of JPs in Maryland

Pluralism in colonial America consisted both in the replication, with little variation, of colony-level government 13 times and in the proliferation of different levels of government within each colony. Small government initially corresponded to small community and therefore was also effective government. Moreover as population grew decision-making authority was devolved.

Initially economic decision-making was exercised by unspecialised agencies. A court system existed at every level of local government but had wide-ranging executive as well as judicial powers. Initially the legislature was also an arm of the executive. Over time, however, the independent assemblies asserted a separation between the two. Steadily the legislature, judiciary and executive emerged as separate arms of government, although rather more slowly within the independent municipal corporations. Ultimately the constitution embodied this separation in its system of checks and balances on a strong central authority. The church, which also controlled a significant area of decision-making, became an increasingly pluralistic church. Other important but separate decision-makers included township proprietors, the militia bands or municipal freemen. The revolution speeded up the proliferation of decision-making units, but the process had begun long before.

A major characteristic of such decision-making was a large degree of participation. The franchise in the election of officers was wide, and the number of office-holders itself impressive. In Connecticut, for example, in 1790 alone the number of office-holders amounted to about one tenth of the population. This was a typical picture. Not surprisingly local government was highly responsive to the needs of the local population. Bockelman's remarks about Pennsylvania might apply to any colony: 'county officials functioned as transmitters of local wishes to provincial authorities and as translators of provincial

143

policy into local reality' (Daniels 1978). In this context pluralism institutionalised and helped to control factionalism.

Inherent in any pluralist structure are strong centrifugal tendencies, indeed such forces threatened to dissolve the overall unity of colonial America. Fortunately the centrifugal were offset by balancing centripetal tendencies; defence needs, common origins and culture and similar institutional arrangements. These forces were sufficiently strong to keep the whole together.

The existence of separate political units is not always an economic advantage, nor was the exact structure in colonial America the most rational. For example, the splitting of the Chesapeake into two political units, Virginia and Maryland, produced some significant negative features (Middleton 1953). Such a separation prevented government control over tobacco production and postponed the introduction of tobacco inspection; it resulted in the failure to build a much-needed lighthouse at the Capes and engendered disputes over fishing and navigation in the Potomac; it undermined cooperation in defence and in customs control, and it hindered uniformity on pilots and ferries.

As we shall see later these disadvantages were more than counterbalanced by the stimulus given to movement into the commercial phase by the unbroken vertical and horizontal chains of decision-making units.

Broadly speaking the north-east was governed locally by the township, the south by the county; the middle colonies occupied an intermediate position. Exact territorial arrangements and the titles of office-holders differed. Even where the structure appeared similar the main locus of decision-making differed.

New England

New England was governed by the township. The township was a unit of government, not a description of population density. Townships contained large rural areas, land often undistributed for long periods, at least in the early period of settlement. On the eve of the Revolution the settled area of New England was divided into some 300 townships. The importance of the township differed between the individual colonies and to some degree over time. Rhode Island consisted of townships which were practically self-governing republics, whereas in Connecticut, at least constitutionally, the towns had no power other than that delegated to them by the government of the colony. Indeed by a system which has been called 'dual localism', the government of the colony kept close supervision over town governments (Daniels 1979). Massachusetts townships were intermediate in their degree of independence between the Connecticut and Rhode Island models. In the early years the degree of control exerted by colony governments was greater than it became later. The increasing harshness of the environment of settled areas and the dispersion of settlement stimulated decentralisation of political power.

Town-meeting government was rooted firmly in the soil of late medieval and early modern England, in manorial courts and parish meetings. 'Through a process that can best be described as "selective borrowing", the new England colonists winnowed out those parts of the English institutional past that were not congenial to the New World conditions and adapted those that were' (Daniels 1979: 64). The Massachusetts Bay Colony was the model for the other New England colonies. A selection occurred from the original selection; the original model was 'twice purified'. Thus a plural system allowed, through a 'second sifting' of English antecedents, a closer adjustment to local conditions (Daniels 1978).

Politically the township consisted of both the town meeting and the town officers. The relative power of each depended upon the frequency of meeting. It does appear that after the first few years the meetings occurred less often, although some evidence exists that the frequency of meetings in eighteenth century Massachusetts increased. The chief officials — the townsmen or selectmen — increasingly became the key figures in each town's political life. In normal times the townspeople seemed willing to allow the selectmen to make decisions for them, often year after year, but the meeting's power was always there and could be and occasionally was asserted. The authority of selectmen was expanded both from above by general enabling acts and from below by delegation from the town meeting.

Economic functions or offices were not initially differentiated although some officials had obvious economic responsibilities, for example, the surveyors of highways, fence viewers, packers and sealers and ratemen. Ad hoc committees often dealt with particular economic problems. Town clerks kept the records crucial to economic life, notably those concerning land transactions or births, deaths and marriages.

One of the basic economic tasks of the township, strictly speaking of the original proprietors, indeed even their raison d'être, was land distribution. The township was an ideal mechanism for distributing the land. The system of land distribution, based on both need and wealth, represented a nice blend of differential status and economic

145

homogeneity. At least initially inequalities in land holding were insignificant. New England was made by parcelling out the land so that communal social interest and individual personal proprietorship could work together in harmony. Religion reinforced the communal aspect. Wealth and status were deferred to in the linking of person and office. The New England system of settlement reflected the need to avoid conflict in the early years of opening up and the resulting tranquillity of those early years is emphasised by many commentators. Even in the eighteenth century harmony seemed to have prevailed over conflict, although the increasing pressure of population upon land and the related growth of commerce were changing the nature of the governors and the governed.

The structure of government in New England was three-tiered; General Court later replaced by Council and Assembly, county and township. Of the three the county was the weakest. In the decision-making hierarchy the individual household grew in importance as dispersed settlement replaced compact townships but the communal habit never disappeared completely. As population grew and commerce increased the importance of central places, new institutional forms of government emerged.

The south

In considering the south attention is focused on the Chesapeake colonies of Virginia and Maryland. Again central government was weak and remote; local government was much more significant. Strong townships on the New England pattern were absent, and the degree of urbanisation was low. In the Chesapeake the main geographic and political unit was the county and the key institution with broad judicial and administrative power, the county court (Wheeler, in Daniels 1978). However the county never quite filled the role of the township.

In contrast to the small household farms in the north, the Chesapeake had as its basic economic unit the plantation, on average larger than the farms to the north because of its access to both indentured white and black slave labour, although the lack of economies of scale meant that in tobacco production large and small plantations co-existed.

Tobacco production was dominated by land abundance and labour scarcity. Soil exhaustion could be avoided by a system of field rotation which allowed at least 20 years for recovery. Buildings in such a system were only temporary, located as centrally as possible within the existing field arrangement. Land looked unkempt since in a mobile agricultural system of this kind, the deterioration of buildings and land was integral to the functioning of the system (Earle 1970: 138).

Geography also encouraged the dispersion of settlement. The labyrinth of rivers in the Chesapeake both facilitated the tobacco trade and set up distinct barriers to local movement and interaction. Nearly all plantations had ready access to a landing, the five-mile maximum in location from a trans-Atlantic landing in All Hallow's Parish, Maryland, not being untypical (Earle 1970). Many of the rivers were navigable by the largest vessels for long distances; the Potomac for 110 miles, the James 100, the Rappahannock 70 and the York-Mattaponi-Pamankey 60. However the importance of overland transport is indicated by the fact that never more than one quarter of plantations owned a boat, but horse ownership rose by 1765 to 90 per cent, and cart ownership to 63 per cent. Geography, in the shape of the intricate estuarine configuration of the Chesapeake, imposed a pattern of commercial dispersion upon Virginia and Maryland.

A liberal land grant system reinforced the influence of tobacco technology and geography. The head-right system allowed 50 acres to be granted cumulatively to merchants, ship captains and plantation owners. Neither township nor county regulated land distribution.

The consistent goals of the colony government, whether it was exercised through governor, councillors or assembly, were a colony of compact settlement and a highly varied and expanding economy supporting a sound political structure which, though offering degrees of affluence for all, would be hierarchical, deferential and orderly (Rainbolt 1974: 6). Geography, land distribution policies, the relative weakness of government, particularly in its middle tiers, and the technology of tobacco production conspired to prevent the achievement of this goal.

However many of the same characteristics which held for New England also applied to the Chesapeake. During the seventeenth century the authority of the county rose relative to that of colony or parish. Justices of the peace wielded their authority in full court sessions, in *ad hoc* courts or as single justices between sessions. Local benches were quite responsive to community needs because they controlled relatively small populations. However the system was highly paternalist and the local benches were largely self-perpetuating. The colony's government was appointed from a list of nominations

147

made by the county court itself. Justices of the peace tended to be men of standing, unpaid.

The county court had wide administrative powers including regulation of the local economy. It appointed officers to open and maintain roads and bridges, it managed financial affairs and recorded numerous transactions. In the eighteenth century it even supervised the tobacco inspection system.

Again there was wide participation in government. Before the eighteenth century high mortality limited the emergence of hereditary power groups. Office-holding was widespread and the franchise, if more limited than in New England, was certainly not narrow. Local government responded to petitions rather than engaged in public planning but the power granted to the justices provided essential flexibility for meeting specific local needs.

With the Chesapeake colonies there were three levels of government: colony, county and parish; and four levels of decision-making if we include the plantations, which grew in influence in the eighteenth century. The parishes usually appeared before the counties and continued to impose the heaviest taxes. The parish existed without a rigid hierarchical structure; resident bishops were absent and diocesan control weak. Steadily the parish shed its economic functions in favour of the county.

Further south, Carolina also enjoyed relatively strong local government, with some differences of nomenclature. Vestries and JPs existed but committees were responsible for roads and other particular projects (Waterhouse, in Daniels 1978). The pattern was broadly similar to that of Chesapeake.

Relative to Russia the Chesapeake colonies, and the south in general, enjoyed a dense system of intermediate units of government; relative to New England there was more polarisation.

The Middle Colonies

The Middle Colonies differed from the two previous regions only in the detailed make-up of local government. Of the four units of local government in Pennsylvania — county, township, borough and city — the county remained the dominant unit (Bockelman, in Daniels 1978). In New York the county emerged as the main unit only after a continuing struggle for popular participation against the quasi-manorial organisation of the patronships (Kim 1978; Varga, in Daniels 1978). Pennsylvania had commissioners and assessors responsible for financial affairs, New York a board of supervisors. One major study of Pennsylvania has strongly argued that effective political power was centred in the countryside (Schweitzer). Moreover because of strong opposition the colony legislature gave up trying to collect taxes, whereas local government bodies had no such trouble in raising revenue. Economic legislation was willingly accepted where it was seen to be in the clear economic interest of the affected groups. Such findings are consistent with our knowledge of other colonies.

The cities

During the colonial period the government of the cities or towns was largely independent of the surrounding rural areas, despite their small size. Total urban population in 1790 was only 201,000. By 1750 14 chartered municipal corporations lined the Atlantic from Albany to Norfolk, the most important of which were New York and Philadelphia. The municipal corporation was absent only in New England. Before the 1730s and 1740s the American borough, like its British ancestor, was primarily a commercial community governed by commercial participants for the service of trade and industry. Merchants and artisans qualified as freemen on the basis of their capital or simply the economic activity they pursued. Freemen monopolised commercial and manufacturing pursuits and dominated municipal councils. Landed freeholders were only slowly admitted during the eighteenth century.

At least before the War of Independence the privileges of the municipal corporations were accepted as inviolable. Only after the War did the newly formed states start to assert their authority over the corporation.

Conclusions

The preceding analysis of the structure of American colonial government lacks the dynamism of our description of the process of enservicement in Russia. However, the maturing of the political system occurred at a different rate in the separate political jurisdictions.

A number of factors made for the rapid creation of mature and stable government in New England. With immigration largely concentrated in the 1630s and consisting mostly of complete, free families, with a low level of mortality, the native population quickly came to

149

dominate political, social and economic life. Few families were disturbed by parental death.

It is also interesting to speculate about the rationale of what Teaford has called the Yankee Anomaly, the integration of urban and rural government with the township as a basic unit. Closed and privileged municipal corporations never existed in New England, not even in Boston and Salem. Massachusetts leaders liked the township form of government and the associated free movement of labour and goods throughout the colony. It may be that good transport accessibility and low commercial risk made the commercial corporation less important, but religious factors must also have played an early and significant part.

By contrast, in the Chesapeake the evolution of political stability and social order was slow. A pronounced asymmetry of circumstance divided the seventeenth and eighteenth centuries. Lockridge talks of 'chaotic individualism' and stresses disorder in the seventeenth century (Lockridge 1981: 84). High mortality and continuing immigration, particularly of servants, largely male, and without capital, prevented the emergence of a native population. There was a high proportion of orphans in the population. In Middlesex County, Virginia, for example, half of the sons lost their fathers before reaching legal maturity or the age of marriage (Rutman, in Tate and Ammerman 1979: 173). The demands of empire and the tobacco economy created further elements of instability.

Jorden notes the significant influence of the harsh realities of sheer survival in the two tidewater colonies, with their low life expectancy and reproduction rates, on the development of political institutions and the evolution of political stability (Jorden, in Tate and Ammerman 1979: 247). Even in times of relative peace, the primary institutions of provincial government — the council, assembly and provincial court — suffered considerable discontinuity in membership and effective service. Tenure was brief, experience a rare commodity, and qualified and sustained political leadership practically non-existent.

In the eighteenth century mortality fell and slaves became the predominant immigrants and the mainstay of the labour force. There emerged a native-born majority in the white population and a ruling group of planter gentry.

In the Middle Colonies the political situation was more fluid, in that immigration of whites was still high in the eighteenth century. However the emphasis on a largely free and balanced family immigration and the low level of mortality outside the immigrant ports made for political stability.

The nature of American towns and cities changed too. The switch in emphasis from external to internal trade demanded close integration of the cities with their hinterland. As a consequence the municipal charter became a controlling instrument of the central authorities rather than a shield of independence. The supremacy of colony or state authority over corporate privilege was strongly asserted, a process beginning in the 1730s and 1740s and being completed within a century. Moreover the growth in population and the reduction in commercial risk caused a change in emphasis in city ordinances from those directly concerned with trade and commerce to those concerned with health, safety and public works.

Despite the tendency to change, we can note a number of key characteristics of a pluralist system. Indeed in the period before major innovations in the nature of bureaucratic organisations created the institutional world of ministries and public corporations, it was difficult to draw a line between what constituted government and what did not. Many services and functions now clearly regarded as public or governmental were carried out by unpaid, part-time, sometimes involuntary, agents rather than full-time paid government servants. In a very real sense this was the age of amateur rather than professional government. A large number of government surrogates, or quasi-government institutions, carried out the main public functions. As we will see later this ambiguity makes it difficult to define and measure the precise level of government revenue and expenditure, and even more significantly in this context to evaluate the density of government.

First, local government was more important than central government. From our point of view this implies that the locus of economic decision-making was in local rather than central government. For example, the frequent concern in the literature with colony-wide taxes belies the repeated assertion that local taxes were often more important (Becker 1980: 36; Daniels 1978: 8).

Secondly, government, even within the colonies, was multi-tiered, possibly the more so the further north along the coast. Three or even four tiers of economic decision-making existed below the colony government.

Thirdly, at each tier a variety of horizontal units existed which were apt to increase as population grew and the economy diversified. Religious and military organisations paralleled the political. Boroughs, towns or cities appeared alongside the counties. Legislative, judicial and executive bodies became distinguished as specialisation of positions increased. Self-help groups began to proliferate at the bottom.

Fourthly, small government corresponded to small communities. Most contact was face-to-face and therefore local. Government accommodated itself to the speed of communication and transport and only grew with population density.

Fifthly, there was wide participation in government. The number of officers represented a high proportion of total population. Many officers were elected and the franchise wide. However, official positions were ranked according to importance and filled according to wealth and status in the local community. Economic interests were well represented. But dense officialdom made for a generally harmonious society.

Sixthly, government was sensitive to local demands, particularly of an economic nature. Government became ideally suited to foster and develop a market system.

Finally, the existence of separate colonies prevented government from fracturing either the vertical chain or the horizontal. Since the colonies had to compete with each other in key areas of policy, dangerously idiosyncratic policies were impossible. For example, all had to distribute land on a fairly liberal basis or fail to sustain significant immigration.

Such was the system institutionalised in the constitution of 1789. New states were later integrated into the existing system.

7

Creation of Markets

The development of a market, although it allowed increased efficiency through specialisation of land and labour, contained elements of additional risk. The subsistence farmer had been at the mercy of the weather; the entrepreneurial farmer was at the mercy of both the weather and the market.

Appleby

The municipal corporation was a community of trade and industry, or organisation moulded by the distinctive needs of commercial life amid a world of subsistence agriculture.

Teaford

COMMERCIAL RISK

It was the very security of the close-knit communities which enabled the market economy to flourish.

Schweitzer, of colonial Pennsylvania

To an observer of modern economic exchange, a market signifies an institution, both impersonal and international, in which multilateral trading in homogeneous products through a process of arbitrage smooths out geographical divergences of price and often through forward markets evens out fluctuations over time. The apparently minor frictions between acts of production and consumption are usually ignored.

In the past, however, the costs incurred after production dwarfed production costs (Shepherd and Walton 1972). Such costs could be broadly divided into four groups — transport, finance, merchanting or transactions, and protection. Transport costs speak for themselves. Financial costs include insurance and banking charges and the costs of foreign exchange. Transaction costs are the search, negotiation and enforcement costs crucial to the establishment and fulfillment of a contract and the efficient operation of a market (North and Thomas 1973). Protection costs are incurred to allow trade to occur without let or hindrance (Lane 1966). A particular kind of service might be provided by a single economic agent or one agent might provide more than one kind of service; in particular the government may provide a significant number of these services. The aggregate of these costs could be called distribution, or commercial, costs. The level of distribution costs reflected to a very significant degree the level of commercial risk.

High commercial costs kept markets local, particular and fragmented. Trade tended to be on a personal, bilateral basis. A number of significant factors — few transactions, time lags in the transfer of information and commodities, indivisibilities in the nature of supply — made the frequent occurrence of market reversals likely but unexpected in exact timing. Indissolubly linked were three characteristics: fragmented and poorly developed markets; frequent and unexpected market reversals; great ignorance, uncertainty and significant commercial risk. Each separately contributed in preventing the specialisation of secondary market institutions, which could ultimately have lowered the elements of distribution costs.

In such an environment the pursuit of profit maximisation is a chimera, simple survival often a precarious business. Moreover misfortune culled both the efficient and inefficient, subverting Alchian's process of natural economic selection which, he claimed, imposed profit maximisation on those failing to pursue this objective consciously. The 'random walk' prevailed.

In practice luck played an important, if decreasing, role in explaining commercial success. Next to luck in importance were personal knowledge and contact through family and friends. The extended kinship family was still a significant factor in the success of mercantile enterprise. A brother as resident representative, a son as supercargo, a nephew as ship captain were invaluable. Even so death or bankruptcy could easily bring a partnership or family firm to a premature end. Risk was an integral feature of commercial activity.

We call the risk characteristic of the commercial phase, commercial risk. There are two components of commercial risk, pioneer and market risk. The former reflects the underdeveloped form of early markets; it impinges on commercial activities in two particular ways, through protection costs and through supply instability.

Protection costs arose because of the need to control violence. F.C. Lane has argues that during the Middle Ages and early modern times protection rents were a major source of the fortunes made in trade; a merchant whose protection costs were lower could make a protection rent. Operating with lower payments for protection was often the decisive factor in the competition between merchants and was achieved by complicated mixtures of public and private enterprise. In practice protection costs could include a variety of imposts; convoy fees, tribute to pirates, higher insurance for voyages into pirate-infested water, bribes or gifts to customs oficials or higher authorities, smuggling costs and the costs of armed protection. Lane attaches great importance to a significant reduction in the proportion of resources devoted to war and policing as a stimulus to growth. Two factors are relevant — the transfer of costs to governments and/or an improvement in the efficiency with which protection was provided.

Market instability is also associated with pioneer risk. Because of the fragmentation of markets and the limited number of transactions any shock, by causing a significant fluctuation in supply or demand, can be a potent source of commercial risk through its impact on price. Disease, famine or war have often had such an impact.

In the pre-industrial period demand for many commodities reflected the size of the potential harvest surplus. Except in the situation of significant net exports of grain and an increase in export prices, a deficient harvest was bound to limit the internal market for all other commodities taken as a whole. The exact impact on particular markets would reflect the differing price elasticities of demand and supply, and the marginal demand propensities of different income groups (Ippolito 1975). The smaller the surplus the greater the impact of a given harvest fluctuation on the demand for non-agricultural commodities. Russia with its small surplus and significant harvest variability was characterised by violent swings in demand.

Commercial risk can arise, therefore, and in the pre-industrial world, where yields were low, frequently did because of the variability of the harvest. However, a stable and assured level of demand is needed for activities which require a significant investment of working or fixed capital. In a fluctuating market assets held in the form of unsold commodities or even debt, represent a hostage to the future.

The second component of commercial risk, market risk, is the risk inherent in any market, where many suppliers and many purchasers operate in ignorance of each others' intentions, and instantaneous action is impossible. Some uncertainty and risk is inherent in such a situation, however well-developed the market. Small fluctuations can through a collective misjudgement lead to inherent instability. Price 'cob-webs' involve major fluctuations in price, and are much more likely when significant time lags occur. Discontinuities in factor supply also promote cobwebs. Improved land tended to appear in discrete amounts, as is well documented for tobacco or cotton plantations (Menard 1978, North 1961). Lumpiness in the size of farm units or in capital investment, time lags in the gestation of investment, could cause surges in supply.

As the first component of risk disappears with market growth specialisation of distributional activities becomes increasingly important. Commercial uncertainty then involves two kinds of economic decision — that of the producer to produce for sale, and that of the merchant who buys in order to sell. The safety-first model helps us to deal with problems of the producer-consumer household (Scott 1976; Wright and Kunreuther 1975). Risk mitigation can be reduced to a problem in activity choice, premised on the need to achieve a given subsistence objective. Each phase is characterised by a different activity; opening up by production of a subsistence good for own consumption, the commercial phase by the production of a cash crop for the market. The model can be used to analyse the transition from opening up to the commercial phase.

In a land-abundant environment the scarce factor is labour and the problem is then one of allocating labour to the different activities. The safety-first model argues that the value of total output is maximised subject to the constraint that the risk of this level falling below target consumption is tolerable. Clearly the closer is target consumption to the subsistence level, the lower will be the tolerable risk level.

During opening up the only relevant variable is the yield of the subsistence crop. During the commercial phase the relevant variables are the yield of the cash crop and the exchange rate between subsistence and cash crops. For the producer commercial risk comprises both natural and market risk, represented here by fluctuations in yield and price. Both average levels of price and yield and the degree of variability in both are relevant to inter-phase movement.

Such a model has limited usefulness, because inter-phase movement involves the increasing divorce of production and consumption. This divorce has two consequences. First, consumers acquire marketable assets, or wealth in many forms. Such asset-holding has a number of significant effects: it reduces the vulnerability of an individual to subsistence effects; it increases his bargaining power, extending his ability to wait and examine competing alternatives; and it strengthens his capacity to resist arbitrary actions from outsiders, to resist for example the transfer of secondary risk. Secondly, specialist merchants appear, whose vulnerability to risk arises solely from market fluctuations rather than any direct subsistence threat.

An economically successful society needs a stable group of potential entrepreneurs, here merchants, with entry into the group sufficiently easy to allow significant innovation to occur. A perpetual renewal of the entrepreneurial group (Pirenne, Wallerstein), or even 'creative gales of destruction' (Schumpeter), destroy the basis for successful economic activity. Continuity in learned skills or accumulated capital is crucial; 'hereditary' merchants are as critical as 'hereditary' workers to phase movement.

The merchant's vulnerability to risk varies enormously according to the nature of the market and his place in it. He is in a better position than the producer to take advantage of, or guard against, the consequences of price fluctuations. The merchant may deliberately pass the risk back whether he works on a commission basis or not. Moreover, as quickly as markets develop so does the capacity of economic agents to manipulate these markets. The profit to be made arises from buying cheap and selling dear — the greater the number of transactions, the smaller the required difference in price. More relevant are deliberate market regulating devices. The typical goal of merchant market activity has always been an oligopolistic one. Most markets have from an early date more oligopolistic than might be conceded.

Any economy requires some minimum of commercial activity, which in the past came to be largely concentrated in the towns or controlled from the towns. Within the towns commercial activity was deliberately organised to limit risk. For most of the colonial period municipal corporations governed the American cities in the interests of commercial activity. Competition was regulated, prices fixed and the quality of output safeguarded. Town government was dominated by commercial interests and most by-laws and ordinances were concerned with trade. The municipal corporation achieved its main objective of containing the level of commercial risk. However it outlived its usefulness when the general level of commercial risk, particularly outside the towns, was reduced.

The Russian merchants were particularly vulnerable, partly because they never benefited from the containment of risk by independent municipal corporations. Historically, Russian merchants were unable to accumulate large and stable fortunes, an important precondition

157

for the foundation of a self-reliant middle class. Almost none of the great merchant families, the *gosti*, that arose in the seventeenth century survived into the eighteenth. As Samuel Baron has so persuasively shown, in the seventeenth century only one great merchant family in four managed to perpetuate its status longer than one generation and almost none longer than two. The rate of attrition among lower merchants, the *gostinnaya* or *sukhonnoya sotnya*, was likely to have been even greater.

As a consequence, demographically the merchants in Russia were very weak (Owen 1981). In 1836 merchant families accounted for less than half of one per cent of the empire's total population, 235,000 in all. The Moscow merchants made up only about five per cent of its population. High mortality was a problem; epidemics such as the plague outbreak of 1654 hit them badly. Merchants often simply changed activity and status, whether rising to better things (and shedding the taint of commerce), or more frequently failing to purchase the certificate that gave them the right to practise trade at the appropriate level.

Secondary risk was probably an even more significant problem. Taxes and extraordinary levies were common. Onerous duties were imposed on the merchant elite in particular, as customs collectors, as supervisors of state enterprises, as the autocrat's factors in trade. Office holding was frequent, above one year in five on average; protracted, in bouts of a year and a half; full time and largely unremunerated. A merchant's own property might be at risk as security for any losses. Generally there was a lack of legal guarantees to protect private property from confiscation or outright theft by the state or powerful magnates.

Moreover the association of the merchants, particularly the gosti, with the government and its exactions put them at risk from below. Merchants were vulnerable to murder in urban uprisings and to the destruction of their property, particularly where their houses included storage facilities. The government was unable to provide adequate security against popular urban upheavals or lawless bands in outlying areas.

Merchants also suffered from the competition of nobles and peasants and from the monopolies of the tsar. Isolation from the main international trade routes and privileges for foreign merchants further restricted opportunities.

Merchants were always careful but in the circumstances it is scarcely surprising that Russian merchants were notorious for extreme caution, defensiveness, a tendency to cheat (Hittle 1979). They rarely risked their capital in long-term investments, preferring short-term gains. They avoided innovation, feared expropriation and distrusted foreigners, the state and other estates.

By contrast American merchant houses were long lived, operating within a relatively stable environment; received legal protection from arbitrary action from both above and below; were relatively free from service obligations. As a consequence they could look much more to the long run, although it must be stressed, all merchants are cautious. Moreover just as government can play a positive or a negative role in risk management, so can the merchant-entrepreneur (Innes). The American merchant was in a much better position to play such a role than his Russian counterpart.

America was not completely free from commercial risk. One commentator has used the term 'variable instability' to describe the position of eighteenth-century Boston and notes the subjection of Boston to a bewildering variety of continuing crises and cataclysmic events (Warden 1976). Perhaps this explains the apparently poor growth performance of Boston in the eighteenth century.

A high level of risk can itself prevent market participation, either by deterring production for the market, or by destroying market participants, financially or physically, through the associated shocks. There is the further danger that risk-reducing activities may prevent the long-run development of the market by reducing the size of a potentially marketable surplus or by making market participation a costly exercise.

To repeat, under the ancient economic regime distribution costs dwarfed production costs. Institutions auxiliary to market operation were critical to its efficient operation. The efficient, and low cost, operation of impersonal markets postdated markets dependent on personal contact and personal knowledge. Once exchange proliferated, economies of scale supported the appearance of specialised auxiliary institutions. A virtuous circle is inherent in any form of economic development. Somebody had to give the market its initial push; this is the significance of government.

RISK, EXCHANGE AND MARKETS

Exchange and markets

The evolution of the institutions of the mercantile economy is

159

largely a matter of finding ways of diminishing risks.

Hicks

There is an extremely intricate relationship between the level of commercial risk, the development of trade and exchange and the creation of markets. The simplified argument advanced here runs as follows. A low level of commercial risk is associated with a high rate of exchange. Reductions in risk stimulate an expansion in exchange. The growth of exchange leads to the creation of markets, both by lowering distribution costs and by promoting the development of auxiliary market institutions. The key independent variable, therefore, is the level of commercial risk.

The likely sources of a decrease in commercial risk are reductions in pioneer risk and, where this is insufficient, direct government action. Already we have noted the role of the government in managing shocks and extending life expectancy. Its direct influence on commercial risk was no less significant. The establishment of a secure environment in which secondary risk was minimised was an important result of the provision of those essential public goods, law and order. Thereby private protection costs were greatly lowered. Government involvement in transport improvement was probably the most significant area of intervention. However the government was also interested in the areas of financing and merchanting, providing reliable media of exchange, regulating the quality of products, laying down laws regulating debt and contract. The following picks out a number of important areas in which government assistance helped either to increase the price of a marketed commodity or to reduce distribution costs. The emphasis is very much on the positive role of the American government in this area.

We start by looking at the reduction in transport costs, although closely associated are reductions in protection and merchanting costs. Transport could be particularly hazardous. Hurricanes or a bad blizzard could wipe out a merchant's capital. Long sea journeys were a very risky business, piracy and privateering, storm, fire, war and disease all threatening their smooth completion.

Some of these risks were reflected in higher freight costs. The often crippling death rates on long voyages reinforced the tendency to carry large crews. Uncertainty of provisioning made necessary the carrying of inflated stocks. Piracy, privateering and war led to significant armaments and even bigger crews. Large numbers of crew members were needed to man the pumps during storms. All these factors reduced the size of cargo relative to ship size, thereby increasing freight rates.

160

In so far as these measures failed to remove all risk, there was a need to incur further costs and to take further measures to manage the risk. The establishment of partnerships and part shares helped to spread risk. However a manageable level of risk was critical to the availability of cheap insurance. By the eighteenth century maritime insurance was available, although expensive in time of war.

On the most important trade route of all, the Atlantic route, a convoy system was established to provide protection against the depradations of enemy ships and privateers (Middleton 1953). Started in 1665 the system was initially haphazard, only becoming regular in 1707. Insurance premiums with the convoy were halved, from between ten and twelve per cent to five per cent during the French and Indian War, removing undue risk of economic losses. However violent fluctuations in marine insurance rates could occur in wartime. Normally peace-time rates were between three and four per cent but these rose to 12-15 per cent on the outward voyage and 20-25 per cent on the homeward between 1744-8, when freight rates including insurance soared from $6-8 per ton to as high as $16.

The America-West Indies routes were the most vulnerable within the Empire, with no convoy protection. Most ships on these routes were small, poorly armed and poorly manned, an easy prey. Peace-time insurance rates from the Chesapeake to the West Indies were three per cent. Towards the end of the French and Indian War they rose to between eleven and twelve per cent. Since the Atlantic route was twice the distance of the West Indies route the risk was at least twice as high.

The features which made the Chesapeake so advantageous for trade also made it vulnerable to the almost continuous danger of attack from an enemy navy, privateers or pirates. In the absence of towns, only a naval force could adequately defend it and after 1684 there was usually a royal warship in the Chesapeake. Fortunately piracy was on the wane after 1720 and more or less ceased in 1727.

In an extreme case lack of naval protection, for example, made insurance unavailable, as in certain areas for the young American republic. High risk ensured that the Russians were less fortunate in the domestic development of insurance. Its absence affected their foreign trade less than might be anticipated since it was dominated by foreigners, who had access to insurance.

Risk, therefore, increased the target rate of return and induced the introduction of risk-spreading devices. It also massively increased the cost of sea transport.

The significance of productivity increase in shipping and its

161

impact on the development of trade has been much discussed (North 1968, Walton 1967, Shepherd and Walton 1972). A large part of this increased productivity reflected a reduction in risk. The reduction in piracy allowed much larger cargoes and smaller armaments. Better provisioning and health, for example the provision of lime juice pioneered by the navy, reduced crew size. A more rapid turnaround of ships allowed a speedier flow of information concerning markets.

The absence of an efficient monetary and credit system also increased the degree of commercial risk. The two most significant problems were the need for an efficient circulating medium of exchange, both internally and externally, and the cost of credit. Scarcity of currency was the main internal problem. A lack of a reliable currency could sharply increase transaction costs. Fluctuations in the value of different currencies, there being, for example over 50 in the Atlantic economy during the eighteenth century (McCusker 1978), could make the difference between a profit or a loss. Debt was such a normal precondition for trading that whole networks of debt were built up, partly for want of an efficient medium of exchange (Price 1980). A number of American colonies devised excellent paper money issues which provided both cheap credit on the security of land and an acceptable medium of exchange. However the British government bitterly resisted this excellent innovation. A high level of commercial risk kept interest rates high, thereby increasing prices and reducing market size. Despite the government's constructive policies, improvement in money markets was slow and steady and even less dramatic than improvements in shipping.

Laws relating to debt might vary in their generosity to debtor and creditor but it was important to the development of commerce that the working of the law was consistent and predictable (Coleman 1974), that the creditor had a fair chance of recovery and that the debtor was not impaired in his ability to make restitution. If a debtor failed financially it was important that losses were minimised, particularly for the individual creditor. Some legal device for spreading the losses was a help; this was the achievement of the bankruptcy laws in America. Vulnerability to a chain reaction was limited by the spreading of risk.

Variation in the quality of a product represents another element of risk. Uneven quality could depress average price and tend to reduce demand. The necessity of quality control is reflected in the series of 'Inspection Laws' passed in the American colonies regulating the quality of all the most important export staples, most notably tobacco and flour. Riga, an important export outlet for Russia, had a similar inspection system from an early date (Knoppers 1976).

The market like the government is a social construct, the product of a particular historical evolution. Often the market is characterised as an exchange whose direct purpose is not an act of consumption by either partner to the exchange; for one or both partners the motive is profit. The transition from exchange to achieve a secure subsistence to exchange for profit is seen as the crucial step in the creation of a market.

In the literature, particularly on colonial New England, a distinction is often drawn between local exchange, the prevalence of rural exchange networks based on land but often involving labour rather than money, as in the 'exchange of local services', or the unloading of subsistence surpluses, and genuine commercial exchange, defined by a conscious profit objective. A society is deemed ruled by the market only if the market is strong enough to direct production. The objectives of profit and security are considered mutually exclusive.

There is no clear line of demarcation between market and non-market exchange. The establishment of such a demarcation has generated a continuing controversy (Henrietta 1978, Clark 1979, Merrill 1977, Mutch 1977, Bushman 1981). Much ink has been spilled in attempts at a definition of market activity.

The argument expressed here is that in an appropriate context of stability the market emerges out of a dense exchange; the transition may be imperceptible. A failure to recognise this generates much artificial conflict and interminable problems of definition.

For example the size of the decision-making unit at the lowest level partly determines the nature of the exchange. Exchange within a largely self-sufficient family farm, or within an estate or plantation, does not involve a market transaction. Considerable movement of supplies occurred over long distances to the St Petersburg and Moscow houses of the nobility, but this is still movement within the framework of the estate.

Some market exchange occurred at all times, involving such necessities as salt, firearms, metal goods or even luxuries when a small cash surplus appeared. There is no doubt that in both societies travelling salesmen, hucksters, pedlars or temporary fairs gave the opportunity for market engagement if only on an intermittent basis. Therefore in one sense the market was ubiquitous; in another sense it was, until very late, of secondary importance since most output was consumed by its producers.

Commitment to market participation might not initially be either permanent or voluntary. For a period flexible economic agents can

163

move in and out of markets at will; they have a choice.

It is interesting to note that the 'small man' was the major source of marketed foodstuffs in both colonial America and nineteenth-century Russia, although large estates did export wheat from the southern steppe. In both areas total marketings consisted of a large number of small surpluses disposed of in a decentralised manner both on local and on distant markets. Schumacher's remarks could apply to central Russia as much as northern America: 'it is apparent that in the Middle Colonies, as in New England, the surplus of an individual farm was small. The narrow margin between surplus and scarcity might readily be wiped out by drought, severe winters, or the inroads of crop enemies.' As Mitchell has written about colonial America, 'Both the extent and growth rate of external trade were out of all proportion to the limited level of agricultural specialisation'.

It is a mistake to identify the market with specialisation and high productivity, and diversification and low productivity with the absence of a market (Mutch 1977: 284). In America the picture is very much one of a mixed agriculture diversified to counteract risk. However a typical peasant farm in Russia was struggling for survival until the nineteenth century and badly linked to the outside world.

Russian peasants, concerned for the most part with achieving a target consumption close to subsistence were often forced into the market to realise enough money to meet their monetary obligations or to procure a few essential items. Colonial Americans had much more room for manoeuvre. For example a series of non-importation agreements which initiated economic warfare with Britain before the start of military hostilities in the War of Independence dramatically reduced the level of market dependence.

The relatively small scale of early international trade, its limitation to high value-to-bulk ratio commodities, the high risk environment in which it occurred, all these factors led to the government regulation of exchange — to administered companies enjoying monopolies and to navigation laws directing trade into particular channels. Thereby returns were kept high and risk reduced. Domestic trade was also closely regulated by governments, particularly municipal governments, who tried to determine prices and fix the actual terms and venue of exchange within real-world markets.

There is also a very close relationship between the evolution of commodity and factor markets. For western Europe the development of factor markets followed fast after that of commodity markets; for America and Russia the delay was much longer.

The freeing of commodity trade resulted from a dramatic improvement in the risk environment. The key relationship is between the sheer weight of exchange, however effected, and market development. The establishment of a market system probably cannot be dated precisely. However economic development depends upon the market as a mechanism by which the necessary specialisation of economic function is brought about. The market solves the problem which the market creates. The market also diffuses the consumption tastes appropriate to each phase.

The next two sections deal with the appearance of factor markets.

Land distribution

Areas of new settlement are characterised by an abundance of virgin land and a scarcity of settlers and therefore labour. The existence of abundant land, even in the context of great demand for that land, does not in itself ensure a free and active land market. This section considers under what circumstances such a market appears.

In an economic sense the land consisted of a bundle of rights to its usufruct, water and mineral rights as well as rights to a share of crop output. In theory each right could be disposed of on a free but separate market. In practice the separation of these rights often represented a major obstacle to market development. Therefore the initial consolidation of such rights as full private property ownership is usually considered a necessary prerequisite to market development. In particular there is a need to protect ownership of improvements in land. Industrial development however requires some specialisation of market operations in the splitting-off of certain rights, as for example the right to water use. In so far as these rights are incompatible, some ranking must be made. The law of eminent domain recognised the threat vested property rights might pose for economic development.

From an economic point of view a clear separation of ownership and sovereignty is necessary. In both America and Russia the land was regarded as the property of the government. Land newly acquired automatically fell into the state domain. In America the land belonged initially to the crown, later but only transiently to the individual colonies and finally to the federal government. In the colonial period the formal rights of the crown were protected by the liability to quitrents, although in practice such quitrents were rarely paid; today by the imposition of local property taxes. In Russia privately held land was held on condition of the fulfillment of service obligations to the government. It is significant that the service obligations and the clearly limited tenure of land emerged with the consolidation of the authority of Muscovy. Land not yet granted to private individuals, the so-called 'black' land, was occupied by state peasants who paid a rental as token of their use of state land. The situation was made more complex by the fact that the imperial family actually controlled land, the fruits of which belonged to them as individuals.

Thus in both countries the ultimate ownership was vested in the government although the rights of control, or the entitlement to the land's usufruct, devolved on others. Even the feudal system had asserted the ultimate ownership of the Crown. The main implication for us is that the government controlled the distribution of the land and through this mechanism indirectly the development and operation of a land market.

Under such a system fusion of ownership and sovereignty was a danger. America inherited a range of options including tenures recognised by English common law which separated various rights to the control and use of land. In colonial America competition for settlers ensured that the terms of land distribution were generous and land tenure was unconditional. Peculiar feudal tenures, such as the one proposed by Locke for South Carolina, were doomed to extinction. Only in the patroonships of New York did a significantly different system survive for any length of time; a quasi-feudal system of land-holding survived into the nineteenth century with its vast estates and patroons. Elsewhere land quickly came to be held in 'free and common socage', a term denoting unencumbered use and free alienation. This is the tenure which came to be known as fee simple.

In Russia the fusion of sovereignty and ownership as writ large. One peculiarity of the Russian system was the persistence of the service obligation attached to land holding; the principle that 'the land must serve' prevailed. Land held on a service tenure first displaced, then fused with allodial holdings. The development of a free market in land was restricted by the increasingly tight adscription of the peasant to the soil. Private ownership was also contrary to the compulsory membership of collectives with its associated imposition of collective obligations and the collective use of the land. These limitations led Madariaga to conclude that the conception of privately owned and exploited land survived only in very small groups such as the *odnodvortsy*, the 'single householders', and farmer soldiers, and that a market in land existed on only a very small scale, usually hidden behind a series of legal fictions (Madariaga 1981: 108).

One major difficulty was the chaotic land law, which combined with the economic importance of land and a growing relative shortage in settled areas led to landgrabbing as a universal phenomenon. There was a land survey in 1684. No new survey was advocated until 1754 although only completed between 1766 and the 1840s. Moreover, as Madariaga noted the basic organising principle was not the property rights of an individual landowner, but the establishment of the amount and the boundaries of the land which belonged to a given village, whether it had one or several owners or belonged to the state (Madariaga 1981: 109).

The full privatisation of land ownership was achieved only very slowly. In practice the land of the serfowners became theirs in 1762 when the service obligation was abolished, in theory when their estates were unravelled from those of the peasants in 1861. For the land held by the peasant or ex-serfs, the assertion of full and unencumbered hereditary ownership of land occurred only in 1906 and 1910, and lasted for a very short period.

The functioning of an efficient land market depended on the assertion and enforcement of full property rights over the land, an assertion not incompatible with some formal but distant shadow of ultimate ownership by the state. It also depended on the speed and terms on which land was distributed, originally by the government.

In colonial America the land was very rapidly and very easily distributed. The exact mechanism varied between the colonies, from the ordered process by which New England town proprietors progressively granted away the land entrusted to them by the General Courts or by which colonial governments deliberately promoted special purposes: through the large patents granted to individuals, who then failed to regulate efficiently the distribution; to the headright system, particularly in Virginia, in which numerous small grants were made, even to indentured servants. Even in Puritan New England it was not long before land was auctioned to raise revenue. Others acquired land claims by investment in the founding colonisation companies or simply by preemption or squatting. Speculation in land became an easy taunt against Easterners but also an essential link in the distribution of land by large owners and the opening up of the land by settlers. Speculation carved up the land into manageable units, even in the colonial period.

Such developments prepared the way for the whole panoply of surveying, land sales at auction and rapid land distribution. Even squatting and preemption were eventually built into the system. The system for both the colonial and federal periods was based on small units, low prices and/or cheap credit.

Russia never saw the evolution of a comparable land market. Up to the end of the eighteenth century the Russian government deliberately sought to fill up the newly acquired territories by granting enormous tracts of land to individual favourites or supporters, who then made use of their control over serf labour to recreate serf society in the new area. Squatting certainly occurred but runaways survived for but a short time beyond the line of the serf system. Even the Cossack bands presented an increasingly stratified social system akin to serfdom as their contacts with the Russian government increased.

Exceptions to serfdom were rare; the North and Siberia were never affected. Catherine also encouraged immigration and set aside land for immigrant settlements. However, serfdom at the same time provided the means to restrict and control the already-settled areas and the means to settle new areas. In theory serfs could not own land or property, indeed for most of Russian history landholding was a monopoly of the nobility. Even after emancipation peasant land was held under a form of communal tenure.

Competitive pluralism encouraged an efficient and active land market in America, whereas monolithic centralism in Russia fudged the distinction between sovereignty and ownership. Free and common socage suited the American pattern of behaviour. The Russians did not have to limit tenure by service, indeed allodial property predated service property. Again practice moulded institutional arrangements. Once institutionalised in the initial formative period, these patterns constantly reasserted their influence, even up to today.

Sovereignty of labour

In a society of new settlement, labour was the scarce factor of production, the ready availability of productive land helping to create the scarcity of wage labour. Both security and profitability encouraged owner-occupier farming. Potential employers could only guarantee control of a labour force by denying labour a choice. It would not be surprising, therefore, if the market for labour was slower to develop than the market for the more abundant factor, land.

Scarcity of labour produces two main tendencies; first, an attempt by employers to control the use of scarce labour, and secondly, a tendency for free labour to become expensive. The latter tendency reinforces the former.

Moreover, the growth of significant commodity markets, by indirectly raising the demand for labour may reinforce both tendencies. It is no accident that the demand for raw cotton revived the declining institution of slavery in the USA, nor that an increased demand for Russian grain reinforced a return to *barshchina*, or labour dues, as a preferred form in which serfowners extracted their obligations from the serfs.

Non-market controls over labour were ubiquitous in the early history of Russia and America. However, two careful qualifications must be made at this point. Not all so-called 'forced' labour was involuntary. A desire for security might lead individuals to sell themselves into some form of slavery or forced labour. An indenture might equally be a means of securing a loan in an imperfect capital market (Galenson 1979).

Secondly, the existence of forced labour was not incompatible with the growth of a market for that labour, sometimes a very sophisticated market as that for slaves, responding sensitively to differences of sex, age, skill and even amenability (Fogel and Engerman 1974). The use of the term free labour is often used to refer to the nature of the relationship between enterprise and worker, in particular whether it was based on contract, not to the personal status of the worker. Serfs on *obrok* often hired themselves out in this way. This allowed the co-existence within a viable economy of a developed labour market and forced labour.

In colonial America, according to Hughes, only between 30 per cent and 50 per cent of the labour force represented free labour (Hughes 1976). Even in this area the whole panoply of medieval restrictions were inherited from Britain. The harsh statute of artificers and apprentices applied. There were even attempts to apply the restrictive guild system. Wage fixing was common. Free labour was subject to various kinds of compulsion; impressment for road work, for military and quasi-military duties, for the night watch, for harvesting. The poor were forced to work and apprentices were bound to their masters for seven years. Such a situation led Hughes to conclude that, 'Even the unfettered sector of the colonial labour force was, by law and custom, liable to rigorous compulsion.' Moreover a strong element of compulsion applied also to labour provided from within the family and continued to be after the other restrictions disappeared. The input of family labour was as much 'forced' as genuinely servile labour and represented an input outside market influence. Reference has also been made to forms of debt peonage implicit in the practice of debt defaulters indenting themselves to creditors (Heyrman).

In the seventeenth century the employment of recognisably servile white labour was very significant. According to the leading authority on indentured servants, A.E. Smith, they accounted for more than half of all white immigrants before 1776 (Smith 1947). Some of these were involuntary indentures — for example, some 34,500 being convicts

— but most were voluntary. The context of indenture was not only the relative demand for and supply of labour in Europe and America but also the high cost of passage relative to income in the principal source areas of Britain in the seventeenth and Palatine Germany in the eighteenth centuries. Some mechanism of credit creation was necessary to finance the flow of immigrants. Sale of labour for a four or seven-year period, or even less for redemptioners, who could meet at least some proportion of the cost of passage, represented such a mechanism. The great shortage and expense of free labour made it profitable for merchants, ship captains and plantation owners to buy such indentures. Most of the indentured servants went to the south, where the greatest demand for labour existed. Clearly such forced labour was both voluntary, for the most part, and compatible with the growing market for indentures.

Slavery became important towards the end of the seventeenth century. Before then America had difficulty in competing with the demand for slaves of the sugar plantations in the West Indies. By 1780 however over half a million, or 20 per cent of the population, were slaves. Although most were concentrated in the south, slavery existed everywhere. The increased demand for labour arising from the growth of the export staples of tobacco, rice and indigo, was a major factor underpinning the increased importance of slavery.

Why was indentured white labour replaced by black slave labour from the end of the seventeenth century? A number of studies have shown that the use of slave labour became more economic on the plantations of the south, both large and small. Hughes argues that the significant factor in the replacement of indentured labour by slaves was a change in labour conditions in Britain. There was, allegedly, a slower rate of growth of the labour force and increasing real wages, at least from the 1660s onwards. Galenson also stressed short-term inelasticities in the supply of indentured labour. On the other hand the abolition of the monopoly of the English Royal African Company in 1698 is said to have lowered the cost of slaves (Lee and Passell 1979: 24). The key issues may however have been a lengthening time horizon of decision-making and a lower possiblity of slave deaths, both reflecting a reduction in risk. The first would allow a longer period during which the lower running costs of the slaves might offset their higher capital cost. Undoubtedly the general belief, and probable reality, that African slaves were more resistant to the disease environment of the south helped to accelerate the replacement of servile white labour by black. Indeed the lower death rate in the relevant period would also have reduced the importance of capital costs. A high rate of natural increase from an early date speeded up the process.

In Russia slavery disappeared relatively quickly. At its height, towards the end of the sixteenth century, slaves represented ten per cent of the population. The vast majority of the slaves were ethnic Russians who operated in a very wide range of employment in government, the military, estate stewardship and as personal servants. It is highly likely that the welfare function was the primary motive for a voluntary servitude. In bad times there was little alternative. In the seventeenth century the use of slaves was steadily reduced and they finally coalesced with the serfs. Slavery's main importance was as a precedent for serfdom, which amongst other functions performed the same welfare role.

Serfdom permeated Russian society and the Russian economy in a way slavery did in only a limited area of the USA. During most of the eighteenth century one half of the population was serfs. Serfdom represented more than a means of controlling the scarce factor of production. Serf ownership, as slave ownership previously, was a source of social status and serfdom extended its influence throughout the economy. The serf was tied not only to his lord but also to the land, where he was part of a collective jointly responsible for certain agricultural operations and for tax payments. There were severe restrictions on mobility unless the serfowner moved the serf. The same limitation on mobility applied to state peasants, who constituted the other significant component of the population.

The lack of market penetration in the Russian village and the lack of interest of most Russian landowners in the efficient operation of their estates prevented first the development of a slave market as economically sensitive as the slave market in the USA, and later restricted the operation of a market for serfs. Where, however, the serf was on *obrok*, that is, where he met his obligations in money rent, he was in practice free to move to maximise his income, and the number of passports issued indicate that he did so on a massive scale. However the sale of movement was lower than it might have been because of the tax represented by the payment of obrok itself.

In theory the ultimate decentralisation in the labour market involves the sovereignty of labour, the free choice by the labourer of his mode and place of employment. There is no guarantee that free labourers will choose to maximise their income rather than ensure their own security. On the other hand it is possible for servile labour to be allocated to the point of highest return. Owners of slaves or serfs may be more responsive to financial returns than the labourers themselves, imposing income maximisation on those who do not willingly seek it. There is, therefore, no *a priori* reason to assume the more

171

efficient allocation of free rather than servile labour.

In both societies free labour was massively expensive. This expense helps to explain the tenacity with which slavery or serfdom was retained. Both servile economies were clearly economically viable on the eve of emancipation. Despite differences in the productivity of free and servile labour, differences which were limited to certain activities, the difference in cost between free and servile labour, both where serfs produced foodstuffs from their own plots and where owners directly supported slaves, was sufficiently large to slow voluntary manumission, even if social pressures had not limited this.

A number of significant issues are raised by the existence of a system of unfree labour and its continuing influence on labour supply, even after emancipation. The main concern has been with its effect on the process of economic development. In the context of our monograph this comes down to asking whether forced labour could be adapted to market penetration or, in our terminology, entry into the commercial phase.

The single answer is yes, although until recently the conventional view has been some variant of the Soviet paradigm which sees the rise of the market or market relations as in some sense incompatible with either serf or slave labour. According to this paradigm, expansion of the new system is predicated upon the availability of free labour and hence on the abolition of serfdom or slavery. The system based on forced labour enters a general crisis becoming moribund, or at the very least, non-viable.

Recent work has rejected this analysis. The profitability of slave or serf labour is no longer seriously disputed (Fogel and Engerman 1974). In a number of ways already indicated, the existence of forced labour may actually have accelerated market penetration. However the issues raised are complex. It is highly relevant that labour in a non-free economic system is the most important form of fixed capital (R.V. Anderson and Gallman 1977). It pays to maximise the utilisation of any fixed capital, which may have two results; first to aid the production of cash crops, but also to increase the potential for self-sufficiency on the estate or plantation. The latter potentiality may not be realised. In Russia the spread of *kustar* industry was allegedly also a reaction to the need to keep serfs employed for long periods of the year. While the short-run impact of this development on market penetration was beneficial, the long-run impact was negative since there is strong evidence that kustar industry outcompeted factory industry. The market stimulus therefore went only so far. It is also significant that in the absence of forced labour in New England and the Middle

Colonies, labour could still seek employment outside agriculture during long slack periods; the typical farm labour regime created a considerable potential supply of free labour for employment in the factories.

SOCIO-ECONOMIC EQUILIBRIA

The fulfillment of family needs ranked above income maximisation as the primary principle of farm production

Bushman

Throughout the period considered the individual family household continued to be the basic economic cell, the main guardian of security and continuity. The two societies had in common the fusion of social and economic spheres within that household, which acted as the main unit of production, reproduction and consumption. However the nature and role of the family household differed markedly in the two societies. By 1800 the American household was typically well-integrated into the market, whereas the typical Russian peasant household was still largely self-sufficient. It would be premature to describe the market system in eighteenth century America as a capitalist system since the basic unit of production was not yet the enterprise, employing family workers outside their household base.

Again we revert to a theme discussed at the start of the book. It would be easy to contrast an economy still feudal and wedded to the household mode of economic transaction and an economy in transition to the capitalist mode with a strong emphasis on market activity. This is a gross oversimplification and inaccurate in key respects.

All producers seek security. What differs is the environment in which that search takes place. A social system adapts to a particular environment of shocks and risk. A high risk environment is likely to yield as the predominant mode of economic transaction the household mode in which Chayanov-type peasants minimise their market involvement. The market is a luxury allowed by a relatively secure and stable environment.

Social historians have usually viewed colonial America's history in the context of a model of communal decline. Like the Marxists, they have viewed commerce as in some sense incompatible with community. Indeed the typical institutions of an organic community are viewed as vestiges of a defunct feudal system, just as Breen has seen localism as a conservative reaction to the Stuart attempt to centralise authority in Britain transmitted across the Atlantic as part of the invisible

173

baggage of the migrants. Both views, together with the religious stress of the Puritans and Quakers have been regarded as a yearning to recreate a lost past and allegedly represent echoes of the medieval period.

Two comments are in order. Community as described by historians of colonial America was, it is true, a legacy of feudalism but not an anachronistic legacy doomed to disappear with economic progress; quite the reverse — community and localism were characteristic features of a society in Britain already the matrix of fast-reaching economic change and closely associated with that change.

Secondly, Bender has quite rightly rejected what he calls 'the law of conservation of historical energy'. Just as market growth does not preclude the development of government, so community is not incompatible with commerce, or the related notion of association; put more formaly *Gemeinschaft* with *Gesellschaft*. It is not a zero-sum game. Indeed there are important elements of community which promote commercial development. It is necessary therefore to analyse the working of each economy, at the level of the family household, in its broad outlines.

The peasant system of Russia had at its centre the family household not only as unit of production and consumption, but also as unit of ownership. Individual property rights did not exist; all the property of the household was familial. According to Hingley the Russians' sense of property is so different to the western conception that the language still does not possess a proper verb for 'to lend' or 'to borrow' (Hingley 1978: 44). Indeed, until the eighteenth century the Russian language even lacked a word for private property (*sobstvennost*) (Hittle 1979: 33). The head of the household managed or administered the property on behalf of the family; he acted as their household representative. Moreover, in the absence of firm property rights there could be no real concept of inheritance. On the death of the head of the household, the *khozyain*, property was partitioned but even the division of the property between the 'heirs' was a late introduction. No individual had a right to a specific share in the property although all enjoyed birth-rights to the usufruct. Primogeniture was unheard of. However in practice the timing and nature of land partition were often arranged to preserve land holdings from fragmentation. Strategic marriages served the same function.

The labour necessary for production was for the most part family labour. The use of hired labour in the peasant economy was insignificant, until the opening of the steppe in the south and the diversification of economic activity in the relatively infertile north. Where land holdings were inadequate and employment opportunities existed outside agriculture family members did leave the household but only on a temporary basis. Income above subsistence needs was usually sent back to the household pool. Considerable mobility could occur where population was sparse, poverty endemic and when repeated shocks occurred. Such mobility was not allowed to disturb the peasant system, even after the beginning of factory industrialisation.

The output of the family farm or factory was devoted almost wholly to direct consumption, for use rather than exchange in the market. The household was largely self-sufficient, selling on the market only in order to pay rent or taxes or to meet the minimum requirements for goods which could not be produced within the household. There was little specialisation. Nor did the peasant *mentalité* include the concept of a wage. Consequently in later competition with the profit-oriented for land, the peasants often overvalued the land, the value of which represented to them, in modern terminology, the capitalisation of gross returns (Chayanov 1966).

The peasant economy largely functioned with only insignificant exchange on local markets and largely without cash, although on occasion these local markets, both for commodities or for whatever land was available, could be quite brisk. Peasant households had a widespread attachment to particular tracts of land. This attachment combined with the importance of real and fictive kin encouraged relative geographical immobility. The bond to the land represented insurance against starvation.

Another significant characteristic of peasant households in Russia was their large size, typically including three generations and a number of daughters-in-law (Ransel 1978). The multiple family household made for stability; the household could function as if economically immune to the births, marriages and deaths occurring within it. By relieving young people approaching marriageable age of the need to establish the means for financial and residential independence, the peasant system of joint families facilitated a pattern of early and nearly universal marriage, something also desired by the landlord to increase the availability of labour and by the community to spread the obligations of tax and recruitment. To a varying degree bailiffs forced large households on the serfs.

Some of the main features of the peasant life cycle strongly influenced the organisation of the family household. Before the nineteenth century women commonly married in their late teens. The imposition by landlords of fines on procrastinators encouraged universal marriage. Family units were rapidly reconstructed by remarriage on the death of one partner. Orphans were adopted or fostered

175

by kin. The system did not allow a long period of disattachment to a household. Early on slavery often solved the problem for the disattached. The high mortality of infants and children was compensated by a very high birth rate, typically over 50 per 1,000.

Partly because women were held in low esteem, partly becaue the children lacked both property and job opportunities to make them independent, the family household was dominated by patriarchal authority. The average age at which a new head of a household took his position was probably 40, by which age the first grandchildren had already been born. Marriage was arranged rather than the result of a romantic attachment. In such a society childhood was short, almost non-existent in the modern sense, and retirement equally curtailed.

Differentiation of households by land or asset holding or by value of output largely reflected the size of a household and the position of its members in the life cycle; demographic differentiation prevailed. Biological or economic accidents could also have an influence. Social differentiation according to economic success was slight, limited by the lack of market involvement.

The structure of peasant communities differed — but the general weakness of most horizontal ties and the lack of economic or social interaction allowed significant differentiation of local characteristics and customs. A social gulf separated the peasantry and other groups in society, particularly the nobility. Town and country were different worlds, a distinction which underpinned the opposition of national laws and local customs. The world outside impinged on peasant society as a pressure from above, from the state for revenue and recruits, from the landlord for cash, commodities and labour. Such pressure varied according to the malignity of a highly unstable and potentially hostile environment and the position of the government or landlord. Such pressure was a strong moulding influence on village life, restricting the freedom of the peasant household to regulate marriage or fertility.

There is no doubt that the multiple extended family system was a major aid in containing risk. The household could be expanded easily by inclusion of the children of the poor. On the other hand labour could be released for outside employment according to local circumstances. The use of the one resource available, labour, was maximised and the continuity of the family ensured.

The pluralist society of America not surprisingly had a number of variants of the market model, major differences characterising the three areas of New England, the Middle Colonies, notably Pennsylvania (although New York had a sub-variant),and the south, particularly the Chesapeake. Much more is known about New England, which explains the disproportionate length of treatment of this area. The other areas are discussed in so far as they diverge from the New England pattern.

New England illustrates the extreme danger of generalisation. Stephen Innes (1983) has subdivided the New England of the seventeenth century into three district settlement zones: the urbanised coastal region, including Boston and Salem; a subsistence farming region, including already carefully studied townships such as Dedham or Andover; and an area of highly commercialised agriculture. The last would include townships in the Connecticut and Merrimack valleys, in Plymouth colony or on Cape Cod. Clearly some of the second group would look very similar to Russian villages — highly communal, egalitarian, non-materialist and self-sufficient. On the other hand a town such as Springfield in the Connecticut valley represented 'the avatar of the new capitalist world' (Innes 1983: 42), with its characteristics of developmentalism, diversification, acquisitiveness, individualism, contentiousness and stratification. Most seem to have tended more in the latter direction.

Moreover, Heyrman has shown the variety of experience even within one of these subdivisions. Gloucester and Marblehead fall in the first group but both illustrate the persistence of a communitarian way of life even within a commercial context, although the latter had greater difficulties in the absence of either a phase of utopian corporatism or even a period of stable, autonomous local development. The following is therefore an over-simplified generalisation of an illusive average.

In New England the individual household farm operated within the context of the township. After a short-lived experiment in communal ownership full private property rights vested in the individual were established, although land ownership was initially in the hands of the town proprietors. Proprietors in the seventeenth century often held back land for later distribution. However, as population increased the communal and undistributed lands disappeared. Early settlement was concentrated; later, in the eighteenth century, it became increasingly dispersed.

Inheritance systems, reflecting the relative abundance of land, and possibly the need to motivate family labour, were initially based on partible inheritance with a double share often going to the first child (Alston and Schapiro 1984). Later, under the influence of population pressure, to avoid fragmentation of land holdings, partible inheritance began to give way to impartible, multigeniture to primogeniture.

177

Far from each family member having a birthright on household property, when a son inherited even the provision for widows had to be spelled out in detail, much to the delight of historians of consumption levels. Wills increasingly sought to prevent the break up of estates. Where possible, superfluous sons were assisted to set themselves up apart from the family farm, on the frontier or locally as a craftsman or professional. Often the youngest rather than the eldest son inherited the farm, frequently taking over before the death of his parents. The inheritor had the right to sell, mortgage, bequeath or alienate the land as he saw fit, unless restricted by specific stipulations in the deed of transfer or will.

Within such a society surplus labour was much more likely to cut its links with the family household. As a consequence there was much more hiring of labour and the emergence of a landless proletariat. In rural areas characterised by fairly dense trade by the middle of the eighteenth century, as many as 30 per cent of the population were landless. Despite the practice of warning off, intended to ease the burden of pauperism on the township, there was considerable mobility.

Alongside the developing labour market there emerged a sophisticated commodity market. Family households were much more dependent on the market for their requirements and as an outlet for surplus production. As a consequence from an early date there was much less self-sufficiency, households being more integrated into both the market economy and the society as a whole. Townships were mutually dependent and closely linked with urban central places. The cash economy was invading the countryside to a significant degree. The economic concepts of wage, rent or profit were much better understood.

Naturally this represented a context of changing risk. While this book emphasises the role of the government in mitigating such risk, the short-run management of risk might very well fall to a small group of merchant-entrepreneurs such as the Willards in the Merrimack valley, the Winthrops in Boston, the Otises in Barnstaple and best known of all the Pynchons in Springfield. Such men provided the credit, technology and leadership to turn a wilderness into a settlement. More to the point they acted as a kind of corporate patron for a region, in Innes' words, 'absorbing price variations and carrying changes in inventories of foodstuffs and soft goods to provide an economic cocoon for the townsfolk or an economic buffer to the outside word' (Innes 1983: 175). They also acted as the employer of last resort. In other words they voluntarily bore more than their fair share of secondary risk. The habits of community cushioned many against the risks of commerce.

Although there is little doubt that age differences could account for a large part of the uneven wealth distribution, the extent of social differentiation was significant and growing. Particularly in urban areas, but also in long settled rural areas, income and wealth differences were increasing. Consequently both the rural and urban society was much more stratified than Russian society.

However the growth of inequality was not a linear process. Warden has pointed out the subjection of Bostonians of the revolutionary generation to a bewildering variety of continuing crises and cataclysmic events. On his account, 'variable instability' rather than 'increasing inequality' or 'economic polarisation' was the chief defining characteristic of Bostonian society (Warden 1976). The instability was sufficient to retard the demographic and economic growth of Boston.

Within New England society the nuclear family predominated. Marriage and fertility rates were much more flexible than in Russia and largely under the control of the immediate family. Recent research suggests that the nuclear family was not a result of, but rather a precondition for economic development. America in general conformed much more to the west European marriage pattern than the Russian. American women typically married in their early 20s, early by western European but late by Russian standards particularly for women. Marriage was by no means universal but much closer to it than in west Europe. As a consequence the birth rate was high, even higher than for Russia. Infant and child mortality was also high, and apt to increase with the growth of cities where children were particularly vulnerable to infectious disease. However a generally low level of mortality, except in the seventeenth century south, kept the natural rate of increase in population well above the Russian level. Family continuity was much more easily assured.

Initially patriarchal authority survived because the head of the household exercised control over land, but as other opportunities were opened up such control diminished. By the end of the colonial period arranged marriages were fast disappearing.

The second variant prevailed in Pennsylvania, although this variant was rapidly converging on the New England model. From the beginning the household farm existed as a separate unit independent of the township, since settlement was always dispersed rather than concentrated. Because of the greater resource endowment and less hostile physical environment, there was much more extensive market involvement, which partly offset the later date of settlement. The

179

greater availability of land reduced the tendency to greater social differentiation but the growing urbanisation associated with market involvement counteracted this influence. Both factors undermined patriarchal authority, which was also weaker because of religious differences.

Demographic characteristics and behaviour were broadly similar to those in New England. The nuclear family predominated, assisted by low mortality and high fertility.

In New York the typical farmer was less often an owner-occupier, more frequently a tenant on the large estates or patroonships. Such an emphasis may have slowed settlements in New York, and it appears to have had some impact on the nature of market involvement. Moreover whereas primogeniture prevailed in colonial New York, multigeniture was the rule elsewhere in the Middle Colonies (Alston and Schapiro 1984).

In the south large plantations and small owner-occupied farms appear side by side. There was little difference between the two in the seventeenth century, and even in the eighteenth century an unbroken continuum of size. Southern society in the seventeenth century represented an interesting combination of high mortality and a stress on the nuclear family. Because broken families and orphanhood were the norm southern society was highly unstable. Only the high returns of tobacco culture, and later rice cultivation, kept this society in existence.

By the eighteenth century Southern society, particularly Chesapeake society, had become much more stable. A reduction in mortality allowed the emergence of a dominant planter gentry. Primogeniture and entail preserved the integrity of the plantation. Considerable social differentiation had become characteristic of these southern societies. Greater stability also allowed the replacement of white indentured or hired labour by slave labour. Authority within the plantations was highly patriarchal with arranged marriages and little mobility. Opportunities for young men were limited by the lack of urban centres and economic diversification.

The economy was export-oriented in the production of cash crops but had strong elements of self-sufficiency, particularly within the poorer white households and the slave economy. In relations with the outside it was very much a cash economy; relations within the plantation, however, were non-monetary. In an economic sense the society was poorly integrated.

Initially the lack of women relative to men and the high level of mortality made for almost universal marriage of women at an early age, a pattern which continued into the eighteenth century. In the seventeenth century many families were expanded by the inclusion of orphans. It is interesting to speculate whether a persistence of the hostile environment of the seventeenth century, with its associated absence of slave labour, might have stimulated the reversion to a multiple or extended family system. The unstable economy of the seventeenth century could not have survived either a curtailment of immigration or a protracted fall in the price of tobacco.

Russian and American households diverged less in their economic motivation and organisation than we might expect. The key difference lay in the environment. The resource endowment and risk level left its powerful imprint on the relationship between household and market. Moreover any complex institutional structure is slow to change, once having evolved. New social formations adapt to the existing structure and reinforce a pro- or anti-market bias. The force of social inertia is very great.

8

Interaction of Government and Markets

MODELS OF GOVERNMENT INTERVENTION

The rulers of Muscovy faced an administrative Hobson's choice: to have local affairs in local hands was to court political disintegration; to maintain centralised control necessarily involved the sacrifice of efficiency, and in many cases the suppression of potentially constructive local initiative.

Hittle

Although there is no one simple mechanism by which governments promote either intra- or inter-phase movement, there are two main models of such promotion in the literature. The first considers direct government intervention in economic activity and the positive linkage effects resulting from such intervention. Traditionally the emphasis has been on public works rather than public goods, on backward rather than forward linkages. However, during both opening up and the commercial phase the significant linkages tend to be forward — that is, services consumed by non-government sectors in the shape of public goods — only during the industrial phase, backward linkages — that is, the demand for non-government produced materials and equipment. Consequently, we call this the public goods model.

The second, the judicial promotion model, considers the way in which the legal rules which influence the non-government sector of the economy are set by the government, in particular the legislature or judiciary. At whatever level, government can indirectly promote the provision of public goods. A municipality, for example, can use waterlot rights to persuade private interests to build public roads or wharfs (Hartog 1979). The judiciary can interpret the law to allow the establishment of public enterprises which wield the power of government enterprises, or to allow the redistribution of costs and benefits in a manner which promotes the kind of economic activities associated with the relevant phases.

A particularly interesting and significant manifestation of this indirect promotion relates to the public service origins of the American business corporation. It became common in America to incorporate all associations whose main function was public service but the definition of the latter was widened from benevolent to business goals. However at the beginning of the federal period both types of organisation effectively performed their services at the local level where they were clearly recognised as beneficent.

The usual justification for government intervention in the economy rests on a divergence between social and private benefits or costs. Indeed some authorities imply that in the absence of such a divergence the need for government would completely disappear (North 1981); market institutions would be an efficient substitute for government in North's Shangri-la. In practice the level of decision-making appropriate to a particular economic activity is one whose jurisdiction contains most of the particular benefits and costs, whether it involves direct government action or a redistribution of costs and benefits through court decisions. Significant discontinuities of investment, or economies of scale, also tend to make appropriate differing areas of jurisdiction. Furthermore, differences in the rate of time discount are important in determining whether particular investments are worthwhile. Such rates tend to decline with the widening scope of jurisdiction. This tendency reflects the fact that the ability to manage risk increases with the size of jurisdiction. The cost of shock management has less significance at a higher level since many shocks are localised in their impact, and good and bad fortune are mutually offsetting. Put another way, it is natural for individuals, but not for governments, to demand a high risk premium.

These three factors — divergence between social and private costs, discontinuities in investment and differing rates of time discount — operate independently in particular economic activities to vary the appropriate government jurisdiction. A dense system of government is more likely to match actual with appropriate jurisdictions.

Transport improvement is a neat illustration of this argument. Commercial development depended greatly on transport improvement. From the point of view of local communities a significant divergence existed between the social and private benefits arising from transport improvement.

For example, a turnpike set up to improve overland transportation might not be profitable, nor be expected to be, but it might raise local land values, improve a community's access to markets, and lower the costs of goods transported into the area. (Pratt: 45).

A given transport route between neighbouring villages might also serve as part of a large number of longer routes. Capital indivisibilities therefore also compounded the problem. A vicious circle existed in which transport improvement was vital to market development but poorly articulated markets made such improvement unlikely without government action. Effective transport improvement at all levels is best implemented by a dense system of government. A dense system of government makes more likely a dense transport network. A quickening of transport, or communication in general, reduces commercial risk both by reducing the impact of natural shocks and by widening, and improving the functioning of, markets, thereby reducing the amplitude of price fluctuations.

Consquently both government policy and structure had a strong influence on inter-phase movement. Indeed policy was very much constrained by structure. Decision-making structures which evolved to cope with the problems of one phase were not neessarily helpful to movement in another phase.

The general picture in America was one in which governments at different levels were able to adjust policies to suit the requirements of their own economic niche. They could achieve this because of the unbroken vertical and horizontal chains of decision-making units.

Although in New England the system of government evolved as an appropriate response to pioneer risk it served also as an excellent mechanism for effecting the transition to the commercial phase. In the Chesapeake commerce was from the beginning crucial to the survival of the colonies, and it is interesting to note that polarisation of decision-making was greater. The relative weakness of county government undermined an effective response from government to the increasingly potent commercial risk. The emphasis in dealing with this risk was thrown back on to the self-sufficient plantations. The south for the most part also lacked the urban centres of the north with their keen sensitivity to local economic requirements. The Middle Colonies displayed a much more complex government structure which, however, was characterised by a dense intermediate government promoting commercial development, particularly for domestic as opposed to external markets, although the latter did help to stimulate the former.

The strong polarisation in Russia inherited from the opening up phase inhibited movement into the commercial phase. Moreover the structure of government did not prove to be flexible enough to adjust effectively to new demands.

Public goods model

Surprisingly for both Russia and America government participation in economic activity before the nineteenth century has been little researched, whether from the revenue or the expenditure side. This neglect has reflected on the one hand the extraordinary difficulty of making any detailed quantitative statements because of inadequate statistical data, and on the other hand an implicit assumption that the significance and nature of that activity was already fully understood.

There is an inherent difficulty in delineating what constitutes an expenditure or tax. This is hardly surprising since much of the relevant exchange took place outside the market. Labour services, or *corvée*, constituted the major part of a citizen's obligations to government, particularly at the local level. For example, in colonial America work on the roads, militia service, office holding without pay — all represented obligations imposed, willingly or not, on the taxpayer.

In Russia the same principle applies with even more pronounced significance. Service was, as we have seen, an essential element of the system. *Barshchina*, or labour dues, required of the serf enabled the serfowner to perform his quasi-governmental duties.

As a consequence it is difficult to calculate the total value of direct taxes, paid in differing forms as labour services, in kind or cash, particularly where local taxation predominated. In principle indirect tax, reflecting the development of the market, was much easier to collect, and in the form of cash. A high level of external trade, as in colonial America, allowed a considerable dependence on customs dues. An alternative, pursued largely in Russia, was to impose internal tolls on trade. There is good evidence that during periods of abortive but rapid trade growth in Russia, at least temporarily indirect taxation grew to be more important as a source of revenue than direct taxation.

For the same reason the evaluation of resources commanded by the government is also difficult because of the great importance of direct labour inputs by those owing a tax-like obligation. It is, therefore, extremely difficult to calculate the levels of economically-oriented expenditure, let alone compare them.

On the other hand the lack of overt interest reflects a tendency in the past to downgrade both the importance of pre-industrial

185

growth and to focus on central government, ignoring the significance of lower decision-making echelons in the government structure during the pre-industrial era.

The tax burden in colonial America was most probably significantly lower than in contemporary Russia, in particular during its formative period. Palmer has provided a set of statistics for 1765 and 1785 which have often been used in the past to show the relative burden of taxation in colonial America and contemporary Britain (Palmer 1959). The data are limited in their coverage, excluding local taxation, a significant omission since the general view is that local taxation revenue exceeded colony revenue. However, inclusion of the value of obligations owed to serfowners and supporting their surrogate government services would also at a minimum double total 'government' revenue in Russia.

On Palmer's evidence the level of central government taxation in Russia in 1785 was very much higher than in colonial America but lower than in post-revolutionary America. The explanation for the change is quite simple. In the colonial period tax rates, particularly direct tax rates, fluctuated markedly according to the requirements of war. Almost as frequently the mechanism of finance came to be a paper-money issue, later contracted or even liquidated with the aid of British subsidies. In many years, notably of peace, there was no taxation. During the colonial period the British government met most of the military expenditures and this explains the marked increase in expenditures after the Revolutionary War. Moreover, many of the military and most of the non-military services provided by government were provided at the local level (Davis and Huttenback 1982, Palmer 1959, Gunderson 1976). After Independence the central budget covered frontier needs and even significant civil tasks, such as exploration or the work of the Corps of Engineers.

For Russia the statistics for calculating the tax rate during the formative period, or for very much later periods, are very limited. Crude approximations, derived from average *per capita* income, itself deduced from the statistics of average land holdings, yields and household size found in the work of R.E.F. Smith (1977) and Blum (1961), and from known tax revenues per head (Hellie 1971, Bushkovitch 1978), suggest that direct taxes alone must have exceeded 20 per cent by a significant amount. Indirect taxes, although limited in scope by lack of market development, would have increased this by a large amount. By contrast Gunderson, using Palmer's figures, calculates the tax burden in America in 1785 at between five and ten per cent of averge *per capita* income.

Evidently the tax burden was much more significant in Russia than in colonial America, a factor accentuated by low income levels and reinforced by the assunption by the British in America of a considerable proportion of military payments. The demands of the Russian central government and of government surrogates preempted a high proportion of discretionary income. In terms of government expenditures the gap may not be as great as the tax revenues suggest, if we take account of British military expenditures.

A number of significant differences stand out. First, in terms of tax raising or expenditures, the American system was much more decentralised than the Russian. Such a decentralised system allowed greater sensitivity to local economic requirements. Funds (or direct labour) were available at the county, township and municipality level to finance local transport improvement, the provision of education, the subsidy of necessary craftsmen.

Secondly, therefore, the share of expenditures going to economically-oriented projects was greater in colonial America than in Russia where administration and the military absorbed a high proportion of such revenue. The dense system of government in America encouraged this tendency. The tendency of the British to cover administrative and military costs freed resources to be used in the pursuit of economic growth (Hughes 1983).

Finally in the long run the extension of the market system and of trade in America had greater potential for revenue-raising than in Russia, where the emphasis kept swinging back to direct, and increasingly more regressive obligations.

Much has been made of the limited revenue-raising capacity of Russia and of fluctuations in this capacity. The manoeuverability of the Russian government in providing public goods was undoubtedly heavily constrained. The tax burden does seem to have been particularly great in the formative period with a stress on the expensive provision of key public goods such as defence and law and order.

In America the significant government involvement in the economy of the early nineteenth century was not new (Goodrich 1960). The tax burden supporting this involvement in the colonial period was unexpectedly small. An emphasis on the role of taxation in the conflict between America and Britain has diverted attention from the economically-significant areas of government activity. Colonial America scored over early Russia in three ways: more resources were available for public goods provision, at least *per capita*; a greater proportion of those resources was available for public goods relevant to commercial phase entry; and the public goods requirement

187

for entry into both phases was less.

Judicial promotion model

The courts responded pragmatically to the needs of the emergent early phase industrial economy, adopting an instrumentalist posture . . . balancing the imperatives of "constitutionalism" (the ideal that "organised power must be useful and just") with the perceived obligation to open the channels of enterprise, to "release entrepreneurial energy", and to expedite material growth.

Scheiber

Russia did not succeed in the eighteenth century (and not, in fact, until well into the nineteenth) in bringing about a "modern" legal consciousness and culture, with regularity of procedures, security of person and property, and respect for the law and its application by autonomous institutions.

Raeff

There were severe limitations on the effectiveness of public goods provision by the government itself in early phase movement. These limits were the constraints on government penetration of the economy, in particular a limited revenue-raising potential and the problems of inadequate bureaucratic organisation. An alternative to the government provision of public goods was their provision by public corporations supported by legal rules which concentrated benefits on these corporations and spread costs outside them. Indirectly the judiciary could allow the subsidy of its activities. Risk was offset and even reduced by such subsidy and by the grant of quasi-monopoly privileges.

Initially legislative, executive and judiciary were fused: law-making and enforcement simply aspects of government. Eventually the system of courts came to rival in its vertical density the administrative bureaucracy of government. Indeed the judiciary can also act as a semi-independent arm of that government. The degree of independence depends upon the method of appointment and the group ethos of the legal profession as well as the formal constitutional rules. Law enforcement is as important as law-making and in common-law countries is sometimes hard to distinguish from it.

From an early date the judiciary had important functions to perform which could promote phase movement. An efficient law enforcement system can act as a protector of order and of the sanctity of property and contract; thereby uncertainty is removed and risk reduced. Arbitrary acts of violence are discouraged and protection against economic loss provided. Equally as important, economic agents require a consistent and rational set of rules regulating the relationship between agents in their different roles. The law can reinforce tendencies to change while containing the change within a predictable pattern.

Thirdly the law has been a significant agent of secularisation, which in its turn has two major results. The monarch has ceased to rule by divine right as God's annointed. Sovereignty ceased to be a personal matter and became a legal quality divorced from a particular person. Such detachment has helped to free the economy from the influence of the monarch's arbitrary whims, or from vulnerability to what we have called secondary risk.

Some secularisation has also aided the measurement of efficiency by material or economic criteria. The law ceased to be primarily concerned with moral or ethical principles and became concerned primarily with the violation of property rights.

It is possible to articulate a three-stage development of the judicial system. Initially legal relations are largely personal and lack due process. In the technical jargon they are dyadic rather than triadic, that is, they involve the injurer and the injured but no impartial third party.

After the emergence of the third party — closely associated with the rise of a strong central government — the rules of judicial procedure are formalised. During this stage the law becomes predictable and acts largely to protect vested rights or interests. Whether they act to protect the rich or the poor — and opinions differ on the actual historical function of the the law — the courts promote security and stability.

Finally during the third stage the law may even actively promote some economic change. The acceleration of economic change may occur independently of the law. In the process of change all sorts of divergent interests need to be reconciled. Both the rich and the poor cease to be homogeneous groups. In the most favourable situations the law may favour innovations against the vested interests of existing property owners. Such an outcome may result from the domination of the courts by those associated with innovation or from the recognition of a higher public interest.

In comparing the role of the legal systems in America and Russia we need to note one obvious difference. Russia's legal system has always been based on civil codes, which are in essence a manifestation of statute law. America by contrast adopted the English common law system. The latter proved to be a much more flexible instrument of adjustment to changing social and economic circumstances during the relevant period. In America the law was interpreted and reinterpreted by those firmly embedded in local communities. Again the low vertical tiers often took the initiative.

In Russia even the movement through the relevant legal stages was imposed from above, in so far as it could be. Worse, as Wortman (1976) writes, 'The belief in the supremacy of the executive and the subservience of the judiciary are elements in the traditional pattern of behaviour that has persisted in Russia through the course of modernisation.' Legal rulings were passed down from above. The legal system consequently lacked the full panoply of the triadic system, that is independent public courts, an oral adversary and jury system and a trained legal profession.

There is no one-to-one relationship between particular structures of judicial influence and economic growth. However, America was poised at Independence to move to the third stage of judicial development. In this stage, first at the state, then at the federal level, eminent domain power was defined as an inherent attribute of sovereignty, to be exercised only for a 'public use or purpose' with 'just' compensation for injured private owners. Moreover, a series of cost-reducing expediting doctrines eased the financial obligations involved in the exercise of this power. The eminent domain power was also devolved to private incorporated companies. Such an instrumental approach reflected once more the density of the vertical tiers and the ability of such a system to contain risk.

GOVERNMENTS AND PHASE MOVEMENT

The performance of an economy reflects the actions of both government and a host of low level economic agents. The preceding section has considered the ways in which government policies might influence economic decision-making. We need now to turn from theory to practice. There is always a gap between government intention and achievement. The structure of government itself influences the kind of policy adopted, but even more it limits the successful implementation of that policy.

The relationship between institutional structure and policy, even at the lowest level of decision-making, is a very close one. The previous two chapters have examined the evolution of both government and market systems within the context of that decision-making. Structure partly reflects policy; for example, markets develop as a result of a multitude of particular exchange decisions. However the institutional structure which emerges develops its own inertia and in its turn comes to constrain decision-making.

The government could play either a positive or a negative role in the transition. If, for example, a government taxes trade in a burdensome and arbitrary manner, this will limit the growth in markets. Unhappily in an unfavourable resource environment the government was still forced to rely upon indirect rather than direct taxes. In Russia there existed a form of cascade tax on trade turnover, that is a cumulative tax levied at key points in the movement of commodities to the market, particularly exports. Such a tax was very obstructive to the free flow of trade. Arbitrary and unpredictable taxation designed to protect the government's financial position against fluctuations in the market could also be a source of secondary risk.

On the other hand there is a positive role for the government. Any action which reduces distribution costs and increases their stability lowers commercial risk. Probably the key action of the government in this field is transport improvement, which extends the scope of a market and by increasing the number of transactions within a given market reduces the potential for price fluctuations. Such an increase in market size also promotes through economies of scale the provision of services necessary to successful market operation.

From the beginning of settlement, government in America was vitally concerned with every aspect of transport improvement — with providing ferries, buildings bridges, constructing and maintaining roads, and later with canal and railway building. Sometimes direct participation was involved, sometimes indirect promotion. The striking feature was involvement at every level of government; indeed local and state governments were more important in this role than the central government.

In Russia there is a similar concern but it is concentrated at the centre and largely concerned with building the main trade arteries. Such a difference was largely explicable by the lack of resources and weakness of middle tiers of government.

Again the pluralism of policy in America acted to promote the transition to the commercial phase. For example, from an early date there was competition for the siting of relevant transport routes. Because of this pluralism we need to consider the relationship between government policy and entry into the commercial phase separately for each region.

191

In New England the weakening of the communal feeling characteristic of the early townships and so conducive to successful pioneering, and the growth of the individualism associated with market participation, largely left undisturbed the existing institutional framework. The township, so well suited to pioneering in New England, was also quick to promote commercial development. Bushman (1967) indicates how a concern with successful pioneering merged into promotion of trade: 'land distribution, road building, supervision of fencing, supplementation of pasturage, the recruitment and subsidy of millers, tanners and blacksmiths, and the destruction of pests made the town's participation in the economy crucial to a farmer's success.' Almost hitting the bull's eye he continues, 'Without aid from the community, few indeed could have produced a surplus and taken it to the market.' Such measures involved both the containment of pioneer risk and the reduction of commercial risk. The quotation lacks only in failing to accord full significance to transport improvement. In this way, although colony government was also important in land distribution, fiscal and monetary policies, most economic policy relevant to commercial development occurred at the township or county level.

The Middle Colonies, characterised by neither the hostile natural environment of New England nor by the malign disease environment of the south, saw an emphasis on the county, or even more on individual settlements in comparatively small owner-occupied farms as the relevant decision-making units. The relatively dense settlement patterns, characterised by a high level of urbanisation, and the nature and specialisation of agricultural production led to rapid market development. Since the main cash crops were subsistence foods market involvement was less risky than it might have been.

The vertical decision-making structure was relatively dense, as in New England. The sensitivity of the New England township to local economic needs was also repeated. Once again the government's most positive role was to improve transport, even more essential with relatively high bulk-to-value commodities. A relatively high level of urbanisation was associated with the demands of the distributional system. Competition between the city ports of New York, Philadelphia and Baltimore became increasingly significant (Bridenbaugh 1964a and 1964b).

In the seventeenth century only the extraordinarily high returns of the tobacco economy offset the ravages of the virulent disease environment of the Chesapeake. From about the start Chesapeake planters were locked into a fluctuating staple economy, particularly vulnerable to market risk. Increasingly the existence of many sellers made for a baffling combination of abundant production and economic hardship. The price of tobacco — the barometer of an extremely erratic trade — fluctuated wildly, in parallel with European wars and financial crises, with production gluts and even with changes in taste.

The market was almost solely an external one. The apparently rapid transition to the commercial phase was made possible by dependence on British commercial institutions. This was to be a pattern repeated by other colonial staples and later by cotton.

The Chesapeake represents an interesting case study in the response to a high level of commercial risk, both at the highest level of decision-making, the Assembly, and at the lowest, the plantation. The attempt to deal with a high level of risk could result in either an extension of market penetration or a retreat from the market. The governments of the Chesapeake colonies aimed at the former but the lack of intermediate levels of government prevented the effective implementation of this objective. On the other hand the plantation, faced with a high level of risk, often retreated into autarky.

The chief policies of the government of Virginia, increasingly opposed by the Imperial government, for whom the revenue from tobacco had become the main consideration, were diversification of economic activity, the curtailment and control of tobacco production, and the provision of urban settlement, in other words measures which, if successful, would have had the effect of mitigating and managing commercial risk. Such policy measures, concentrated into periods of depressed tobacco prices, had little success. Given the rudimentary organisation of government most of the schemes were unworkable.

A whole series of particular measures were designed to promote diversification — tax incentives, discouragement of raw material export, bounties, public enterprise. The range of commodities involved was wide, including silk, hemp and flax, naval stores, wine as well as the more predictable iron, timber, cotton or wheat. Unhappily the emphasis was often on the most inappropriate.

The second aim — curtailment and control over tobacco production — took the form of 'stints', embargoes and cessation schemes, all largely ineffective. Repeated town acts, the third type of measure, were no more successful. Only Norfolk as an economic centre had genuinely urban pretensions, and at a lower level Annapolis or Williamsburg as political centres.

The lack of an efficient government bureaucracy reduced the effectiveness of colonial policy. Part-time officials might save a positive purpose, particularly where strong intermediate levels of government existed, but less so at the highest levels. There is no doubt that colony government in the Chesapeake was deliberately used as a significant source of private income. Meagre revenue underpinned the spasmodic nature of government intervention, defence representing a major call on this revenue.

Divided political control over the Chesapeake was a mixed blessing. It could slow the beneficial introduction of tobacco inspection, but in Rainbolt's words, it represented 'the creation of checks against precipitous economic experimentation which, however benevolently motivated, would have disrupted and harmed the economy of the area'.

At the lowest level the product of the reactions to the trans-Atlantic economy of boom and bust was the increasingly self-sufficient plantation. A significant response to commercial risk was the transformation of the plantation from a specialised agricultural sector dependent on Europe to a diversified and potentially self-sufficient settlement. The most important changes were, as with government policies, concentrated during the tobacco depressions.

With the repeated onset of depression, flexible or intermediate plantations increased in numbers relative to rigid plantations. Nevertheless depression prosperity was largely restricted to the ten or twenty per cent of great planters. In such plantations diversification took the form of wheat or corn production, increased livestock numbers, the planting of orchards and cider production, the growing of textile fibres, and an improved capability in home manufacture and repair. These tendencies set the pattern. The rise in the level of autarky reinforced the dispersal of settlement.

The Russian government's role in the movement into the commercial phase was weak. Particularly in the eighteenth century mercantilist policies were part of the government's attempt to modernise or westernise Russia, Peter by compulsion and Catherine by persuasion. However in practice the government as a potent source of secondary risk actually hindered the expansion of trade.

Peter gave temporary stimulus to external trade by his creation of St Petersburg on the Baltic Sea. More long lasting was the westernisation of the tastes of the gentry, but the impact of this demand was limited by the relatively small numbers involved. Deliberate attempts were also made to improve the transport system, particularly in building canals linking the Volga with the new outlet into the Baltic. Most of these projects were not completed until the beginning of the nineteenth century.

Catherine sought to decentralise the locus of economic decision-making and to promote the operation of the free market. Internal

194

tolls had been abolished in the 1750s. Catherine encouraged the development of a free market, even seeking to emphasise the independent role of the law and of the towns. However, the failure to reform basic institutions and the limitation of the reforms to a largely propaganda role made most of the changes of little practical significance.

Poor resources, a sparse population and 'thin' government denied Russia the kind of government action which promoted such movement in much of colonial America. For example, a common complaint of the *nakazy* submitted by the nobles to Catherine's Legislative Commission of 1767, in practice largely a propaganda exercise, was that the Russian government took from the provinces but failed to provide anything in return, at least anything of visible economic significance. Specifically they took revenue and recruits but failed to provide roads, bridges, granaries, banks, schools, hospitals, chemists, surveyors, judges and police, in short the whole paraphernalia of public goods necessary not only to limit the impact of pioneer risk but also to reduce the level of commercial risk below the crucial threshold. Incidentally the nobles' instructions characterised the provincial administrations in Russia as 'incompetent, ineffective and altogether inadequate'. The government's role in the abortive attempts at transition into the commercial phase was ambiguous, largely because of the weakness of the middle tiers of government.

METROPOLIS AND PERIPHERY

Governments seek to promote and control individual trade decisions, just as traders seek to influence government policy covering trade. We have considered the role of the government in this process; it is time to consider the trade decisions. The present section therefore considers the role of exchange and the market in the economic development of Russia and America during the early modern period.

Exchange can occur at three main levels beyond merely local trade; international, inter-regional and intra-regional trade. Each of these types of trade involves exchange between a metropolis and a periphery. Although exchange can also occur between metropolises or even between peripheries, the significance of such trade is secondary in the transition into or out of the commercial phase.

Market exchange reflects comparative power as much as comparative advantage. The more powerful partner can often impose the conditions of exchange on the weaker partner. We need to distinguish therefore between genuine market exchange involving a two-way

195

flow of commodities and a parasitic one-way flow based solely on non-economic pressures.

Moreover commodity flows are often reinforced by factor flows, by migration and capital movement. Despite frequently separate treatment the two kinds of flow are inextricably linked. For example, immigration into America could only be sustained if a standard of living could be supported which offered an improvement on European levels, a standard sustainable only by the import of consumption goods and therefore by a strong commercial base. Equally the new exporting areas could only be opened up with the aid, indirect sometimes, of migrant labour and imported capital.

The links between international, inter-regional and intra-regional exchange are critical to the commercial transition. The search for an export staple, suggestive of a strong commercial orientation, might be very important to this transition but only if the associated trade is 'plugged' into domestic exchange. Only under rather special conditions does trade promote the transition to the industrial phase. Indeed a successful transition often reduces the dependence on international trade, as it did in Russia and America.

The nature of the commodity flow reflects the different factor endowment which itself is the main defining feature of metropolis and periphery. The metropolis, characterised by an increasing density of poplation, experiences a dwindling supply of land and natural resources *per capita*. The diversification of economic activity associated with the increase in population assists in maintaining income levels, or even raising them, and also in generating capital. Expanding markets lead to economies of scale in sectors of the economy outside agriculture. However, in conditions of diminishing returns the rise in population, and in income, raises demands for land-intensive (resource-intensive) commodities, thereby raising their prices relative to those of non-agricultural commodities, themselves experiencing increasing or constant returns to scale.

On the other hand the periphery has a sparse population and an abundant supply of relatively empty land. The domestic market for all commodities is limited by the small population. Both labour and capital tend to be in scarce supply.

In such a context trade can occur, with the metropolis exporting capital or labour-intensive commodities in exchange for land or resource-intensive goods. Whether trade actually takes place depends on the relative level of prices in metropolis and periphery and on the level of distribution costs. If the price in one centre exceeds that in the other by more than the level of distribution costs, then a profitable

196

exchange can be made. The greater the demand and the lower the relevant bulk/value ratio together with associated distribution costs, the more likely is this to occur. Increases in income and population, combined with improvements in distribution, represent an even more favourable context for a flourishing trade.

Since in practice factor price equalisation does not occur as theory would suggest, the different factor endowments of the metropolis and periphery not only create a favourable setting for trade in commodities but also for migration and capital movements. Indeed since production in the periphery may require new settlement and investment a flow of migrants and capital may be a precondition for successful exchange.

However, the growth of trade and the increasing flow of capital and migrants did not occur in a steady and ordered manner. Large annual fluctuations were common, reflecting the instabilities inherent in an environment of significant commercial risk. The most regular pattern of fluctuations in America was probably one of long cycles lasting 20 years or so. According to the work of Brinley Thomas there was an inverse investment cycle on the two sides of the Atlantic.

The argument rests on two assumptions; first, that population growth in both source and destination country accelerated and decelerated significantly according to the level of migration: secondly that a large component of investment consisted of population-sensitive construction, the infrastructure necessary for 'opening up' new areas.

The argument runs as follows. When external migration was high, investment rose in America and declined in Britain, particularly in the construction and domestically-oriented sectors of industry, if not the export sector. When external migration was low, and domestic migration in Britain high, investment in America declined and in Britain rose.

During the upswing in America imports were high, and the barter terms of trade tended to deteriorate. During the downswing imports were high, as supply adjusted with a time lag to previous investment and demand was expanded by the domestic boom in Britain. Hence the barter terms of trade improved.

As Brinley Thomas writes, 'one may summarise the process as an inter-regional competition for factors of production within the Atlantic economy, with the old world and the new world alternating in the intensive build-up of resources'. On the whole Britain tended to dominate, particularly as movements of demand in Britain determined movements in the barter terms of trade. Over time, however, the Atlantic economy was growing in relative size. In 1700 there were 20 Englishmen for every American (over 5m to 0.25m), but in 1775 only three to one (7.8m to 2.5m) and by the end of the century less than two to one (9.6m to 5.3m).

Fortunately for the health of the Atlantic economy, Britain alternated between pumping in investment funds and purchasing imports. The level of resource use was kept high and the degree of commercial risk thereby reduced.

Britain and Western Europe would be defined as the metropolis, and America and Russia as parts of the periphery, indeed competitive parts in that they sought export outlets for similar commodities. The relative position of Russia and America to take advantage of these trading opportunities differed. The Russians were hindered by their lack of export outlets. The establishment of an outlet through Archangel led to an abortive commercial flowering in the late sixteenth and early seventeenth centuries; it was by no means an ideal outlet because of its remoteness. The permanent opening of the Baltic in the early eighteenth century, of the Black Sea in the late eighteenth century, had a more lasting impact, although once more the impact was delayed until improvement of the waterways in the early nineteenth century and the construction of the railways, particularly in the 1860s, reduced the cost of transporting commodities to the export outlets.

Russia was closer to the Western European metropolis by the relevant sea routes, although winter closure was a major problem for Russia. However, the export-producing areas were much closer to water outlets in colonial America. In the pre-railway era the high cost of overland movement severely limited the length of economic transportation; overland movement was many times more expensive than waterborne carriage. The overland component of transport was significantly greater for Russia.

During the seventeenth and eighteenth centuries before the canal and railway ages, major productivity advances in transportation were largely concentrated on sea carriage. One general index of shipping productivity indicates a rate of advance of at least 0.8 per cent per annum, largely accounted for by a reduction in risk, with the elimination of piracy and the greater certainty of full loads (Shepherd and Walton 1972).

The impact of this should not be underestimated. On the Atlantic route the productivity gains from improved distribution cut the real resources needed by more than half over the century before the American Revolution (Lee and Passell 1979: 25). The improvement partly explains the rise in importance of the Atlantic trade, although it is also partly explained by that rise. It is clear that this productivity increase favoured the American relative to the Russian trade.

An enormous fall in the share of distribution costs in total costs occurred on the Atlantic route. In the early eighteenth century high-value English manufacturers sold in America at a mark up of as much as 80 to 140 per cent above English price; by 1750 this was down to 45 to 75 per cent; and in the late colonial period 15 to 25 per cent. The percentage mark up on tobacco going the other way, from Philadelphia to Amsterdam, declined from 82 per cent to 51 per cent between 1720–4 and 1770–2.

Such a relative improvement in distribution costs, in the context of a favourable resource and risk environment, largely accounts for the massive rise in the significance of the American trade. The great reciprocal demand for manufactured goods is the other key factor, again weak in the Russian case.

During the eighteenth century there occurred an 'Americanisation' of British foreign trade. In 1700 80 per cent of English exports went to Europe and only ten per cent to North America and the West Indies; by the era of Independence, the share of exports going to Europe was down to 40 per cent and the share taken by North America and the West Indies was up to 42 per cent. The West Indies link was important to the American colonies, supporting as it did a high level of export of provisions, timber and horses, a trade which could not at the time have been sustained with the relatively distant Europe. indirectly this link supported the export of sugar from the West Indies to Britain. Moreover the returns in specie and bills of exchange helped cover the American deficit in the British trade.

Detailed statistics on changes in immigraton or capital inflow are lacking but there seems little doubt that a long cycle of the sort described above existed. Menard (1978) has given an excellent description of a largely self-contained price-and-production cycle for Chesapeake tobacco, upon which the shocks of war, weather and metropolitan recession were superimposed.

By contrast Russia was much less involved in the international economy, largely because of transport difficulties poor natural environment and a low level of demand for imports. In the absence of major staples, trade was relatively slow to develop. Migration was much less significant than for America, and capital import relatively weak, despite a continuing reliance on foreign technology. Russia therefore benefited much less from the international metropolis/periphery interaction.

In Russia the inter-regional links were far more significant than the international. Given an improvement in transportation, the potential for trade between forest and steppe was enormous. The south came to concentrate on food production and the less fertile north on the sale of commercial services and industrial commodities. This clear regional division of labour makes its first appearance in the second half of the eighteenth century.

The growing exchange of commodities was accompanied by a movement of migrants and capital to the south, particularly into the Ukraine and New Russia. From 1724 to 1795, between 60 and 100,000 male immigrants moved into this steppe region. The whole population of left bank Ukraine rose from 910,000 to 1,697,000. In 1795 the population of left bank Ukraine was 1,738,000 and of New Russia 684,000. If we assume conservatively that only half represented an increase in indigenous population since 1724, this gives a total increase of over two million, which is about as large as the increase for the American colonies as a whole over the same period.

In America the main inter-regional trade in the colonial period was between New England and the Upper South. New England imported as much as 25 per cent of its food needs; it provided commercial services for all other areas.

Much more important in America was the growth of exchange between the rapidly growing urban areas on the coast, New York, Philadelphia, Baltimore and Boston and their hinterlands. Again the main exchange was foodstuffs, and raw materials for commercial and industrial commodities. In Russia the relationship between Moscow and St Petersburg and their hinterland was very different. The flow of food and raw materials into the cities was largely based on non-economic pressure. Lack of income and market penetration limited rural demand for commercial services or industrial goods. The relationship was therefore largely parasitic.

A key factor in the development of the domestic market was the growth of proto-industrial activity. Such activity implies an exchange of industrial and agricultural goods. Those stimuli which promoted industrialisation also encouraged market development: a dense marketing system with a large number of distribution centres and good transport access, and more particularly, a productive agriculture able to produce a surplus. However, proto-industrialisation often occurred in relatively infertile areas where population was pressing on the land, creating a plentiful supply of cheap labour. Such was clearly the case in eighteenth-century New England and the central provinces of Russia at a similar date. The nature of the labour regime could also have a significant effect on labour supply. The combination of grain-based agriculture and short growing seasons could make labour available in plentiful supply during the off-season. Women and children were prominent in the new activities.

Such considerations kept rural costs below urban costs. This was particularly the case in Russia, where desperately high urban mortality rates and low fertility rates, depressed by the presence of a large transient population, slowed the development of a permanent industrial proletariat, firmly urban-based, and thereby discouraged the growth of urban industry right through to 1917.

In America the labour regime in the agriculture of New England and the Middle Colonies allowed significant surplus labour to be employed outside agriculture at low cost, initially temporarily, later permanently. In the south, where the slaves produced foodstuffs as a product complementary to cotton, proto-industry was much less evident.

The main role of proto-industrialisation was to extend the market system in rural areas where the majority of the population lived. The interaction of market and industrial activity allowed for significant gains in productivity as specialisation increased and existing labour could be more intensively employed.

The nature of export staples was crucial in determining whether external trade promoted phase movement. Equally important in phase movement, particularly entry into the industrial phase, was the nature of proto-industrialisation. Small-scale industry had an amazing resilience and could actually represent a major barrier to factory industrialisation. The weighing of positive and negative factors determined whether proto-industry persisted or whether it was merely a transitional phase.

There are significant positive features including the stimulus given to market development, the conditioning of consumers to the purchase of industrial commodities on that market, what has been called the primary accumulation of capital and finally the acquisition of relevant entrepreneurial and labour skills.

On the other hand there could exist a number of serious negative features. The easing of constraints on marriage as employment opportunities expanded acted to increase labour supply further and keep that labour cheap. Consequently there might be little incentive to mechanise production with the factory system; that is, to substitute capital for labour. Levine has christened this tendency industrial 'involution'.

Tugan-Baranovskii has also pointed out that domestic industry in Russia was often directly competitive with factory industry. The share scale of *kustar* industry confirms this belief. There are good reasons why this might be the case. Milward has pointed out that uncertainty of productive process or market possibilities made serfowners inclined to release their serfs on *obrok* for outside employment rather than directly employing them on *barshchina* within factories located on their estates. In this way they transferred risk to the serf.

However Milward ignored a much more important source of risk; fluctuations in the harvest which could cause violent swings in the demand for industrial commodities. An assured market, as in a government contract, was a great boon. The crux of the problem lies in the need to employ capital as fully as possible; a failure to do so increases fixed costs per unit of output enormously. Factory industry involves large fixed investment in plant, equipment and buildings. *Kustar* industry, with its low requirements for fixed capital, was much more flexible and competitive in a high risk environment. Russian demand conditions relative to those in America seriously disfavoured the factory system.

The successful transition from proto-industry to factory system also depended on the existence of complementary raw materials and power sources, particularly coal. Needless to say, areas of *kustar* industry in Russia were not so endowed.

TRADE: HANDMAIDEN OR TYRANNICAL MISTRESS?

[It is] difficult to overemphasise the importance of the commercial sector . . . ; the economic success of the nineteenth century actually stemmed from roots stretching well back into the colonial period.

Shepherd and Walton

Except for initially helping to provide capital, foreign trade had a relatively small influence on American industrialisation.

Cochran

There has been a tendency to emphasise the significance of external trade to the economic development of the American colonies and to note the relationship between abortive commercial developments and the lack of important economic advance in Russia. Such a view, strongly held by many commentators on American and Russian economic history, requires significant modification.

Two major qualifications must be made immediately. First,

excessive concentration on the easily quantifiable can strongly distort the general view. In the long run the less visible local trade is more important than the more obvious external or inter-regional trade.

Secondly, while external trade does create economic opportunities, their full exploitation depends upon the resources and institutional framework of the relevant society. For example, excessive dependence on an export staple may create an overspecialised, and externally vulnerable, economy. While prices are high good returns might compensate for the vulnerability to commercial risk. A fall in prices highlights all the economic weaknesses. Trade can, therefore, act either as a stimulus or as a fetter on economic development. The fetter argument, advanced in terms of colonial dependency for both colonial America and pre-revolutionary Russia, has had some strong adherents.

Some historians have argued strongly that Imperial control imposed a major economic burden on America. Various attempts have been made to quantify this burden. From the perspective of this book the potential for obstruction was great in slowing either inter- or intra-phase movement. The Proclamation Line could have slowed the opening up of areas to the west of the Appalachians, or the Navigation Acts imposed a trading pattern on America based on Britain as the entrepôt. Restrictions on paper money issue might also have limited commerce in general. The bans on certain kinds of manufacturing, as for example iron fabrication or hat making, could have slowed entry into the industrial phase. In practice all these factors had a minor impact.

The restrictions on settlement or manufacturing were removed before they could bite. In the absence of Imperial control, trading patterns would have differed little from those which actually prevailed. Defence subsidies, bounties and assured markets more than compensated for any trade distortion.

The main features of the fetter argument as applied to Russia point to the domination of external trade and capitalistic investment by foreigners and the preponderance in that trade of a small number of relatively unprocessed commodities as exports and of expensive manufactured goods as imports. Technical dependence reinforced the subservient relationship.

However a logical implication of their resource position was for America and Russia to export largely unprocessed foodstuffs and raw materials, and to import manufactured goods and capital, even technical knowledge. Since both America and Russia developed sufficient political clout to resist the conversion of economic intervention

203

into political intervention, comparative advantage rather than power relations dictated the pattern.

The claims made for the beneficial impact of trade are also enormous, as a recent review of colonial economic history shows. Shepherd and Walton (1979) noted that existence in early America of a strong commercial base, which was 'the chief stimulus to market expansion, economic specialisation, capital accumulation and advancing productivity', and the main source of 'essential capital, entrepreneurial talent, and know-how for this budding industrialisation'. More relevant to the present analysis is their argument that foreign trade played the leading role in developing the institutional arrangements and other elements of a viable market system.

However, whether or not foreign trade plays this role depends upon the links between the different levels of trade and the nature of export staples. For example, recent work has played down the role of cotton exports in American economic development by denying the strength of the inter-regional trade links described by North.

Our definition of different generation staples allows us to consider the role of trade in promoting phase movement. One of the major weaknesses of traditional staple analysis is its lack of a properly dynamic treatment. Such a weakness can be removed by the association of a different generation of staples with each economic phase. The key question to ask here concerns the potential role of second generation staples in Russia and America in promoting movement into the industrial phase.

Two difficulties have emerged in using the staple approach. First, it is often unclear whether the staple generates phase movement or phase movement causes the staple to grow in importance. There is probably no hard-and-fast rule on this. Secondly, the key element consists in any 'automatic' link between different phases. What causes an economy to move from one generation of staples to another? The exact nature of particular staples has a strong influence on movement. An important part of this section is therefore a checklist of characteristics which promote or fail to promote inter-phase movement.

There are a number of dynamic mechanisms which promote movement from one phase to another. Settlement itself, by improving knowledge of the natural environment and its resources, helps to promote the appearance of second-generation staples. Such staples often involve a long process of adjustment and learning. Similarly, an increase in population, by diminishing the availability of land per head and by encouraging the establishment of property rights, pushes the economy from first to second generation staples.

The developments associated with second generation staples bring a change in relative factor supply, and therefore relative factor prices. Initially such changes may encourage the use of more labour-intensive processes but eventually, through the support of higher income levels and generation of more capital, the choice of more capital-intensive processes. Technical change, particularly in so far as it lowers transport costs, also has a dramatic impact on the nature of export staples.

The weakness in development of second generation staples in Russia before 1800 limited their potential stimulus to phase movement, although the inter-regional movement of grain began to supplement the role of flax and hemp. In the eighteenth century iron and linen exports were the most significant, in the nineteenth century grain. In America a number of second generation staples appeared during the colonial period — tobacco, rice, indigo, grains. In both economies staples of this kind dominated whole regions.

The physical nature of the staples may have an important role to play in phase movement. For example, the perishability of a product was highly relevant when transport was slow, simple and costly. Often a product had to be converted into a non-perishable form before dispatch. Wheat had to be converted into flour, bread or biscuits when exported to the tropics. This conversion was an important factor in the provisions trade between the Middle Colonies and the Upper South, and the West Indies, generating considerable industrial activity in that area. Necessary processing, which is significantly weight — or volume — reducing, may be concentrated at the point of production. Examples include cotton-ginning, various timber processing activities, or the crushing of gold-bearing quartz.

The role of transport in the relationship between staple and phase is ambiguous. Too high a bulk/value ratio, particularly where the transport component in total costs is also high, can prevent a given commodity from becoming a staple at all. Over time a reduction in transport costs widens the hinterland of a metropolitan market for a given commodity and also extends the range of feasible staples at a particular point. For a given region or economy the progression of relevant staples is likely to be from high value/bulk ratio to low, but the impact in terms of promoting other economic activities is also likely to increase. The progression from tobacco, to cotton, to grain in the United States is not accidental.

However, a highly bulky commodity might also require considerable transporting and warehousing inputs and slow movement may involve a dense network of provisioning points for the transporters. Lemon describes the evolution of such a dense network in south-west Pennsylvania in the late colonial period (Lemon 1967b).

Supply side considerations are not the only relevant factor. The whole marketing system affects the impact of the staple. Where the demand for a staple is concentrated the activities associated with distribution are also likely to be concentrated, usually in that main market. The great weight of distribution costs relative to production costs explains the significance of the entrepôt role. Tobacco was an example of concentrated demand and dependence on an external entrepôt. Many of the benefits of the staple seep outside.

These kind of influences are often much more important than the so-called linkage effects, often quantified in the simple form of the overall contribution to national income made by the staple sector. Such linkages are better spelled out in specific terms as demand for equipment and materials, as uses of final product and influences on capital or labour markets. The net impact depends on how many of these links are established abroad.

A number of linkages centre on the factor intensity of the productive process. All export staples are by definition resource-intensive but they differ in their use of other factors. Some staples encourage the opening up of vast new areas by being large 'consumers' of land. The products of the cattle and sheep sectors have such an influence.

Staples also differ in their labour or capital intensity of production. The more labour intensive is production, the greater the encouragement given to settlement. Often this tendency is related to the existence of economies of scale. Some staples, such as cotton or sugar or rice, lend themselves to the plantation type of organisation. Others are much more based on small units. Staples even differ in the degree of labour skill required. Before significant mechanisation and the opening up of steppe and prairie, grains tended to be produced in small units by farmers with a wide range of skills. Consequently grain production was associated with close settlement.

Factor intensity also has two other indirect influences. First, there is the impact on international factor movements. Staple growth may promote either the import of capital or immigration, or indeed both, sometimes directly, sometimes indirectly. The import of human capital had a very significant impact on the American economy.

Secondly, factor intensity of production affects income distribution. The more capital intensive the production, the greater is the share of income likely to go to those providing the capital. If foreign ownership of capital is significant, then the income generated will largely seep out; the greater the risk, the greater the seepage. Domestically a labour-intensive method of production associated with a more even income distribution tends to increase the potential demand for industrial commodities.

The term export staple logically could refer equally to an export to a nearby metropolis as to an export to a metropolis abroad. In practice the former may give greater stimulus to phase movement. In analysing the impact of an export staple we need to look not only at the level and growth of the relevant trade but also at the diversification of exports and at the location of distribution and processing activities. The movement to third generation staples is more likely to arise the closer the association of a staple with a high level of population density, itself usually associated with significant development of financial institutions and commercial services in the producing country. Frequently international trade in staples occurs with the assistance of the market auxiliary institutions of another economy; sometimes with little other assistance.

Our comparison yields examples of each of the possible outcomes Russia displays weak staple growth, both externally and internally, at least before the nineteenth century. The colonial south had strong staple growth with a significant element of external dependence. New England and the Middle Colonies had either a strong bias towards domestic staples or strong links between the international and internal exchange.

The diversification of staples is a crucial link in the inter-generation and inter-phase movement. Second generation staples are particularly vulnerable to declining income and price elasticity of demand. However their influence in extending market penetration, if temporarily only in stimulating a demand for imports, is crucial to the establishment of third-generation staples and the beginnings of industrialisation.

Part 4
Conclusion

9

A General Model of an Uncertain and Insecure World

This book can be regarded either as an analysis of America in the Russian mirror and of Russia in the American mirror; or alternatively, as a generalisation about the nature of economic development based on two important case studies, the generalisation emerging from the particular comparison.

Under the heading of general remarks this chapter will summarise the main conclusions of the comparison. Under the heading of continuity and discontinuity, it will try to generalise these conclusions as a new theoretical framework for understanding the process of economic development. It will conclude with broad interpretative comments on the later development of Russia and America in the context of the preceding conclusions and generalisations.

A sample of only two makes perilous the task of generalisation since an extended comparison may negate these conclusions. However it is comforting that in a number of important respects the general conclusions conform to a new set of tentatively formed views about economic development.

GENERAL REMARKS

Modern economic development does not begin and end with the so-called industrial revolution. Many economies grew impressively in the pre-industrial era. Both economies considered here have displayed strong secular impulses to expansion. Such impulses originated in the growth of population within a large area of cultivable land containing a wide variety of resources and in technical and organisational improvement within the international economy, particularly in economics linked to Russia and America. Moreover before significant industrialisation, American income levels were already amongst the highest in the world.

Among economic historians the implicit basis of analysis of economic development has begun to change significantly. There has been a growing tendency to interpret economic development as in some way the normal state of affairs, rather than as an exceptional experience, and to recognise that the change of approach requires a further shift away from explaining the onset of economic development by the satisfaction of certain necessary prerequisites, or by the appearance of a unique set of favourable economic and social features, to the need to explain its absence by the presence of significant obstacles to that economic development. Even where the obstacles have not prevented development they have certainly shaped the institutional framework of that development.

In one school of thinking there has been a tendency to find these obstacles in the external economy, a tendency understandable in terms of the human propensity to blame somebody else for one's own failings, but unjustified in that the sheer marginality of these economic links makes such a stress rather puzzling (O'Brien 1980). Again the particular Russian and American experiences reinforce the need to get the focus of interest back onto domestic factors.

It is necessary to consider obstacles which are strictly speaking non-economic, in this context geographical or political. By excluding consideration of such factors the now-dominant school of the new economic history has failed to confront properly the issue of development. The economic dynamism of any society is largely determined by a complex interaction between physical and human environments. Consequently the narrow focus of the new economic historian must be widened.

Although in one sense or another both America and Russia have been considered resource-rich countries — that is, a favourable natural environment has stimulated economic advance — there is little doubt that the advantage both in terms of resource endowment and vulnerability to risk lay with America. Translated into different terminology, America was favoured by high potential average income per head both in absolute terms and relative to Russia; it was also less likely to experience instability in that income.

More specifically, with regard to phase movement the agricultural potential of America was greater, both in terms of meeting subsistence needs and in generating a surplus which could be marketed. A good natural transport infrastructure aided commercialisation. By contrast Russia's movement into the commercial phase was hampered by an inappropriate combination of climate, soil and inaccessibility reinforced by an unstable environment. In addition Russian industrialisation was hampered by poor location of relevant raw materials, a lack of 'soft energy' sources and of an indigenous supply of raw cotton.

Moreover the much greater frequency of harvest failure and famine, of epidemic and of violence in Russia relative to America led to immediate destruction of scarce human capital but also to a risk environment which discouraged investment in all kinds of capital.

A society which has accommodated to a small and unstable surplus, and to frequent shocks and high risk, may require some trauma to break that accommodation and considerable means to do so quickly; a society which has accommodated to a large surplus and relatively rapid growth requires only slight 'ecological' pressure to redirect economic activity to reinforcing existing growth. It takes little imagination to place Russia as an example of the former and America of the latter. Although the physical environment did not prevent the economic development of Russia and America it did have a powerful influence often obscured by its early provenance.

Of course every society has available to it an institutional and attitudinal inheritance from source countries or even its own past. Russia and America shared a European inheritance but the exact nature of that inheritance differed sharply. America not only participated as one member, and an increasingly important member, of a multi-cell state-system, largely based on the Atlantic world, but even in microcosm aped that structure internally during the colonial period. Eastern Europe diverged from the Western European model because it did not share its feudal background of decentralised power. In significant ways Russia was intermediate between Europe and Asia. While it was not an 'oriental despotism' of the hydraulic Wittfogelian type, or even the modified Jonesian variety, it was clearly not fully European. It showed some characteristics of both; it participated in the economic and political successes of Europe but with a marked distortion of the relevant social and political structure and system of economic management.

Since institutions and attitudes can be modified to suit a particular environment, areas of new settlement are not invariably 'fragments' of the source country in arrested development. The institutions and attitudes evolve in their own particular way, as happened in America. Oddly Russia's periphery conformed much more to the Hartz model. The notion of a formative period has allowed us to expand the Hartz model to take account of environmental factors.

The Hartz model is but one version of the diffusionist model, whose central contention is that political and economic systems, most notably those associated with the industrial revolution, are exported from country to country by some seemingly irresistable process. One variant of the diffusionist approach already considered briefly sees the interaction as hindering rather than promoting economic development. Significant unease has developed with this model. The important shift in emphasis is to focus attention on the domestic response rather than the external stimulus.

The key relationship in the maintenance of economic development is that between the structure of government and that of economic institutions. In the past the complementarity of the relationship between government and market has often been obscured. However the institutional structure of a society is hard to change, except in further elaboration of the principles underpinning the existing structure. The forces of social inertia have to be reckoned with, although it must be granted that inertia can refer to the momentum of a body already in motion.

A consideration of the political factor in economic history may therefore reveal the nature of the obstacles limiting economic development and clarify the relative significance of elements of continuity or discontinuity in the two societies. The next section dwells at some length on the political factor.

CONTINUITY AND DISCONTINUITY

The excessive attention devoted to the Russian Revolution in 1917, and the consequent specialisation of historians' interest in isolated Tsarist and Soviet periods, highlights the tendency to exaggerate the importance of discontinuous as against continuous elements in history. The discontinuous is clearly more dramatic, and therefore more interesting. Similarly a stages approach to economic history, even the adoption of the label 'industrial revolution', tends to stress the importance of decisive turning points. History rarely in practice displays such marked discontinuities. More recently attention has been drawn to continuities, an emphasis less surprising when the field of analysis is widened to include institutional structures and attitudinal sets.

In this book it has been argued that deep (or in North's terminology, fundamental) institutions are moulded during a critical formative period. Change, thereafter, is usually limited to reform of the surface, or secondary, institutions, which rarely amounts to fundamental restructuring. Once the basic principles of organisation of an economy are established it becomes difficult to change them; socio-economic equilibrium is established.

The risk environment is one of the chief moulding influences on attitudes and institutions. The central theme of this book is that risk reduction is a necessary precondition for phase movement, although the nature of relevant risk changes with the phase. Entry into a particular phase depends on the reduction of the aggregate risk characteristic of that phase below a threshold level, defined according to the unique characteristics of particular economies. A desire for security, particularly in the context of a high level of risk, is a significant force making for social inertia.

The role of government is critical to risk mitigation and/or management and therefore to economic development. The government can play either a positive or a negative role, as so well illustrated by E.L. Jones in *The European miracle*. The American government played a very positive role on the West European pattern. The Russian government, faced with a much higher aggregate level of risk, was successful in dealing with pioneer risk but at the cost of developing a structure and policies unconducive to entry into the commercial and industrial phases. In terms of managing a high level of risk, the Russian government has been very successful but the costs in terms of pressure on the population has been high.

It is possible to develop a model which explicitly conceptualises our ideas and explains the speed of phase movement and more specifically how much government intervention such movement demands. The degree of government intervention might be produced by the interaction of two ratios influencing motivation. Such ratios are notional but illustrative of a method of analysis; they indicate the strength of the external stimulus and the domestic response.

First, there is a ratio of the income *per capita* of the leader economy to the actual income *per capita* of the country studied. This ratio is sometimes called the degree of relative backwardness (Gerschenkron 1962); it is a measure of a particular kind of power risk which becomes increasingly important with phase movement, vividly illustrated by recent obsession with growth league tables. The income *per capita* of the leader reflects the technology, institutional framework and resource position of that economy. Actual income per head reflects the existing technology, resources and institutions in the economy under study.

A second ratio contrasts the potential income *per capita* with actual income. We might call this the degree of achievement of potential. Potential income reflects the use of available resources and relevant

215

technology within an ideal institutional framework and factor supply situation. It also takes account of instability in the environment.

As a general rule governments are concerned about the degree of relative backwardness, individuals about the possibilities for profit or higher income; therefore the former, at least implicitly, often explicitly, looks to the level of backwardness and changes in this ratio, the latter to the level of, and changes in, the degree of achievement of potential.

In terms of the two ratios Russia and America were in strikingly different situations at the end of the eighteenth century. Russia was a country more or less reaching its full potential but lagging behind other countries because of its resource position; that is, it was characterised by extreme relative backwardness and a high degree of achievement of potential. Moreover it was characterised by significantly high levels of risk and, because of limited resources, by a relatively low level of the risk threshold.

America on the other hand constituted a 'forward' economy but one with very favourable resources even at the existing technological level; that is, America was characterised by a low degree both of relative backwardness and of achievement of potential. Moreover actual risk was low and threshold risk levels high.

Three stages of government reactions to backwardness can be distinguished. The first stage is one in which a 'preliminary' consciousness of backwardness, or dependence, becomes significant, a consciousness experienced by key government and other important interest groups. The mechanism of transmission may be dramatic, for example military defeat, or more gradual, as through economic demonstration effects. Indeed we could argue that the consciousness of backwardness is equivalent to becoming aware of a vulnerability to particular kinds of aggregate risk, a presentment of significant and more widespread power risk. Income superiority may not be adequate to avoid such a feeling; a lag in inter-phase movement itself constitutes backwardness or dependence, since the latter threatens the former.

The second stage involves the adoption and implementation of key reforms by the government in order to remove significant obstacles to economic development. Some of the measures represent a direct attempt to mitigate or manage risk, others an attempt to remove institutional adaptation to a previously high risk environment. Some of the reforms may be dramatic, such as the emancipation of the serfs, others may involve the rearrangement of surface institutions, such as the laws relating to the nature of business enterprise.

If the economic system is still unresponsive, a third stage may involve — and that may be the case if it is already close to achieving its potential income — the deliberate forming of a strategy of phase movement, in particular industrialisation, with a coherent programme of fiscal, monetary and commercial policies; this stage may culminate in a high level of direct government participation in the economy. Ultimately an economy may be fully controlled, at least in theory, and planned by the government.

The emancipation of the serfs and slaves in the 1860s illustrates the difficulty of fundamental change, despite the symbolic importance attached to the act in both historiographies. The lateness of the reform relative to our analysis simply helps to reinforce the main conclusion. It is enlightening to start with what the reforms failed to do — they failed to change the nature of existing organisation of production or the commodities produced, or even to reform significantly the immediate conditions of labour supply. Undoubtedly they failed to disturb the conditions under which risk was concentrated on the former serfs or slaves. In both cases the reform ran counter to the interests of the strongest group in the countryside, principally the owners who were reluctant participants. In Russia the reform had to be carried out by the ex-serfowners, in America it was imposed from outside. The ex-slave or serf owner managed to adapt the reforms to their own interests; in the one case stripping away the land or increasing cash payments, in the other replacing the slave relationship by an overtly racist relationship (Ransom and Sutch 1977). In both cases, after emancipation the ex-slaves lacked full civil rights and full *de jure*, or indeed *de facto*, ownership of the land. The economic system based on slave or serf labour had been perfectly viable and for the owner highly desirable (Fogel and Engerman 1974). After emancipation the agricultural sector, divested of labour, entered a long period of stagnation. The former owners sought to recreate its main features as exactly as possible: *plus ça change, plus c'est la même chose*.

Classification by phase indicates the existence of key transitional periods, that is, some increase in discontinuous elements. There may be critical moments when stressed areas are about to move into a new phase, or when they may miss out on the opportunities available. However the weight of social inertia determines how those critical moments, or *Sternstunden* in Gerschenkon's terminology, are confronted.

A critical movement may be heralded by a disadvantageous movement in the ratio referred to above; by an increase in relative backwardness or by a decrease in the achievement of potential. The latter may reflect either an increase in potential income, as transaction costs decline in a context of better provision of public goods, or a decline in actual income as population pressure on resources increases. A dense population may be threatened by greater harvest fluctuations, outbreaks of epidemic disease, urban fires and violent outbreaks. Temporarily the level of commercial risk may rise. There may be more market reversals and an increase in their significance as the level of debt rises.

Relative backwardness impinged on the government and associated interest groups at key stages in the history of America and Russia. The relevance of income or output per head was less significant than differences in the phase, or in a dependency relationship. America experienced such a crisis in the 1760s and 1770s, despite relatively high income levels. Russia experienced a repetition of such crises at varying intervals, but most dramatically under Peter the Great and after the Crimean War.

The symptoms of stress are vividly illustrated by the problems of two regions in particular, although in both cases there is some controversy concerning the exact level of stress. The two examples are New England before the War of Independence (Lockridge 1970; D.L. Jones 1981; Gross 1976; Hall 1982) and the central agricultural region of Russia from the 1870s (Egiazarova 1959). Both regions display the same deteriorating economic conditions. A sustained rise in population began to change the relationship between people and resources. The average size of land holdings apparently declined precipitately as the distribution of available land was completed. Diminishing returns and falling income levels characterised such a period. Competition from new areas of settlement exacerbated the difficulties.

The options available to a stressed area are three; regression into Nurkse's 'low-level equilibrium trap', maintenance of the *status quo* with an adjustment to the existing situation, or movement into a new phase. The first follows from a failure of population increase to moderate and the continuation of existing production methods. Adjustment might result from a reduction of population growth which in this context would involve a reduction in birth rates and an increase in emigration. The third, most successful option, would involve either an intensification of agriculture or a diversification of economic activities, comprising commercialisation or proto-industrialisation. A positive response might combine the latter two options.

A successful transition to the commercial phase depends upon a positive interaction of the resource and risk environment, and an appropriate institutional structure. A good resource position makes for a low risk threshold and a dense government structure. On its own, dense government helps to lower actual risk. A good resource position and a low risk environment prompts a high level of exchange and market development.

In New England the double safety valve of migration and commercialisation allowed a positive response. The nature of the nuclear household and impartible inheritance encouraged the former; good income levels and transport facilities encouraged the latter. Although reactions in these two areas was swift, other responses were much slower. Up to about 1840 change in agricultural production methods was slow, the increase in agricultural productivity slight; however there was some diversification to livestock. Proto-industrialisation occurred more rapidly and factory industrialisation began as early as the 1820s. Fertility levels began to decline only well into the nineteenth century.

It is possible to revive at least part of a diffusionist model since the problem-solving mechanism, having evolved in a stressed area, is available to be exported elsewhere. The merchants who established the institutional patterns appropriate to the commercial phase also operated outside New England (Hall 1982).

The centre of Russia saw the same combination of commercialisation and migration, but in a more limited way. Migration was very often temporary rather than permanent; the link with the village was never broken. The evolution of a proper market system was hindered by the reinvigoration of forced labour by commerce and the brittleness of market demand.

Phase movement however was by no means invariably accompanied by an abrupt transition. The emphasis on critical moments and stressed areas implicitly exaggerates the significance of discontinuous elements. Moreover choice of option was greatly influenced by the weight of the past.

Bibliographical Review

This bibliographical review represents a personal evaluation of the relevant literature, not an attempt at an exhaustive listing of useful books and articles. I could devote a whole book to a discussion of the methodological approach appropriate for an economic historian. Not to put too fine a point on it economic history is in a mess. The new economic history is based on faulty foundations; even its most prominent exponent has become an apostate (North 1981). Moreover the Marxist historians have also argued themselves into a corner, divorcing theory from the real world in a notably un-Marxian way (Thompson 1978).

Attempts by economic historians to generalise about the modern experience of secular economic development have petered out. Only one offers some potentially valuable insights into a possible generalising approach (Gerschenkron 1962, 1968, 1970). Even Gerschenkron made no concerted attempt to construct a comprehensive model nor even a sustained analysis of a particular case study.

The theoretical case for comparative history has been well put by Bloch (1953) with a more recent comment by Sewell (1967). Direct attempts to compare the historical experience of Russia and America are few, particularly for the early period. Most comparative treatments refer to the contemporary situation with little historical treatment (W.H. Parker 1972). The only significant exception to this is a work which is largely political history (Dukes 1970).

There are a number of broad interpretative works which have proved stimulating. Blum's book on rural Russia before Emancipation (1961) has proved a never-ending source of new insights. Pipes (1974), Hellie (1971, 1977) and R.E.F. Smith (1959, 1977) have particular standpoints which demand attention. The Birmingham School in general, of which Smith and Shanin (1972) are leading members, offers an alternative to Marxist interpretation by placing the stress on the peasant economy à la Chayanov.

The potential of the new economic history in the area of American history is best seen in the volume edited by L.E. Davis *et al* (1972) and in Hughes (1983). However that promise has only partially been fulfilled. Recent textbooks on the colonial period, such as those of Shepherd and Walton (1979) and Perkins (1980) rest heavily on quantitative works and consequently lack balance. More adventurous and therefore more interesting are the older works of Henretta (1973) and Bruchey (1965).

COVERAGE AND CONCEPTS

Recent work has rightly tended to deprecate the very concept of an industrial revolution. Relevant economic and social change had begun long before the traditional dating of the transition. Theories of modernisation implicitly resurrect that discontinuity and induce a self-fulfilling approach (Brown 1976; Black 1975). The minimum requirements of an operational stages approach have already been set out neatly and concisely (Kuznets 1965). The best comment on Russia as a feudal economy is still by Szeftel in Coulborn (1965), although an opposing point of view is to be found in P. Anderson (1974).

In the economic and historical literature, concern with uncertainty or risk is a very rare bird indeed. Economists have considered the issue within the very limited framework of inventory analysis, a pathway opened up by Keynes. Economic historians have dabbled with the 'safety first' model (Wright and Kunreuther 1975). There are one or two impressive examples of direct reference to risk to explain particular kinds of economic behaviour (McCloskey 1976). However, nobody has taken up an early plea for a sustained analysis of historical experience in terms of risk (Easterbrook 1954). The best example of such an approach lies in the field of social history (Scott 1976), although in this case the social setting is one of conflict rather than cooperation.

STYLISED FACTS

There is a rather obvious asymmetry in depth of treatment between early American and early Russian economic history. In almost every area of interest in American history there is a multitude of secondary works, although surprising and therefore rather irritating gaps still exist, particularly for the colonial peeriod. Local taxation is a good example. On the other hand Russian history is still largely virgin steppe, unworked either by its own historians or by English-writing experts.

The above remarks apply particularly to the area of demography. The new techniques of family reconstitution or backwards projection (Wrigley and Schofield 1981) have been used on Russian data only very tentatively (Ransel 1978; Hoch 1982b). Almost all commentators rely on a rather dated authority (Rashin 1956), and to a lesser extent on more recent work (Kabuzan 1963). Attempts to calculate native numbers begin in a comprehensive way with the 1897 census (Rowland and Lewis 1976). Before this only isolated figures exist.

By contrast the American demographic picture, even for the colonial period has been much better outlined. Twenty years ago there were only intelligent guesses on colonial demography (Potter 1965). Today particular parts of the picture have considerable detail (D.S. Smith 1972; Vinovskis 1972). Many of the raw data have been collected (Greene and Harrington 1966 reprint). One part of the picture for which the detail has become very much stronger involves native numbers. The old authority (Mooney 1928) has been revised (Cook 1973; Dobyns 1966; Jennings 1975). Moreover the whole nature of the relationship between white settlers and natives is seen in a new light (Jennings 1975; Jacobs 1971; Martin 1978; or more dispassionately Russell 1980).

The frontier thesis was an American invention (Turner 1962 reprint). Although subjected to frequent criticism it still offers much of substance (Walsh 1981); a continuing elaboration of the original themes has seen to that (Billington 1968, 1974). There is even a detailed study of frontier demography (J.E. Davis 1977). Similar claims for the frontier's importance in Russia have been made (Sumner 1944; Klyuchevsky 1960 reprint), but little has been done to develop the broad arguments, except for one or two regions. There is much on the difficulties of assimilating specific frontier areas (McNeill 1964; Donnelly 1968), particularly Russian America (Gibson 1976; Kushner 1975).

Again the level of market involvement in colonial America has been a focus of controversy and research; at a theoretical level (Mutch 1977; Merrill 1977; Henretta 1978; Bushman 1981), at an aggregate statistical level (Shepherd and Walton 1972; Klingaman 1971), and at a regional level (Lemon 1967a; Mitchell 1977; Grant 1961). Such studies are generally lacking for Russia, although Lenin's remarks on the creation of a national market at a comparatively early date have been much quoted (Lenin 1964 reprint). Grain marketings have been the only specific area of study (White 1976; Gregory 1980), but for a much later date. There are studies on the balance of payments position of the two economies at early dates (Shepherd and Walton 1972; Attman 1981a, 1981b), and attempts to give rather a premature dating to the growth of inter-regional trade (North 1961, Blum 1961).

Good statistics on wealth holding are now available for colonial

America. These can be used to calculate the level of income per head and even the growth of that income (A.H. Jones 1978, 1980). Similar statistics for Russia start only in 1861 (Goldsmith 1961; Gregory 1982).

OF GARDENS AND DESERTS

The literature touching indirectly on the relationship between population and resources is enormous. The sparseness of direct treatments does not reflect a unanimity of opinion; there are widely divergent views on the nature of the relationship. Some stress the autonomy of population (Boserup 1981; Wilkinson 1973), others the autonomy of resources (Rosenberg 1972; Christensen 1981). It is easy to assert *a priori* the importance of resources, much more difficult to prove their significance. The negative impact of the Russian natural environment is sometimes made explicit (Pipes 1974), the positive impact of the environment more often taken for granted in America, although some do spell out its benignity (Cochrane 1979). One or two authorities still fall into the trap of the static inventory-listing approach to resources (W.H. Parker 1972), but most consider resources in the context of contemporary technology (Rosenberg 1972).

Simple descriptions of the physical matrix are not hard to find but never quite do what is required. As textbook expositions Estall (1972) and Cole (1967) suffice, although Hooson (1970) is much more concise. On climate Lydolph, and Bryson and Hare have done the relevant work in the *World survey of climatology* series, volumes 7 and 11. A comparative classification by climatic type on the Köppen system has been made (W.H. Parker 1972).

Because of the lack of good crop data it is difficult to compare agricultural productivity directly for the relevant period. The data for wheat provide the material for such a comparison in the late nineteenth and twentieth centuries (Timoshenko 1937, 1942, 1943, 1944). Fortunately there is an attempt to argue the responsibility of natural factors for crop yield differences in the twentieth century (N.C. Field 1968). Most of the assertions concerning the relative incidence of famine rest on literary rather than statistical evidence (Kahan 1968; Dando 1976, 1980).

It is easier to get a comparative picture on meat consumption. A reasonable range of calculations can be found for colonial America (Lemon 1967a; McMahon 1981; B.G. Smith 1981). Russian data are more fragmented (Christian 1980; Hoch 1982; Blum 1961; Smith and

Christian 1984), but can be integrated into a 'typical' picture.

There is an extensive literature on the role of export staples although it appears to be about to die for lack of new ideas. The classifications by generation of staple is, as far as I can tell, my own. Detailed work on first-generation staples is available (on furs, R.H. Fisher 1975; Moloney 1967; T.E. Norton 1971; on fishing, Morris 1979; on timber, Algvere 1966; Carroll 1973).

There are good accounts of the inadequacies of the natural transport infrastructure in Russia (Haywood 1969) and even an interesting comparison of the introduction of the steamboat on the main waterways of the two areas, the Mississippi and the Volga (Haywood 1981). References to the natural transport infrastructure in America are again scattered.

An early article pointed out the difficulties associated with the location of coal and iron in Russia (Baykov 1954). The endowment of America with coal and iron has been considered in the context of the application of coke-smelting and the steam engine, at least outside transport (Hunter 1929, Temin 1964a). The relative abundance of soft energy sources in America is something now being made much more of (Greenberg 1980, 1982).

SHOCKS AND DISASTERS

Jones has played the pioneer in putting the emphasis in economic history on disasters or shocks and at the same time helped us to classify such events (F.L. Jones 1977, 1978 and 1981a). Explicitly, a catalogue of Russian disasters (Kahan 1968) and implicitly, an analysis of two case studies, the plague outbreak of 1770 (Alexander 1980) and the Pugachev rising of 1773–5 (Alexander 1969), have stressed the significance and frequent incidence of shocks in Russian history.

Most work has been on epidemic disease as a type of shock. Generally contrasting positions on the autonomy of disease have been adopted (McKeown 1976; McNeill 1977). The importance of plague in Russian history has been a particular focus of interest (Kahan 1979; L.N. Langer 1975, 1976; McNeill 1964; D.H. Miller 1976; Alexander 1980). An analysis of the cholera epidemic of 1829–30 supplements our understanding of Russia's vulnerability to such an outbreak (McGrew 1965).

There is a most useful general study on epidemics in colonial America (J. Duffy 1953). This review can be supplemented by local or regional studies; for example, on New York (J. Duffy 1968), on

Boston (Blake 1959), on Philadelphia (D.B. Smith 1978) or on the Mississippi Valley (Harstad 1959-60, 1960a, 1960b, 1963). The relative healthiness of New England is made much of in a series of local studies (Demos 1970; Greven 1970; Lockridge 1970; S. Norton 1971) and in review articles (D.S. Smith 1972; Vinovskis 1972, 1979). The early unhealthiness of the south is emphasised (Duffy 1953; Clowse 1971; D.B. and A.H. Rutman 1976; Tate and Ammerman 1979). A study on the impact of malaria on the demographic behaviour of a Virginian parish illustrates the potential for a high incidence of disease, even in America (D.B. Smith 1978). An interesting debate concerns the causes of a high mortality in the very early years of settlement (D.B. and A.H. Rutman 1976; Earle 1979; Kupperman 1979).

Reference to the frequent incidence of famine in Russia is commonplace but more systematic treatments are rare (Kahan 1968; Dando 1976, 1980). Russia's vulnerability to Malthusian population pressure is best illustrated by conditions in the sixteenth century (Mankov 1951; Blum 1961). There is an interesting discussion on the Russian diet (Christian 1980, Smith and Christian 1984).

Acts of violence are difficult to deal with as a type of shock. There is no literature on levels of domestic violence comparable with that on England (Gurr 1981; Stone 1983). A high level of violence is assumed for Russia. The best treatments of violence relate to subjugation of native peoples and to foreign wars (McNeill 1964; Hellie 1971, 1977). The size of the army is an indirect index of the threat (Prucha 1967; Duffy 1981). Particular studies of individual wars can be most useful (Leach 1966).

PIONEER RISK

Figures on average life expectancy provide some notion of the typical person's vulnerability to shocks, physical rather than financial. Again the data are fragmentary for early periods. Likewise the picture for America is more complete than for Russia (compare Meeker 1972; Vinovskis 1971,1972; Demos 1970; Greven 1970; Lockridge 1970; D.H. Fischer 1978; with Rashin 1956; Hoch 1982b). For the want of anything better crude mortality rates can be used (Potter 1965; Heer 1968).

The different responses of government to shocks are dealt with in general terms by E.L. Jones (1977, 1978). Specific responses are described in many of the works already referred to (on disease

Duffy, Blake, Alexander and McGrew; on famine Dando and Kahan; on violence McNeill and Hellie 1971). There is an interesting debate on the efficiency of the Russian government's response to the 1891 famine (Robbins 1975; Simms 1976, 1977; Hamburg 1978).

CREATION OF GOVERNMENT

The nature of the relationship between government and market is the key issue in this and the following two sections. All of the main points of view — the Marxist;the pure neoclassical (North 1979); those based as a clear distinction between spontaneous and induced economic development (Crisp 1976); those focussed on government as an economic interest group in its own right (Gerschenkron 1971) — have valid perspectives but do not tell the whole story.

The concept of the degree of penetration of the economy helped bind the material together (Grew 1978). An analysis of Europe's multi-cell state system (E.L. Jones 1981a) is relevant to consideration of colonial America and the appropriate size of political unit.

There are sound general discussions on the role of government in American colonial economic life (Hughes 1976, 1977). The lack of imperial government penetration is noted elsewhere (Becker 1980). The nature of the pluralist system of government emerges in a multitude of individual case studies, particularly for New England (Zuckerman 1970; Cook 1976; Gross 1976; Breen 1980), and in the generalising work of Daniels (1978, 1979). There are also a number of good sources on government in the south (Earle 1970; Rainbolt 1974; Tate and Ammerman 1979). Particular treatment has been accorded to urban government (Teaford 1975; Bridenbaugh 1964a, 1964b).

My first suspicions of a tendency to under-government in Russia were confirmed by excursions into political history (Starr 1972; Yaney 1972). Russia's failure to create a proper bureaucracy is made much of (Madariaga 1981; Raeff 1982). The influence of compulsory service on government structure is often emphasised (Yaney 1972; Hellie 1977). The dominance of the executive and a tendency to treat the economy as the tsar's private patrimony is stressed elsewhere (Pipes 1974). The story of the enserfment, or enservicement, of the peasant has been many times told (Hellie 1971; Culpepper 1965; R.E.F Smith 1968; Blum 1961). The enservicement of the city dweller has at last received a full historical treatment (Hittle 1979). Finally the unamenability of the service system to reform is illustrated by the emancipation of the gentry (R.E. Jones 1973).

THE CREATION OF MARKETS

A lot of attention has been devoted over the years to the proper definition of a market (for recent examples see Merrill 1977; Henretta 1978; Clark 1979). However nobody has formalised the treatment of risk and its influence on market participation. The analysis has to be derived from studies of merchants, either as a group or as individuals (Bushkovitch 1975, 1980; Hittle 1979; Owen 1981; Rieber 1982; Bailyn 1964), or of particular areas (Warden 1976; Innes 1983; Heyrman 1984) or specific routes (Middleton 1953; Pares 1968; Kirchner 1966; Attman 1973, 1979).

The importance of distribution costs relative to production costs, particularly with respect to international trade, has been clearly shown (Shepherd and Walton 1972). Transactions and protection costs have been analysed at the theoretical level (North and Thomas 1973; Lane 1966), but not at the practical level. The opposite applies to transport and financial costs concerning which there has been a legion of practical studies (Walton 1967; North 1968; Ferguson 1953; McCusker 1978; Becker 1980; Rothenberg 1981), whereas the theoretical studies are relevant to only the nineteenth century. There are good analyses of discontinuities of supply (Menard 1978; North 1961).

The importance of the process of proto-industrialisation for market development is emphasised by Perlin (1983). In a recent work de Vries (1984) has noted the enormous scale of proto-industrial development in early modern Europe. Rudolph (1980, 1985) and Tryon (1966 reprint) show its ubiquity in Russia and America.

The literature on factor markets is much better adapted to our purposes. The land distribution system in colonial America is well researched (on New England, Akagi 1924, and a host of local studies; on New York, Kim 1978; on Pennsylvania, Lemon 1972; on the Chesapeake, Tate and Ammerman 1979; on North Carolina, Merrens 1964; on South Carolina, Clowse 1971). There is a good reference book on the legal issues of landholding in colonial America (Harris 1970). For Russia, by necessity the tenurial system has been dealt with alongside the growth of serfdom (Blum 1961; Hellie 1971).

The prevalence of forced labour in the colonial American economy is well attested (Hughes 1976, 1977). There are good treatments both on indentured labour (A.E. Smith 1947; Galenson 1979) and on slavery (Fogel and Engerman 1974; Genovese 1976), which thankfully give a balanced view in combination. The transition from indentured to slave labour is not fully explained (Heavner 1978; Galenson 1979). Hellie has written an exhaustive, if exhausting, treatment on

227

Russian slaves (1982). There are a vast number of works on serfdom.

The concept of a socio-economic equilibrium, even a dynamic equilibrium, is implicit in the fundamental and secondary institutions of North and Thomas (1973). There has been a close resemblance to my deep and surface institutions. The former define the relevant transitional mode (Polanyi 1957). Chayanov and his disciples are most helpful on the peasant mode, Marx on the market mode.

INTERACTION OF GOVERNMENT AND MARKETS

Taxation data for early America and Russia are incomplete. Given their limitations, the data of Palmer (1959) are greatly overused. Recent studies have provided more detail but still only at the topmost level of government (Becker 1980). The degree of military subsidy from Britain and its significance have been evaluated (Davis and Huttenback 1982). There is a study considering the influence of the frontier on the distribution of government expenditures, at least for the nineteenth century (Davis and Legler 1966). Relevant information from an earlier period has to be ferreted out of authorities already dated (Gipson 1931) and from local studies.

On Russia there are sources of fragmentary information on indirect tax (Bushkovitch 1978; Zlotnick 1979), on direct taxation (Blum 1961) or both (Hellie 1971) but all of this only amounts to very tentative estimates of the tax burden when combined with the work of R.E.F. Smith (1977). The expenditure side is even less well documented for both economies.

The role of the legal system in economic change has recently become an increasingly interesting focus of interest. Hurst (1964, 1977) is the pioneer in this field and Scheiber (1971, 1972–3, 1973, 1975, 1980, 1981) the main publicist. Some grandiose claims have been made (Horvitz 1977). Unhappily nearly all this work is concentrated on post-Independence America. The reason why the legal system was poised to play an economically instrumental role at Independence and the use of the law in the colonial period is either ignored or controversially treated (Nelson 1975; and the review by H.B. Zobel in the *NEQ* 1977). There are one or two brief but interesting hints (Hartog 1979).

For Russia the subordinate role of the law is made explicit in a number of studies (Kaiser 1980; Pipes 1974; Wortman 1976; Raeff 1982). Pipes takes up the issue of the relationship between law and economic activity.

There are reasonable studies of 'modernising' policies in early modern Russia (Blanc 1974 on Peter the Great; and Madariaga 1981 on Catherine). The more successful but less dramatic nature of government intervention in much of America is illustrated by Bushman (1967). Even colonial America has its failures (Rainbolt 1974). The positive results of competitive government emerge clearly in the literature (Bridenbaugh 1964a and 1964b; Goodrich 1960).

Shepherd and Walton (1972) have done a thorough job on colonial America's external trade, also presenting a rigorous and largely non-controversial model of the relationship with Britain. B. Thomas (1978) has offered a more controversial, but very interesting, model of factor flows and their link with commodity movements. (Blum (1961) and North (1961) make much of an early inter-regional trade, criticised as premature by Lindstrom (1978) and Munting (1979). Lindstrom has rightly pointed out the importance of the cities and their trade with an immediate hinterland. Bater's work on St Petersburg (1976) offers a good contrast. Thankfully there is some research on early Russia's external trade (Attman 1981b; Kirchner 1966).

A seemingly continuous flow of work stressed the creation of underdevelopment by trade and factor movements (Wallerstein 1974; Frank 1978; Stavrianos 1981; Wolf 1982). The Imperial burden argument for colonial America has been rejected (Walton 1971). For a later date Sontag (1968) rejects the dependency argument for Russia.

GENERAL MODEL

Most of the relevant topics are dealt with under other chapter headings, the major exception being stressed areas and critical movements. Gerschenkron talked of *Sternstunden*. The classic article on New England as a stressed area is by Lockridge (1968). Others have taken up the theme (Gross 1976; D.L. Jones 1981; Hall 1982). The same argument has been advanced for Central Russia (Egiazarova 1959; Hamburg 1978).

There are many examples of the failure of reform. The failure of Emancipation both to improve the lot of the peasants and of agriculture as a whole is discussed in Ransom and Sutch (1977) and in Gerschenkron (1965) and Field (1976).

Bibliography

Abbreviations

AER	American Economic Review
AH	Agricultural History
AHe	American Heritage
AHR	American Historical Review
AJS	American Journal of Sociology
AQ	American Quarterly
BHA	Biology and Human Affairs
BHR	Business History Review
BLR	Buffalo Law Review
CA	Current Anthropology
CG	Canadian Geographer
CJE	Cambridge Journal of Economics
CJEPS	Canadian Journal of Economics and Political Science
CSS	California Slavic Studies
CaSS	Canadian Slavic Studies
D	Demography
E	Economica
EDCC	Economic Development and Cultural Change
EEH	Explorations in Economic History (formerly Explorations in Entrepreneurial History)
EFN	Ecology of Food and Nutrition
EH	Economy and History
EHR	Economic History Review
EIHS	Essex Institute Historical Collections
GR	Geographical Review
HB	Human Biology
HM	Historical Methods
IS	Istoriya SSSR
JAH	Journal of American History
JEBH	Journal of Economic and Business History
JEEH	Journal of European Economic History
JEH	Journal of Economic History
JGO	Jahrbücher für Geschichte Osteuropas
JIH	Journal of Interdisciplinary History
JPE	Journal of Political Economy
JPS	Journal of Peasant Studies

JSH	Journal of Social History
JSoH	Journal of Southern History
JUH	Journal of Urban History
LE	Land Economics
LPS	Local Population Studies
MSESS	Manchester School of Economic and Social Studies
MVHR	Mississippi Valley History Review
NEQ	New England Quarterly
PAH	Perspectives in American History
PHR	Pacific Historical Review
PP	Past and Present
PS	Peasant Studies (formerly Peasant Studies Newsletter — PSN)
PoS	Population Studies
PSQ	Political Science Quarterly
R	Review
REH	Research in Economic History
RH	Russian History
RHR	Radical History Review
RR	Russian Review
SEHR	Scandinavian Economic History Review
SH	Social History
SR	Slavic Review
WLR	Wisconsin Law Review
WMH	Wisconsin Magazine of History
WMQ	William and Mary Quarterly
WP	World Politics
WS	Wheat Studies

Adams, D.R. (1980) 'American neutrality and prosperity, 1793–1808: a reconsideration', *JEH 40*, 713–37

Akagi, R.H. (1924) *The town proprietors of the New England colonies: a study of their development organisation, activities and controversies 1620–1770*, Philadelphia: University of Pennsylvania Press

Alexander, J.T. (1969) *Autocratic politics in a national crisis: the imperial government and Pugachev's Revolt 1773–5*, Bloomington and London: Indiana University Press

—— (1980) *Bubonic plague in early modern Russia: public health and urban disaster*, Baltimore: John Hopkins University Press

Algvere, K.V. (1966) Forest Economy in the USSR, An analysis of Soviet competitive potentialities. Studia Forestalia Suedia NR 39

Alston, L.J. and Schapiro, M.O. (1984), 'Inheritance laws across colonies: causes and consequences'; *JEH 44*, 277–87

Anderson, M. (1980) *Approaches to the history of the western family, 1500–1914*, London: Macmillan

Anderson, P. (1974) Passages from Antiquity to Feudalism and Lineages of the Absolutist State. London: New Left Books

Anderson, R.V. and Gallman, R.E. (1977) 'Slaves as fixed capital: slave labour and southern economic development'; *JAH 64*, 24–46

Anderson, T.L. (1975) *The economic growth of seventeenth-century New England: a measurement of regional income*, New York: Arno Press

—— (1979) 'Economic growth in colonial New England: "statistical renaissance" ', *JEH 39*, 243–57

—— and Thomas, R.P. (1978) 'The growth of population and labour force in the seventeenth-century Chesapeake', *EEH 15*, 290–312, 368–87

Appleby, A.,B. (1978) *Famine in Tudor and Stuart England*, Liverpool: Liverpool University Press

Atack, J. and Bateman, F. (1981) 'Egalitarianism, inequality and age: the rural north in 1860', *JEH 41*, 85–95

Attman, A. (1973) *The Russian and Polish markets in international trade, 1500–1650*, Gothenburg: Institute of Economic History of Gothenburg University

—— (1979) *The struggle for Baltic markets: powers in conflict 1558–1618*, Gothenburg: Institute of Economic History of Gothenburg University

—— (1981a) *The bullion flow between Europe and the East, 1000–1750*, Gothenburg: Institute of Economic History of Gothenburg University

—— (1981b) 'The Russian market in world trade, 1500–1860', *SEHR* and *EH 29*, 177–202

Bailyn, B. (1964) *The New England merchants in the seventeenth century* New York: Harper and Row

Bairoch, P. (1969) *Revolution industrielle et sous-development*, Paris: Mouton

Ball, D.E. and Walton, G.M. (1976) 'Agricultural productivity change in eighteenth-century Pennyslvania', *JEH 36*, 102–17

Baron, S.H. (1969) 'The town in 'feudal' Russia', *SR 28*, 116–22

—— (1970) 'The Weber thesis and the failure of capitalist development in early modern Russia', *JGO 8*, 320–36

—— (1972) 'The transition from feudalism to capitalism in Russia: a major Soviet historical controversy', *AHR 77*, 715-29

—— (1973) 'Who were the *gosti*?' *CSS 7*, 1-40

—— (1983) 'Entrepreneurs and entrepreneurship in sixteenth/seventeenth century Russia', in Guroff, G. and Carstensen, F.V. (*qv*), 27-58

Bater, J.H. (1976) *St Petersburg: industrialisation and change*, London: Edward Arnold

—— (1978) 'Some dimensions of urbanisation and the response of municipal government: Moscow and St Petersburg', *RH 5*, 46-53

Baykov, A. (1954) 'The economic development of Russia', *EHR 7*, 137-49

Becker, R.A. (1980) *Revolution, reform and the politics of American taxation, 1763-83*, Baton Rouge and London: Louisiana State University Press

Berthoff, R.T. (1971) *An unsettled people: social order and disorder in America*, New York: Harper and Row

Bidwell, P.W. and Falconer, J.I. (1925) *History of agriculture in the northern United States, 1620-1860*, Washington: Carnegie Institution of Washington

Billington, J.H. (1966) *The icon and the axe: an interpretative history of Russian culture*, New York: Knopf

Billington, R.A. (1968) Frontier, in C. Vann Woodward (ed.), *The comparative approach to American history*, New York: Basic books

—— (1974) *Westward expansion: a history of the American frontier*, New York: Macmillan

Biraben, J.N. (1975-6) *Les hommes et la peste en France et dans les pays européens et mediterraneans*, Paris: Ecole pratique des Hautes Etudes, Centre de Recherches historiques

Bjork, G.C. (1964) 'The weaning of the American economy: independence, market changes and economic development', *JEH 24*, 541-60

Black, C.E. (ed.) (1960) *The transformation of Russian society: aspects of social change since 1861*, Cambridge, Mass.: Harvard University Press

—— (1975) *The modernisation of Japan and Russia: a comparative study*, New York: Free Press

Blackwell, W.L. (1968) *The beginnings of Russian industrialisation*, Princeton, N.J.: Princeton University Press

—— (1980) 'Geography, history and the city in Europe and Russia', *JUH 6*, 357-65

Blake, J.B. (1959) *Public health in the town of Boston 1630-1822*,

Cambridge, Mass.: Harvard University Press

Blanc, S. (1974) The economic policy of Peter the Great, in Blackwell, W.L. (ed.), *Russian economic development from Peter the Great to Stalin*, New York: New Viewpoints

Bloch, M. (1953) Towards a comparative history of European societies, in Lane, F.C. and Riemersma, J.C. (eds), *Enterprise and secular change*, Homewood, Illinois: Richard D. Irwin

Blum, J. (1957) 'The rise of serfdom in Eastern Europe', *HR 62*, 807–36

—— (1961) *Lord and peasant in Russia from the ninth to the nineteenth century*, Princeton, N.J.: Princeton University Press

—— (1978) *The end of the old order in rural Europe*, Princeton, N.J.: Princeton University Press

Boserup, E. (1981) *Population and technological change: a study of long-term trends*, Chicago: University of Chicago Press

Boyer, P. and Nissenbaum, S. (1974) *Salem possessed: the social origins of witchcraft*, Cambridge, Mass.: Harvard University Press

Brady, D.S. (1972) 'Consumption and the style of life', in Davis, L.E. *et al* (*qv*) 61–89

Breen, T.H. (1980) *Puritans and adventurers: change and persistence in early America*, New York and Oxford: Oxford University Press

Brenner, R. (1976) 'Agrarian class structure and economic development in pre-industrial Europe', *PP 80*, 30–75

Bridenbaugh, C. (1964a) *Cities in the wilderness: the first-century of urban life in America, 1625–1742*, New York: Capricorn Books

—— (1964b) *Cities in revolt: urban life in America, 1743–76*, New York: Capricorn Books

Brown, R.D. (1976) *Modernisation: the transformation of American Life, 1600–1805*, New York: Hill and Wang

Bruchey, S. (1958) 'Success and failure factors: American merchants in foreign trade in the eighteenth and early nineteenth centuries', *BHR 32*, 272–92

—— (1965) *The roots of American economic growth, 1607–1861: an essay in social causation*, London: Hutchinson University Library

Bryson, R.A. and Hare, F.K. (1974) 'Climates of North America', in *World Survey of Climatology*, vol. 11, Amsterdam, New York: Elsevier Scientific Publishing Co

Bushkovitch, P.A. (1975) 'The merchant class of Moscow, 1580–1650', PhD thesis: Columbia University

—— (1978) 'Taxation, tax farming and merchants in sixteenth-century Russia', *SR 3*, 381–98

—— (1980) *The merchants of Moscow, 1580–1650*, Cambridge: Cambridge University Press

Bushman, R.L. (1967) *From Puritan to Yankee; character and social order in Connecticut, 1690–1765*, Cambridge, Mass.: Harvard University Press

—— (1981) 'Family security in the transition from farm to city, 1750–1850', *Journal of Family History 6*, 238–56

Carefoot, G.L. and Sprott, E.F. (1969) *Famine on the wind: plant diseases and human history*, London: Angus and Robertson

Carroll, C.F. (1973) *The timber economy of Puritan New England*, Providence, R.I.: Brown University Press

Cassedy, J.H. (1969) *Demography in early America: beginnings of the statistical mind, 1600–1800*, Cambridge, Mass.: Harvard University Press

Chandler, A.D. (1972) 'Anthracite coal and the beginnings of the industrial revolution in the US', *BHR 46*, 141–81

—— (1977) *The visible hand: the managerial revolution in American business*, Cambridge, Mass.: Harvard University Press

Chayanov, A.V. (1966) *The theory of peasant economy*, Thorner, D., Kerblay, B. and Smith, R.E.F. (eds), Homewood, Illinois: American Economic Association Translation Series

Christensen, P. (1976) 'Land, labour and mechanisation in the *antebellum* United States economy', PhD thesis: University of Wisconsin

—— (1981) 'Land abundance and cheap horsepower in the mechanisation of the *antebellum* United States economy', *EEH 18*, 309–29

Christian, D. (1980) 'Food and the condition of the peasantry in nineteenth-century Russia', unpublished paper: Macquarie University

Clark, C. (1979) 'Household economy, market exchange and the rise of capitalism in the Connecticut Valley, 1800–60', *JSH 13*, 169–89

Clawson, M. (1966) 'The land system of the United States: an introduction in the history and practice of land use and land tenure', unpublished paper

Clemens, P.G.E. (1980) *The Atlantic economy and colonial Maryland's eastern shore: from tobacco to grain*, Ithaca and London: Cornell University Press

Clifton, J.M. (1981) 'The rice industry in colonial America', *AH 3*, 266–83

Cloudsley-Thompson, J.L. (1976) *Insects and history*, London: Weidenfeld and Nicolson

Clowse, C.D. (1971) *Economic beginnings in colonial South Carolina*,

Columbia: University of South Carolina Press

Cochran, T.C. (1981) *Frontiers of change: early industrialism in America*, New York and Oxford: Oxford University Press

Cochrane, W.W. (1979) *The development of American agriculture: a historical analysis*, Minneapolis: University of Minnesota Press

Cole, J.P. (1967) *Geography of the USSR*, London: Penguin Books

Coleman, P.J. (1974) *Debtors and creditors in America: insolvency, imprisonment for debt, and bankruptcy, 1607-1900*, Madison: State Historical Society of Wisconsin

Confino, M. (1969) *Systèmes agraires et progrès agricole; l'assolement triennal en Russie aux 18ᵉ-19ᵉ siecles*, Paris: Mouton

Cook, E.M. (1976) *The fathers of the towns*, Baltimore and London: John Hopkins University Press

Cook, S. (1973) 'The significance of disease in the extinction of the New England Indians', *HB 45*, 485-508

Coulborn, R. (ed.) (1965) *Feudalism in history*, Hamden, Conn.: Archon Books

Crisp, O. (1976) *Studies in the Russian economy before 1914*, London: Macmillan

Critchley, J.S. (1978) *Feudalism*, London: George Allen and Unwin

Crosby, A.W. Jr. (1965) *America, Russia, hemp and Napoleon; American trade with Russia and the Baltic, 1783-1812*, Columbus: Ohio State University Press

— (1965) 'Virgin soil epidemics as a factor in the aboriginal depopulation', *WMQ 33*, 289-99

— (1972) *The Columbian exchange: biological and cultural consequences of 1492*, Westport, Conn.: Greenwood Publishing Co

Culpepper, J.M. (1965) 'The legislative origins of peasant bondage in Muscovy', PhD diss.: Columbia University

Curtin, P.D. (1968) 'Epidemiology and the slave trade', *PSQ 80*, 190-216

Czap, P. (1978) 'Marriage and the peasant joint family in the era of serfdom', in Ransel (ed.) (*qv*)

Dando, W.A. (1976) 'Man-made famines: some geographical insights from an exploratory study of a millenium of Russian famines', *EFN 4*, 219-34

— (1980) *The geography of famine*, London: Edward Arnold

Daniels, B.C. (ed.) (1978) *Town and county: essays on the structure of local government in the Atlantic colonies*, Middletown, Conn.: Wesleyan University Press

— (1979) *The Connecticut town growth and development, 1635-1790*, Middletown, Conn.: Wesleyan University Press

—— (1980) 'Economic development in the colonial and revolutionary Connecticut: an overview', *WMQ 37*, 429–50

Davidson, B.R. (1981) *European farming in Australia: an economic history of Australian farming*, Amsterdam, Oxford and London: Elsevier Scientific Publishing Co

Davis, J.E. (1977) *Frontier America, 1800–40: a comparative demographic analysis of the settlement process*, Glendale, Calif.: A.H. Clark and Co

Davis, L.E. and Legler, J. (1966) 'The government in the American economy, 1815–1902: a quantitative study', *JEH 26*, 514–52

—— and Easterlin, R.A. and Parker, W.N. (eds) (1972) *American economic growth: an economist's history of the United States*, New York: Harper Row

—— and Huttenback, R.A. (1982) 'The cost of empire', in Ransom, Sutch and Walton (eds) 41–71

de Vries, J. (1984) *European urbanisation, 1500–1800*, London: Methuen and Co Ltd

Demos, J. (1970) *A little commonwealth: family life in Plymouth Colony*, New York: Oxford University Press

Diamond, S. (1958) 'From organisation to society: Virginia in the seventeenth century', *AJS 63*, 457–75

—— (1967) 'Values as an obstcle to economic growth: the American colonies', *JEH 27*, 561–75

Dobyns, H.F. (1966) 'Estimating aboriginal American population: an appraisal of techniques within a new hemisphere estimate', *CA 7*, 395–416

Domar, E.D. (1970) 'The causes of slavery or serfdom: a hypothesis', *JEH 20*, 18–32

Donnelly, A.S. (1968) *The Russian conquest of Bashkiria 1552–1740: a case study in imperialism*, New Haven: Yale University Press

Dubos, R. and J. (1953) *The white plague: tuberculosis, man and society*, London: Victor Gollancz Ltd

Duffy, C. (1981) *Russia's military way to the west: origins and nature of Russian military power, 1700–1800*, London: Routledge and Kegan Paul

Duffy, J. (1951) 'The passage to the colonies', *MVHR 38*, 21–38

—— (1953) *Epidemics in colonial America*, Baton Rouge: Louisiana State University Press

—— (1968) *A history of public health in New York City, 1625–1866*, New York: Russell Sage Foundation

Dukes, P. (1970) *The emergence of the super powers: a short comparative history of the USA and the USSR*, New York: Harper and Row

Dunn, R.S. (1972) 'The social history of early New England', *AQ 24*, 661–79

Earle, C.V. (1970) 'Evolution of a tidewater settlement system: All Hallow's Parish, Maryland, 1650–1783', Chicago: University of Chicago, Department of Geography research paper no. 170

—— (1976) 'Staple crops and urban development in the eighteenth-century south', *PAH 10*, 7–78

—— (1978) 'A staple interpretation of slavery and free labour', *GR 68*, 52–65

—— (1979) 'Environment, disease and mortality in early Virginia', in Tate and Ammerman (eds)

—— and Hoffman, R. (1980) 'The foundation of the modern economy: agriculture and the costs of labour in the United States and England, 1800–60', *AHR 85*, 1055–94

Easterbrook, W.T. (1954) 'Uncertainty and economic change', *JEH 14*, 346–60

Eaton, H.L. (1970) 'Early Russian censuses and the population of Muscovy, 1550–1650, PhD thesis: University of Illinois

Eckaute, D. (1965) 'Les brigands en Russie du 17e au 19e siècle: mythe et realité, *Revue d'histoire moderne et contemporaire 12*: 161–202

Egiazarova, N.A. (1959) *Agrarnyi krizis Kontsa XIX veka v Rossii*, Moscow: State Publishing House

Egnal, M. (1975) 'The economic development of the thirteen continental economies, 1720–75', *WMQ 32*, 191–222

Esper, T. (1969) 'Military self-sufficiency and weapons technology in Muscovite Russia', *SR 28*, 185–208

Estall, R.C. (1972) *A modern geography of the USA: aspects of life and economy*, London: Penguin Books

Farnie, D.A. (1962) 'The commercial empire of the Atlantic, 1607–1783, *EHR 15*, 205–18

Fedor, T. (1975) *Patterns of urban growth in the Russian empire during the nineteenth century*, Chicago: Department of Geography, University of Chicago

Felix, D. (1979) '*De gustibus disputandum est*: changing consumer preferences in economic growth', *EEH 16*, 260–96

Ferguson, E.J. (1953) 'Currency finance: an interpretation of colonial monetary practices', *WMQ 10*, 153–80

Field, D. (1976) *The end of serfdom; nobility and bureaucracy in Russia, 1855–61*, Cambridge, Mass.: Harvard University Press

Field, N.C. (1968) 'Environmental quality and land productivity: a comparison of the agricultural land base of the USSR and

North America', *CG 12*, 1–14

Fischer, D.H. (1978) *Growing old in America*, Oxford, London and New York: Oxford University Press

Fisher, R.H. (1975) *The Russian fur trade, 1550–1700*, Ann Arbor: University Microfilms

Fishlow, A. (1964) '*Antebellum* inter-regional trade reconsidered', *AER 44*, 352–62

—— (1965) *American railroads and the transformation of the antebellum economy*, Cambridge, Mass.: Harvard University Press

—— (1966) 'Levels of nineteenth-century American investment in education', *JEH 26*, 418–36

Fleming, D. and Bailyn, B. (eds) (1971) *Law in American history*, Boston, Toronto: Little, Brown and Co

Flinn, M.W. (1974) 'The stabilisation of mortality in pre-industrial Western Europe', *JEEH 3*, 285–318

Fogel, R.W. (1964) *Railroads and American economic growth: essays in econometric history*, Baltimore: John Hopkins University

—— and Engerman, S.L. (1974) *Time on the cross: the economics of American negro slavery*. Boston: Little, Brown and Co

Frank, A.G. (1978) *World accumulation, 1492–1789*, London: Macmillan

Frieden, N.M. (1977) 'The Russian cholera epidemic, 1892–93, and medical professionalism', *JSH 10*, 538–59

Friedman, L.M. (1973) *A history of American law*, New York: Simon and Schuster

Fuhrmann, J.T. (1972) *The origins of capitalism in Russian industry and progress in the sixteenth and seventeenth centuries*, Chicago: Quadrangle Books

Galbraith, J.T. (1979) *The nature of mass poverty*, London: Penguin Books

Galenson, D.W. (1977) 'Immigration and the colonial labour system — an analysis of the length of indenture', *EEH 14*, 360–77

—— (1979) *White servitude in colonial America: an economic analysis*, New York: Cambridge University Press

—— (1981) 'White servitude and the growth of black slavery in colonial America', *JEH 41*, 39–49

Gallman, R. (1972) 'The pace and pattern of American economic growth', in Davis *et al*, *American Economic Growth*, 15–60

Galton, D. (1971) *Survey of a Thousand Years of Beekeeping in Russia*, London: Bee Research Association

Genovese, E.D. (1976) *Roll, Jordon, roll*, New York: Vintage Books

Gerschenkron, A. (1962) *Economic backwardness in historical perspective*, Cambridge, Mass.: Harvard University Press
—— (1963) 'The early phases of industrialisation in Russia: afterthoughts and counter-thoughts', in W.W. Rostow (ed.), *The economics of take-off into sustained growth*, New York: St. Martin's Press
—— (1965) 'Agrarian policies and industrialisation: Russia, 1861–1917', in Postan, M.M. and Habakkuk, H.J. (eds), *The Cambridge Economic History of Europe, Vol. 6*, Part II, Cambridge: Cambridge University Press
—— (1968) *Continuity in history and other essays*, Cambridge, Mass.: Harvard University Press
—— (1970) *Europe in the Russian mirror*, New York: Cambridge University Press
—— (1971) 'Soviet Marxism and absolutism', *SR 30*, 853–69
Gibson, J.R. (1969) *Feeding the Russian fur trade: provisionment of the Okhotsk seaboard and the Kamchatka peninsula, 1639–1856*, Madison, Milwaukee and London: University of Wisconsin Press
—— (1976) *Imperial Russia in frontier America. the changing geography of supply of Russian America, 1784–1867*, New York: Oxford University Press
Gilbert, G. (1977) 'The role of breadstuffs in American trade, 1770–90, *EEH 14*, 378–87
Gipson, L.H. (1931) *Connecticut taxation, 1750–75*, Tercentenary Commission of the State of Connecticut Committee on Historical Publications
Goldin, C.D. and Lewis, F.D. (1980) 'The role of exports in American economic growth during the Napoleonic Wars, 1793–1807', EEH 17, 6–25
Goldsmith, R.W. (1961) 'The economic growth of Tsarist Russia, 1860–1913' *EDCC 9*, 441–75
Goodrich, C. (1960) *Government Promotion of American Canals and Railroads*, New York: Columbia University Press
Gottfried, M.H. (1936) 'The first depression in Massachusetts', *NEQ 9*, 665–78
Grant, C.S. (1961) *Democracy in the Connecticut frontier town of Kent*, New York
Gray, R. and Wood, B. (1976) 'The transition from indentured to involuntary servitude in colonial Georgia', *EEH 13*, 353–70
Greenberg, D. (1980) 'Energy flow in a changing economy, 1815–80', in Frese, J.R. and Judd, J. (eds), *An emerging independent American economy 1815–75*

—— (1982) 'Reassessing the power patterns of the industrial revolution: an Anglo-American comparison', *AHR 87*, 1237–61

Greene, E.S. and Harrington, V. (1966 reprint) *American population before the federal census of 1790*, Gloucester, Mass.: Peter Smith

Gregory, J.S. (1968) *Russian land, Soviet people: a geographical approach to the USSR*, London: George C. Harrap and Co Ltd

Gregory, P.R. (1980) 'Grain marketings and peasant consumption, Russia, 1885–1913', *EEH 17*, 135–64

—— (1982) *Russian national income, 1885–1913*, Cambridge: Cambridge University Press

Grenfell Price, A. (1963) *The western invasions of the Pacific and its continents: a study of moving frontiers and changing landscapes 1513–1958*, Oxford, Clarendon Press

Greven, P. (1970) *Four generations: population, land and family and colonial Andover, Massachusetts*, Ithaca, New York: Cornell University Press

Grew, R. (ed) (1978) *Crises of political development in Europe and the United States*, Princeton, N.J.: Princeton University Press

Gross, R.A. (1976) *The Minutemen and their world*, New York: Hill and Wang

Gunderson, G. (1976) *A new economic history of America*, New York: McGraw-Hill Book Co

Guroff, G. and Carstensen, F.V. (1983) *Entrepreneurship in imperial Russia and the Soviet Union*, Princeton, N.J.: Princeton University Press

Gurr, T. (1981) 'Historical trends in violent crime: a critical review of the evidence', *Crime and Justice: an annual review of research 3*, 295–353

Habakkuk, H.J. (1962) *American and British technology in the nineteenth century*, Cambridge: Cambridge University Press

Haines, M.R. (1977) 'Mortality in nineteenth-century America: estimates from New York and Pennsylvania census data, 1865 and 1900', *D 14*, 311–31

Hajnal, J. (1965) 'European marriage patterns in perspective', in Glass, D.V. and Eversley, D.E.C. (eds), *Population in history*, London: E. Arnold

Hall, P.D. (1982) *The organisation of American culture, 1700–1900: private institutions, elites and the origins of American nationality*, New York: New York University Press

Hamburg, G.M. (1978) 'The crisis in Russian agriculture: a comment', *SR 37*, 481–90

241

Hamm, M.F. (ed.) (1976) *The city in Russian history*, Lexington, Kentucky: University Press of Kentucky
—— (1977) 'The modern Russian city: an historiographical analysis', *JUH 4*, 39-76
Harris, C.D. (1970) *Cities of the Soviet Union*, Chicago: University of Chicago Press
Harris, M. (1970) *Origin of the land tenure system in the United States*, Westpoint, Connecticut: Greenwood Press
Harstad, P.T. (1959-60) 'Sickness and disease on the Wisconsin frontier: malaria, 1820-50', *WMH 43*, 83-96
—— (1960a) 'Sickness and disease on the Wisconsin frontier: cholera, 1820-50', *WMH 43*, 203-20
—— (1960b) 'Sickness and disease on the Wisconsin frontier: smallpox and other diseases, 1820-50', *WMH 43*, 253-63
—— (1963) Health in the Upper Mississippi River Valley, 1820 to 1861, PhD thesis: University of Wisconsin
Hartog, H. (1979) 'Because all the world was not New York City: governance, property rights and the state in the changing definition of a corporation, 1730-1860', *BLR 28*, 91-106
Hartz, L. (1964) *The founding of new societies; studies in the history of the United States, Latin America, South Africa, Canada and Australia*, New York: Harcourt, Brace and World
Haxthausen-Abbenburg, A.F.L.M., Baron von (1968) *The Russian empire: its people, institutions and resources*. Translated by R. Farie, New York: Da Capo Press
Haywood, R.M. (1969) *The beginnings of railway development in Russia in the reign of Nicholas 1, 1835-42*, Durham, North Carolina: Duke University Press
—— (1981) 'The development of steamboats on the Volga River and its tributaries, 1817-56', *REH 6*, 127-92
Heavner, R.O. (1978) *Economic aspects of indentured servitude in colonial Pennsylvania*, New York: Arno Press
Heer, D.M. (1968) 'The demographic transition in the Russian Empire and the Soviet Union', *JSH 1*, 193-240
Heilbronner, H. (1962) 'The Russian plague of 1878-9', *SR 21*, 89-112
Hellie, R. (1971) *Enserfment and military change in Muscovy*, Chicago: University of Chicago Press
—— (1977) 'The structure of modern Russian history: towards a dynamic model', *RH 4*, 1-22
—— (1978) 'The stratification of Muscovite society: the townsmen', *RH 5*, 119-75

—— (1979) 'Muscovite slavery in comparative perspective', *RH 6*, 133–209

—— (1982) *Slavery in Russia, 1450–1725*, Chicago: University of Chicago Press

Henretta, J. (1973) *The evolution of American society, 1700–1815: an interdisciplinary analysis*, Lexington, Mass.: Heath

—— (1978) 'Families and farms: *mentalité* in pre-industrial America' *WMQ 35*, 3–32

Herlihy, P. (1978a) Russian grain and the Mediterranean markets, 1774–1861, PhD thesis: University of Pennsylvania

Herlihy, P. (1978b) 'Death in Odessa: a study of population movements in a nineteenth-century city', *JUH 4*, 424–32

Heyrman, C.L. (1984) *Commerce and culture: the maritime communities of colonial Massachusetts, 1690–1750*, New York and London: W.W. Norton and Company

Hicks, J. (1969) *A theory of economic history*, London: Oxford University Press

Higgs, R. (1971) *The transformation of the American economy, 1865–1914: an essay in interpretation*, New York: Wiley

—— (1973) 'Mortality in rural America, 1870–1920: estimates and conjectures' *EEH 10*, 177–95

—— (1975) 'Urbanisation and inventiveness in the United States, 1870–1920', in Schnore (ed) (*qv*), 247–59

—— (1979) 'Cycles and trends of mortality in 18 large American cities, 1871–1900', *EEH 16*, 381–408

—— and Settler, H.L. (1970) 'Colonial New England demography: a sampling approach', *WMQ 27*, 282–94

Hilliard, S.B. (1972) *Hog meat and hoecake; food supply in the Old South, 1840–60*, Carbondale: Southern Illinois University Press

Hindle, B. (1975) *America's wooden age: aspects of its early technology*, Tarrytown, New York: Sleepy Hollow Restorations

Hingley, R. (1978) *The Russian mind*, London: Bodley Head

Hirst, P.Q. (1975) 'The uniqueness of the west', *Economy and Society 4*, 446–75

Historical Statistics of the United States: Colonial Times to 1957 (1960) Washington DC: Government Printing Office

Hittle, M.J. (1979) *The service city; state and townsmen in Russia, 1600–1800*, Cambridge, Mass.: Harvard University Press

Hoch, S.L. (1982a) 'Serf diet in nineteenth-century Russia', *AH 56*, 391–414

—— (1982b) 'Serfs in imperial Russia: demographic insights', *JIH 13*, 221–46

—— and Augustine, W.R. (1979) 'The tax censuses and the decline of serf population in imperial Russia, 1833–58', *SR 38*, 403–25

Hofstadter, R. (1956) 'The myth of the happy yeoman', *AHe 7*, 43–53

Hollingsworth, J.R. (1978) 'The United States', in Grew, (ed) (*qv*), 163–96

Hooson, D.J.M. (1970) 'The geographical setting', in Auty, R. and Obolensky, D. (eds), *An introduction to Russian History*, Cambridge: Cambridge University Press

Horvitz, M.J. (1977) *The transformation of American law, 1780–1860*, Cambridge, Mass.: Harvard University Press

Hughes, J.R.T. (1976) *Social control in the colonial economy*, Charlottesville, Virginia: University Press of Virginia

—— (1977) *The government habit: economic controls from colonial times to the present*, New York: Basic Books

—— (1983) *American economic history*, Glenview, Illinois: Scott, Foresman and Company

Hunter, L.C. (1929) 'The influence of the market upon technique in the iron industry in Western Pennsylvania up to 1860', *JEBH 1*, 241–381

Huntingdon, S.P. (1966) 'Political modernisation: America *vs* Europe', *WP 18*, 378–414

Hurst, J.W. (1964) *Law and the conditions of freedom in the nineteenth-century United States*, Madison: University of Wisconsin Press

—— (1977) *Law and social order in the United States*, Ithaca: Cornell University Press

Hutchinson, W.K. and Williamson, S. (1971) 'The self-sufficiency of the *antebellum* south: estimates of the food supply', *JEH 13*, 591–612

Hyde, C.K. (1977) *Technological change and the British iron industry*, Princeton, N.J.: Princeton University Press

Innes, S. (1983) *Labour in a new land-economy and society in seventeenth-century Springfield*, Princeton, New Jersey: Princeton University Press

Innis, H.A. (1954) *The cod fisheries: the history of an international economy*, Toronto: University of Toronto Press

Ippolito, R. (1975) 'The effects of the agricultural depression on industrial demand in England , 1730–50', *E 42*, 298–312

Jacobs, W.R. (1971) 'The fatal confrontation: early native-white relations on the frontiers of Australia, New Guinea and America: a comparative study', *PHR 40*, 283–309

—— (1972) *Dispossessing the American Indian: Indians and whites on the colonial frontier*, New York: Scribners

—— (1974) 'The tip of an iceberg: pre-Columbian Indian demography and some implications for revisionism', *WMQ 31*, 123–32

James, J.A. and Skinner, J.S. (1985) 'The resolution of the labour-scarcity paradox', *JEH 45*, 513–40

Jennings, F. (1975) *The Invasion of America: Indians, colonialism and the cant of conquest*, Chapel Hill: University of North Carolina Press

Jensen, A.L. (1963) *The maritime commerce of colonial Philadelphia*, Madison, Wisconsin: The State Historical Society

Jones, A.H. (1978) *American colonial wealth, documents and methods*, 3 volumes, New York: Arno Press

—— (1980) *Wealth of a nation to be: the American colonies on the eve of the revolution*, New York: Columbia University Press

Jones, D.L. (1981) *Village and seaport: migration and society in eighteenth-century Massachusetts*, Hanover and London: University Press of New England

Jones, E.L. (1964) *Seasons and prices: the role of weather in English agricultural history*, London: Allen and Unwin

—— (1968) 'Agricultural origins of industry', *PP 40*, 58–71

—— (1974) 'Creative disruptions in American agriculture 1620–1820', *AH 48*, 510–28

—— (1977) 'Societal adaptations to disaster', *BHA 42*, 145–9

—— (1978) 'Disaster management and resource saving in Europe 1400–1800', in Maczak, A. and Parker, W.N. (eds), *Natural Resources in European History*, Washington, DC: Resources for the future, 114–38

—— (1979) 'The environment and the economy', in Bourke, P. (ed), *The New Cambridge Modern History 13*, companion volume; Cambridge: Cambridge University Press, 15–42

—— (1981a) *The European miracle: environment, economies and geopolitics in the history of Europe and Asia*, Cambridge: Cambridge University Press

—— (1981b) 'Demographic and educational interaction in nineteenth-century Europe and the modern third world', in Zajda, J. (ed), *Education and society in the 1980s*, Melbourne: James and Nicholas, 224–32

Jones, R.E. (1973) *The emancipation of the Russian nobility 1762–85*, Princeton, N.J.: Princeton University Press

—— (1977) 'Jacob Sievers, enlightened reform and the development of a "third estate" in Russia'. *RR 36*, 424–37

Kabuzan, V.M. (1963) *Narodonaselenye Rossii XVIII — pervoy polovine XIXv (po materialiam revizii)*, State Publishing House: Moscow

Kahan, A. (1966) 'The costs of westernisation in Russia: the gentry and the economy in the eighteenth century', *SR 25*, 40–66

— (1968) 'National calamities and their effect upon food supply in Russia (an introduction to a catalogue)', *JGO 16*, 358–73

— (1979) 'Social aspects of the plague epidemics in eighteenth-century Russia', *EDCC 27*, 255–66

Kiser, D.H. (1980) *The growth of the law in medieval Russia*, Princeton, N.J.: Princeton University Press

Keep, J.L.H. (1956–7) 'Bandits and the law in Muscovy', *SR 35*, 201–21

Kerblay, B. (1966) A.V. Chayanov, life, career, works in Chayanov (*qv*)

Kim, S.B. (1978) *Landlord and tenant in colonial New York: manorial society 1664–1755*, Chapel Hill: University of North Carolina Press

Kirchner, W. (1966) *Commercial relations between Russia and Europe 1400–1800*, Bloomington: Indiana University Press

Kleimola, A.M. (1979) 'Up through servitude: the changing condition of the Muscovite elite in the sixteenth and seventeenth centuries', *RH 6*, 210–29

Klingaman, D.C. (1969), 'The significance of grain in the development of tobacco colonies', *JEH 29*, 268–78

— (1971) 'Food surpluses and deficits in the American colonies, 1768–72', *JEH 31*, 553–69

— (1972) 'The coastwise trade of colonial Massachusetts', *EIHS* 217–34

— (1975) *Colonial Virginia's coastwise and grain trade*, New York: Arno Press

Klyuchevskii, V.D. (1960 reprint) *A history of Russia*, New York: Russell and Russell

Knoppers, J.V. (1976) *Dutch trade with Russia from the time of Peter I to Alexander I: a quantitative study in eighteenth-century shipping*, Montreal: Inter-university Centre for European Studies

Koopmans, J.C. (1957) *Three essays on the state of economic science*, New York: McGraw-Hill

Kovalchenko, I.D. (1959) *Krestyane i Krepostnoye Khozyaystvo Ryazanskoy i Tambovskoy Guberniy v Pervoy Polovine XIX veka*, Moscow: State Publishing House

— (1959) 'Dinamika urovnya zemledelcheskovo proizvodstva Rossii pervoy polovine XIXv', *IS 1*, 58–86

―― (1964) 'O tovarnosti zemledeliya v Rossii v pervoy polovine XIXv', in *Yezhegodnik po agrarnoy istorii vostochnoy yevropy*, 1963, g, Vilnius

―― (1973) 'Agrarnyi rynok i kharakter agrarnovo stroya evropeyskoy rossii v kontse XIX — nachale XX veka', *IS 2*

―― and Milov, L.V. (1969) 'O printsipakh issledovaniya protsessa formirovaniya vserossiyskovo agrarnovo rynka [XVIII–XVv]', *IS 6*

Kulikoff, A. (1979) 'The economic growth of the eighteenth-century. Chesapeake colonies', *JEH 39*, 275–88

Kupperman, K.O. (1979) 'Apathy and death in early Jamestown', *JAH 66*, 24–40

―― (1980) *Settling with the Indians: the meeting of English and Indian cultures in America, 1580–1640*, London: J.M. Dent and Sons Ltd

―― (1982) 'The puzzle of the American climate in the early Colonial period', *AHR 87*, 1262–89

Kushner, H.I. (1975) *Conflict on the north-west coast: American-Russian rivalry in the Pacific north-west, 1790–1867*, Westport: Greenwood Press

Kuznets, S. (1965) 'Notes on the take-off', in *Economic growth and structure-selected essays*, London: Heinemann, 213–35

Land, A.C. (1965) 'Economic base and social structure: the northern Chesapeake in the eighteenth century' *JEH 25*, 639–54

―― (1967) 'Economic behaviour in a planting society: the eighteenth-century Chesapeake, *JSoH 33*, 469–85

―― (1969) 'The tobacco staple and the planter's problem: technology, labour and crops', *AH 43*, 69–89

Landes, D. (1969) *The unbound Prometheus*, Cambridge: Cambridge University Press

Lane, F.C. (1966) *Venice and history*, Baltimore: John Hopkins Press. Espec. Chap 23, 'The economic meaning of war and protection', 383–98; and Chap. 25, 'Economic consequences of organised violence', 412–28

Langer, L.N. (1975) 'The Black Death in Russia: its effects upon urban labour', *RH 2*, 53–67

―― (1976) 'Plague and the Russian countryside: monastic estates in the late fourteenth and fifteenth centuries', *CaSS 10*, 351–69

―― (1979) 'The historiography of the pre-industrial Russia city', *JUH 5*, 209–40

Langer, W.L. (1975) 'American foods and Europe's population growth, 1750–1850', *JSH 10*, 51–66

Large, E.C. (1940) *The advance of the fungi*, New York: H. Holt and Co

Laue, T.H. von (1960) 'The state and the economy', in C. Black (ed.) (*qv*)

Leach, D.E. (1966) *The northern colonial frontier, 1607–73*, New York: Holt, Rinehart and Winston

Lebergott, S. (1984) *The Americans: an economic record*, New York and London: W.W. Norton and Co

Lee, S.P. and Passell, P. (1979) *An economic view of American history* New York and London: W.W. Norton & Co

Lemon, J.T. (1967a). 'Household consumption in eighteenth-century America and its relationship to production and trade: the situation among farmers in south-eastern Pennsylvania', *AH 41*, 59–70

—— (1967b) 'Urbanisation and the development of eighteenth-century south-eastern Pennsylvania and adjacent Delaware', *WMQ 24*, 501–42

—— (1972) *The best poor man's country: a geographical study of early south-eastern Pennsylvania*, Baltimore: John Hopkins Press

Lenin, V.I. (1964 reprint) *The development of capitalism in Russia*, Moscow: Progress Publishers

Levine, D. (1977) *Family formation in an age of nascent capitalism*, New York, San Francisco and London: Academic Press

Levy, L.W. (1957) *The law of the Commonwealth and Chief Justice Shaw*. Cambridge, Mass.: Harvard University Press

Lewis, W.A. (1954) 'Economic development with unlimited supplies of labour', *MSESS 22*, 139–41

—— (1977) *The evolution of the international economic order*, Princeton, N.J.: Princeton University Press

—— (1978) *Growth and fluctuations*, London: Allen and Unwin

Lillard, R.G. (1973) *The great forest*, New York: Da Capo Press

Lindstrom, D. (1978) *Economic change in the Philadelphia region, 1810–50*, New York: Columbia University Press

—— (1979) 'American economic growth before 1840: new evidence and new directions', *JEH 39*, 289–302

—— and Sharpless, I. (1978) 'Urban growth and economic structure in *antebellum* America', *REH 3*, 161–216

Littlefield, D.C. (1981) *Rice and slaves: ethnicity and the slave trade in colonial South Carolina*, Baton Rouge and London: Louisiana State University Press

Lockridge, K.A. (1968) 'Land, population and the evolution of New England society, 1630–1790', *PP 39*, 62–80

—— (1970) *A New England town: the first hundred years, Dedham, Massachusetts, 1636–1736*, New York: Norton

—— (1981) *Settlement and unsettlement in early America: the crisis of political legitimacy before the revolution*, Cambridge: Cambridge University Press

—— and Kreider, A. (1966) 'The evolution of Massachusetts town government, 1640–1740', *WMQ 23*, 549–76

Loehr, R.C. (1952) 'Self-sufficiency on the farm'. *AH 26*, 37–41

Longworth, P. (1969) *The Cossacks*, London: Constable

Lurie, J. (1972) 'Speculation, risk and profits: the ambivalent agrarian in the late nineteenth century', *AH 46*, 269–278

Lyashchenko, P. (1949) *A history of the national economy of Russia*, New York: Octagon Books

Lydolph, D.E. (1976) *Climates of the Soviet Union (World survey of climatology vol. 7)*, Amsterdam, New York: Elsevier Scientific Publishing Co

—— (1977) 'The agricultural potential of the *nonchernozem* zone', chap. 4 in Laird, R.D., Hajda, J. and Laird, B.A. (eds), *The Future of Agriculture in the Soviet Union and Eastern Europe*, Boulder, Colorado: Westview Press

Madariaga, I. de (1981) *Russia in the age of Catherine the Great*, London: Weidenfeld and Nicholson

Maddison, A. (1982) *Phases of capitalist development*, Oxford, New York: Oxford University Press

Main, G.L. (1982) *Tobacco colony: life in early Maryland, 1650–1720*, Princeton, N.J.: Princeton University Press

Main, J.T. (1965) *The social structure of revolutionary America*, Princeton, N.J.: Princeton University Press

Mak, J. (1972) 'Intra-regional trade in the *antebellum* west: Ohio, a case study', *AH 46*, 489–97

Mankov, A.G. (1951) *Tseny i ikh Dvizheniye v Russkom Gosudaistve XVI veke*, Moscow: State Publishing House

Martin, C. (1978) *Keepers of the game: Indian-animal relationships and the fur trade*, Berkeley: University of California Press

Massie. R.K. (1981) *Peter the Great: his life and world*, New York: Knopf

Matossian, M.K. (1984) 'Mould poisoning and population growth in England and France', JE 44, 669–686

McClelland, P.D. (1969) 'The cost to America of British imperial policy', *AER 59*, 370–81

McCloskey, D.N. (1976) 'English open fields as behaviour towards risk', *REH 1*, 124–70

McColley, R. (1973) *Slavery and Jeffersonian Virginia*, Urbana: University of Illinois Press

McCusker, J.J. (1978) *Money and exchange in Europe and America, 1660–1775: a handbook*, London: Macmillan

MacFarlane, A. (1978) *The origins of English individualism: the family, property and social transition*, Oxford: Blackwell

McGrew, R.E. (1965) *Russia and the cholera, 1823–32*, Madison and Milwaukee: University of Wisconsin Press

McKay, J.P. (1970) *Pioneers for profit*, Chicago: University of Chicago Press

McKeown, T. (1976) *The modern rise of population*, New York: Academic Press

McMahon, S.F. (1981) 'Provisions, laid up for the family: toward a history of diet in New England 1650–1850', *HM 14*, 4–21

McManis, D.R. (1975) *Colonial New England — a historical geography*, New York, Oxford: Oxford University Press

McNeill, W.H. (1964) *Europe's steppe frontier, 1500–1800*, Chicago: University of Chicago Press

—— (1977) *Plagues and peoples*, Oxford: Blackwell

—— (1980) *The human condition an ecological and historical view*, Princeton, N.J.: Princeton University Press

Medick, H. (1976) 'The proto-industrial family economy: the structural function of household and family during the transition from peasant society to industrial capitalism', *SH 3*, 291–316

Meeker, E. (1972) 'The improving health of the United States, 1850–1915', *EEH 9*, 353–73

—— (1974) 'The social rate of return on investment in public health, 1880–1950', *JEH 34*, 392–421

Menard, R.R. (1978) 'The tobacco industry in the Chesapeake colonies, 1617–1730: an interpretation', *REH 5*, 109–77

Mendels, F.F. (1972) 'Proto-industrialisation; the first phase of the industrialisation process', *JEH 32*, 241–61

Merrens, H.R. (1964) *Colonial North Carolina in the eighteenth century: a study in historical geography*, Chapel Hill: University of North Carolina Press

Merrill, M. (1977) 'Self-sufficiency and exchange in the rural economy of the United States: cash is good to eat', *RHR 7*, 42–71

Meyendorff, J. (1981) *Byzantium and the rise of Russia: a study of Byzantino-Russia relations in the fourteenth century*, Cambridge: Cambridge University Press

Middleton, A.P. (1953) *Tobacco coast: a maritime history of Chesapeake Bay in the colonial era*, Newport News, Virginia: Mariners' Museum

Millar, J.R. (1969)'A reformulation of A.V. Chayanov's theory of the peasant economy', *EDCC 18*, 219–229

Miller, D.H. (1976) 'State and city in seventeenth-century Moscovy', in Hamm, M.F. (ed) (*qv*)

—— (1977) 'Russian urban development and the "myth" of backwardness', *JUH 4*, 117–26

Miller, N. (1962) *The enterprise of a free people: aspects of economic development in New York State during the canal period, 1792–1838*, Ithaca, N.Y.: Cornell University Press

Milov, L.V. (1974) 'Paradoks khlebnykh tsen i kharakter agrarnovo iynka Rossii v XIX veke', *IS 1*

Mitchell, R.D. (1977) *Commercialism and the frontier: perspectives on the early Shenandoah Valley*, Charlottesville, Virginia: University Press of Virginia

Moloney, F.X. (1967) *The fur trade in New England, 1620–76*, Hamden, Connecticut: Archon Books

Mooney, J. (1928) 'The aboriginal population of America north of Mexico', *Smithsonian Miscellaneous Collections, LXXX*, Washington DC

Morgan, E.S. (1971) 'The first American boom: Virginia' 1618–30, *WMQ 28*, 169–98

—— (1975) *American slavery, American freedom: the ordeal of colonial Virginia*, New York: Norton

Morris, J.M. (1979) *America's maritime heritage: maritime developments and their impact on American life*, Washington: University Press of America

Munting, R. (1979) 'Mechanisation and dualism in Russian agriculture', *JEEH 8*, 752–58

Mutch, R. (1977) 'Yeoman and merchant in pre-industrial America', *Societas 7*, 279–302

Nelson, W.M. (1975) *Americanisation of the common law: the impact of legal change on Massachusetts society, 1760–1830*, Cambridge, London: Harvard University Press

Nettels, C.P. (1962) *The emergence of a national economy 1775–1815 (vol II of The economic history of the United States)*, New York: Holt, Rhinehart and Winston

Neumark, S.D. (1957) *Economic influences on the South African frontier, 1652–1836*, Stanford, California: Stanford University Press

Niemi, A.W. Jr. (1969) 'A further look at inter-regional canals and economic specialisation, 1820–40', *EEH 7*, 499–520

Nifontov, A.S. (1974) *Zernovoye proizvodstvo Rossii vo vtoroy polovine XIX veka*, Moscow: State Publishing House

North, D.C. (1961) *The economic growth of the United States,*

1790–1860, Englewood Cliffs, New Jersey: Prentice Hall
—— (1968) 'Sources of productivity change in ocean shipping 1600–1850', *JPE 76*, 953–70
—— (1979) 'A framework for analysing the state in economic history', *EEH 16*, 249–59
—— (1981) *Structure and change in economic history* , New York, London: W.W. Norton & Co
—— and Davis, L.E. (1971) *Institutional change and American economic growth*, Cambridge: Cambridge University Press
—— and Thomas, R.P. (1973) *The rise of the western world: a new economic history*, Cambridge: Cambridge University Press
Norton, S. (1971) 'Population growth in colonial America: a study of Ipswich, Massachusetts', *PoS 25*, 433–52
Norton, T.E. (1971) *The fur trade in colonial New York, 1686–1776*, Madison: University of Wisconsin Press
Nugent, W. (1981) *Structures of American social history*, Bloomington: Indiana University Press
O'Brien, P.K. (1980) 'European economic development: the contribution of the periphery', *EHR 2nd ser. 35*, 1–18
Owen, T.C. (1981) *Capitalism and politics in Russia: a social history of the Moscow merchants, 1855–1905*, Cambridge and London: Cambridge University Press
Palmer, R.R. (1959) 'The age of democratic revolution: a political history of Europe and America', *Vol 1, The challenge*, Princeton, N.J.: Princeton University Press
Papenfuse, E.C. Jr (1972) 'Planter behaviour and economic opportunity in a staple economy', *AH 46*, 297–311
Pares, R. (1968) *Yankees and Creoles: the trade between North America and the West Indies before the American revolution*, Hamden: Archon Books
Parker, W.H. (1972) *The superpowers: the United States and the Soviet Union compared*, London: Macmillan
Perkins, W.J. (1980) *The economy of colonial America*, New York: Columbia University Press
Perlin, F. (1983) 'Proto-industrialisation and pre-colonial South Asia', *PP 98*, 30–95
Pintner, W.M. (1978) 'Russia', in Grew (ed.) (*qv*), 347–82
—— and Rowney, D.K. (eds) (1980) *Russian Officialdom: the bureaucratisation of Russian society from the seventeenth to the twentieth century*, Chapel Hill: University of North Carolina Press
Pipes, R. (1974) *Russia under the old regime*, London: Penguin Books
Polanyi, K. (1957) *The great transformation*, Boston: Beacon Press

—— (1977) 'The economistic fallacy', *R 1*, 9–20

Portal, R. (1951) *L'oural au 18ᵉ siècle*, Paris: A. Colin

—— (1965) 'The industrialisation of Russia', in M.M. Postan and H.J. Habakkuk, (eds), *The Cambridge economic history of Europe vol. 6, part 2*, 801–74, Cambridge: Cambridge University Press

Post, J.D. (1977) *The last great subsistence crisis in the western world*, Baltimore: John Hopkins University Press

Potter, J. (1965) 'The growth of population in America, 1700–1860' in Glass, D. and Eversley, D.E. (eds), *Population in history: essays in historical demography*, London: Edward Arnold, 631–88

Powell, S.C. (1963) *Puritan village: the formation of a New England town*, Middletown: Wesleyan University Press

Pred, A.R. (1973) *Urban growth and the circulation of information the United States system of cities, 1790–1840*, Cambridge, Mass.: Harvard University Press

—— (1975) 'Large-city interdependence and, the pre-electronic diffusion of innovations in the United States', in Schnore, L.F. (ed.) *The new urban history: quantitative explorations by American historians*, Princeton, N.J.: Princeton University Press

Price, J.M. (1980) *Capital and credit in British overseas trade: the view from the Chesapeake, 1700–76*, Cambridge and London: Harvard University Press

Primack, M.L. (1962) 'Land clearing under nineteenth-century techniques: some preliminary calculations', *JEH 22*, 484–97

—— (1965a)'Farm construction as a use of farm labour in the US, 1850–1910', *JEH 25*, 114–25

—— (1965b) 'Farm capital formation as a use of farm labour in the US, 1850–1910', *JEH 26*, 348–62

Prucha, F.P. (1967) *Broadax and bayonet: the role of the United States army in the development of the north west, 1815–60*, Lincoln: University of Nebraska Press

Raeff, M. (1982) 'Seventeenth-century Europe in eighteenth-century Russia', *SR 41*, 611–19

Rainbolt, J.C. (1974) *From prescription to persuasion: manipulation of the seventeenth-century Virginia economy*, Port Washington, New York: Kennikat Press

Ransel, D.L. (ed.) (1978) *The family in imperial Russia: new lines of historical research*, Urbana, Chicago and London: University of Illinois Press

Ransom, R.L. (1967) 'Inter-regional canals and economic specialisation in the *antebellum* United States', *EEH 5*, 12–35

—— and Sutch, R. (1977) *One kind of freedom: the economic*

consequences of emancipation, Cambridge, New York: Cambridge University Press

——, Sutch, R., and Walton, G.M. (eds) (1982) *Explorations in the new economic history — Essays in honour of Douglass C. North*, New York, London: Academic Press

Rashin, A.G. (1956) *Naseleniye Rossii za 100 let*, Moscow: State Publishing House

Rieber, A.J. (1982) *Merchants and entrepreneurs in imperial Russia* Chapel Hill: University of North Carolina Press

Riefler, R.F. (1979) 'Nineteenth-century urbanisation pattern in the United States', *JEH 39*, 961-74

Robbins, R.G. (1975) *Famine in Russia 1891-2*, New York: Columbia University Press

Rosenberg, C.E. (1962) *The cholera years: the United States in 1832, 1849 and 1866*, Chicago: University of Chicago Press

Rosenberg, N. (1972) *Technology and American economic growth*, New York: Harper and Row

—— (1973) 'Innovative responses to materials shortages', *AER 63*, 111-18

—— (1975) 'America's rise to wood-working leadership', in Hindle (ed.) (*qv*) 37-62

Rostow, W.W. (1960) *The stages of economic growth*, Cambridge, Mass.: Harvard University Press

Rothenberg, W.B. (1981) 'The market and the Massachusetts farmer, 1750-1855', *JEH 41*, 283-314

Rothstein, M. (1966) '*Antebellum* wheat and cotton exports: a contrast in marketing organisations and economic development', *AH 40*, 91-100

Rowland, R.H. and Lewis, R.A. (1976) *Nationality and population changes in Russia and the USSR: an evaluation of census data, 1897-1970*, New York: Praeger

Rozman, G. (1976) *Urban networks in Russia, 1750-1800, and premodern periodisation*, Princeton, N.J.: Princeton University Press

Rubinstein, N.L. (1957) *Selskoye Khozyaystvo Rossii vo Vtoroy Polovine XVIII v.*, Moscow: State Publishing House

Rudolph, R.L. (1980) 'Family structure and proto-industrialisation in Russia', *JEH 40*, 119-22

—— (1985) 'Agricultural structure and proto-industrialisation in Russia: economic development with unfree labour', *JEH 45*, 47-69

Russell, H.S. (1976) *A long, deep furrow: three centuries of farming in New England*, Hanover, New Hampshire: University Press of New England

—— (1980) *Indian New England before the Mayflower*, Hanover, New Hampshire: University Press of New England

Rutman, D.B. (1967) *Husbandmen of Plymouth — farms and villages in the old colony, 1620–92*, Boston: Beacon Press

—— and Rutman, A.H. (1976) 'Of agues and fevers: malaria in the early Chesapeake', *WMQ 33*, 31–60

—— , Wetherell, C., and Rutman, A.H. (1980) 'Rythms of life: black and white seasonality in the early Chesapeake', *JIH 11*, 29–53

Scheiber, H.N. (1971) 'The road to Munn: eminent domain and the concept of public purpose in the state courts', in Fleming and Bailyn (*qv*), 329–402

—— (1972–3) 'Government and the economy: studies of the "commonwealth" policy in nineteenth-century America', *JIH 3*, 135–51

—— (1973) 'Property law, expropriation, and resource allocation by government: the United States, 1789–1910', *JEH 33*, 232–51

—— (1975) 'Instrumentalism and property rights: a reconsideration of American "styles of judicial reasoning" in the nineteenth century', *WLR 1*, 1–18

—— (1980) 'Public economic policy and the Americal legal system: historical perspectives', *WLR 6*, 1159–89

—— (1981) 'Regulation, property rights and definition of "the market": law and the American economy', *JEH 41*, 103–11

Schnore, L.F. (ed.) (1975) *The new urban history: quantitative explorations by American historians*, Princeton, N.J.: Princeton University Press

Schofield, R.S. (1972) ' "Crisis" mortality', *LPS 9*, 10–21

Schumacher, M.G. (1975) *The northern farmer and his markets during the late colonial period*, New York: Arno Press

Schweitzer, M.M. (1985) 'Contracts and custom: economic policy in colonial Pennsylvania', *JEH 45*, 463–5

Scott, J.C. (1976) *The moral economy of the peasant: rebellion and subsistence in south-east Asia*, New Haven and London: Yale University Press

Sen, A. (1977) 'Starvation and exchange entitlements: a general approach and its application to the great Bengal famine', *CJE 1*, 33–59

Sewell, W.H. Jr. (1967) 'Marc Bloch and the logic of comparative history', *History and Theory 6*, 208–18

Shanin, T. (1972) *The awkward class*, Oxford: Oxford University Press

—— (ed.) (1971) *Peasants and peasant societies*, London: Penguin Books

Shepherd, J.F. (1970) 'Commodity exports from the British North American Colonies to overseas areas, 1768–72: magnitudes and patterns of trade', *EEH 8*, 5–76

—— and Walton, G.M. (1972) *Shipping, maritime trade and the economic development of colonial North America*, Cambridge: Cambridge University Press

—— and Walton, G.M. (1976) 'Economic change after the American revolution: pre- and post-war comparisons of maritime shipping and trade', *EEH 13*, 397–422

—— and Walton, G.M. (1979) *The economic rise of early America*, Cambridge and New York: Cambridge University Press

—— and Williamson, S.H. (1972) 'The coastal trade of the British North American colonies, 1768–72', *JEH 32*, 783–810

Sheridan, R.B. (1960) 'The British credit crisis of 1772 and the American colonies', *JEH 20*, 161–86

Siegelbaum, L. (1980) 'The Odessa grain trade: a case study in urban growth and development in Tsarist Russia', *JEEH 9*, 113–52

Simms, J.Y. (1976) 'The impact of the Russian famine of 1891–2: a new perspective', PhD thesis: University of Michigan

—— (1977) 'The crisis in Russian agriculture at the end of the nineteenth century: a different view', *SR 36*, 377–98

Smith, A. (1976 reprint) *An inquiry into the nature and causes of the wealth of nations*, Oxford: Clarendon Press

Smith, A.E. (1947) *Colonists in bondage: white servitude and convict labour in America 1607–1776*, Chapel Hill, North Carolina: University of North Carolina Press

Smith, B.G. (1977) 'Death and life in a colonial immigrant city: a demographic analysis of Philadelphia', *JEH 37*, 863–89

—— (1981) 'The material lives of labouring Philadelphia, 1750–1800', *WMQ 38*, 163–202

—— (1978) 'Mortality and family in the colonial Chesapeake', *JIH 8*, 403–27

Smith, D.S. (1972) 'The demographic history of colonial New England' *JEH 32*, 165–83

Smith, R.E.F. (1959) *The origins of farming in Russia*, Paris: Mouton

—— (1968) *The enserfment of the Russian peasantry*, Cambridge: Cambridge University Press

—— (1977) *Peasant farming in Muscovy*, Cambridge and New York: Cambridge University Press

—— and Christian, D. (1984) *Bread and salt: a social and economic history of food and drink in Russia*, Cambridge: Cambridge University Press

256

Soltow, J.H. (1965) *The economic role of Williamsburg*, Charlottesville, Virginia: University of Virginia Press

Sontag, J.D. (1968) 'Tsarist debts and Tsarist foreign policy', *SR 27*, 531-3

Spring, D.W. (1975) 'Railways and economic development in Turkestan before 1917', in Symons and White (eds), 46-74

Starr, S.F. (1972) *Decentralisation and self-government in Russia, 1830-70*, Princeton, N.J.: Princeton University Press

Stavrianos, L.S. (1981) *Global rift: the third world comes of age*, New York: Morrow

Stettler, H.L. (1970) 'The New England throat distemper and family size', in Klarman, H. (ed.) *Empirical studies in health economics*, Baltimore: John Hopkins University Press

Stiverson, G.A. (1977) *Poverty in a land of plenty: tenancy in eighteenth-century Maryland*, Baltimore and London: John Hopkins University Press

Stone, L. (1983) 'Interpersonal violence in English society, 1300-1980', *PP 101*, 22-3

Strassman, W.P. (1959) *Risk and technological innovation: American manufacturing methods during the nineteenth century*, Ithaca, New York: Cornell University Press

Sumner, B.H. (1944) *Survey of Russian history*, London: Duckworth

Sydenham, D. (1980) 'Rewards of practice: medical incomes in eighteenth-century America', South Carolina, unpublished paper

Symons, L. and White, C.M. (eds)(1975) *Russian transport: an historical and geographical survey*, London: Bell and Sons Ltd

Szeftel, M. (1965) 'Aspects of feudalism in Russian history', in Coulborn, R. (ed.) (*qv*) 167-84

Tate, T.W. and Ammerman, P.L. (eds) (1979) *The Chesapeake in the seventeenth century — essays on Anglo-American society*, Chapel Hill: University of North Carolina Press

Taylor, P.S. (1954) 'Plantation agriculture in the United States: seventeenth to twentieth centuries', *LE 30*, 141-52

Teaford, J.C. (1975) *The municipal revolution in America: origins of modern urban government 1650-1825*, Chicago and London: University of Chicago Press

Tegoborskii, M.L. (1855-6) *Commentaries on the productive forces of Russia*, (2 volumes), London: Longman, Broom, Green and Langman, reprinted by Johnson Reprint Corp, (1972)

Temin, P. (1964a) 'A new look at Hunter's hypothesis about the *antebellum* iron industry', *AER 54*, 344-51

—— (1964b) *Iron and steel in nineteenth-century America: an economic enquiry*, Cambridge, Mass.: Massachusetts Institute of Technology Press

—— (1975) *Causal factors in American economic growth in the nineteenth century*, London: Macmillan

Thomas, B. (1972) *Migration and urban development: a reappraisal of British and American long cycles*, London: Methuen

—— (1973) *Migration and economic growth: a study of Great Britain and the Atlantic economy*, Cambridge: Cambridge University Press

—— (1978) 'The rhythms of growth in the Atlantic economy of the eighteenth century', *REH 3*, 1–46

Thomas, R.P. (1965) 'A quantitative approach to the study of the effects of British imperial policy upon colonial welfare: some preliminary findings', *JEH 25*, 615–38

Thompson, E.P. (1978) *The poverty of theory and other essays*, London: Merlin

Thomson, B.F. (1977) *The changing face of New England*, Boston: Houghton Mifflin Co

Thorner, D. (1966) 'Chayanov's concept of peasant economy', in Chayanov (*qv*), xi–xxiv

Thurow, L.C. (1983) *Dangerous currents: the state of economics*, Oxford: Oxford University Press

Timoshenko, V.P. (1932) *Agricultural Russia and the wheat problem*, Stanford University, California: Food Research Institute

—— (1937) 'World wheat acreages, yields and climates', *WS 13*

—— (1942) 'Variability of wheat yields and outputs: (Part 1) cycles or random fluctuations', *WS 18*

—— (1943) 'Variability in wheat yields and outputs: (Part 2) regional aspects of variability', *WS 19*

—— (1944) 'Inter-regional correlation in wheat yields and outputs', *WS 20*

Toumanoff, P. (1981) 'The development of the peasant commune in Russia', *JEH 41*, 179–84

Treadgold, D.W. (1957) *The great Siberian migration*, Princeton, N.J.: Princeton University Press

Tryon, R.M. (1966 reprint) *Household manufacturers in the United States, 1640–1860*, New York: A.M. Kelley

Tugan-Baranovsky, P. (1970 reprint) *The Russian factory in the nineteenth century*, Homewood, Illinois: R.D. Irwin

Turner, F.J. (1962 reprint) *The frontier in American history*, New York: Holt, Rinehart and Wisdom

Vance, R.B. (1929) *Human factors in cotton culture: a study in the social geography of the American south*, Chapel Hill: University of North Carolina Press

Vedder, R.K. (1976) *The American economy in perspective*, Belmont, California: Wadsworth Publishing Co Inc

Vinogradoff, E.D. (1975) 'The "invisible hand" and the Russian peasant', *PSN 4*, 6–19

Vinovskis, M.A. (1971) 'The 1789 life table of Edward Wigglesworth', *JEH 31*, 570–90

—— (1972) 'Mortality rates and trends in Massachusetts before 1860', *JEH 32*, 184–213

—— (ed:) (1979) *Studies in American historical demography*, New York, London: Academic Press

Volin, L. (1970) *A century of Russian agriculture: from Alexander II to Krushchev*, Cambridge: Harvard University Press

Vucinich, W.S. (ed.) (1968) *The peasant in nineteenth-century Russia*, Stanford: Stanford University Press

Wallace, D.M. (1970 reprint) *Russia*, New York: Praeger

Wallerstein, I. (1974) *The modern world system: capitalist agriculture and the origins of the European world-economy in the sixteenth century*, New York: Academic Press

Walsh, M. (1981) *The American frontier revisited*, London: Macmillan

Walton, G.M. (1967) 'Sources of productivity change in American colonial shipping, 1675–1775', *EHR 20*, 67–78

—— (1971) 'The new economic history and the burden of the navigation acts', *EHR 24*, 533–42

Warden, G.B. (1976) 'Inequality and instability in eighteenth-century Boston, a reappraisal'; *JIH 6*, 585–620

Watkins, M.H. (1963) 'A staple theory of economic growth', *CJEPS 29*, 141–84

Weeden, W.B. (1890) *Economic and social history of New England, 1620–1789* (2 volumes), Boston: Houghton Mifflin

Whartenby, F.C. (1977) *Land and labour productivity in United States: cotton production, 1800–40*, New York: Arno Press

White, C.M. (1975) 'The impact of Russian railway construction on the market for grain in the 1860s and 1870s, in Symons, L. and White, C.M. (eds.) *Russian transport: An historical and geographical survey*, London: Bell and Sons Ltd

—— (1976) 'The concept of social saving in theory and practice', *EHR 29*, 82–100

Wilkinson, R.G. (1973) *Poverty and progress: an ecological model of economic development*, London: Methuen

Williams, D.A. (1969) 'The small farmer in eighteenth-century Virginian politics', *AH 43*, 91–105

Wolf, E.R. (1982) *Europe and the people without history*, Berkeley: University of California Press

Wood, P.H. (1974) *Black majority negroes in colonial South Carolina from 1670 through the Stono Rebellion*, New York: Alfred A. Knopf

Wortman, R.S. (1976) *The development of a Russian legal consciousness*, Chicago and London: University of Chicago Press

Wright, G. (1978) *The political economy of the cotton south: households, markets and wealth in the nineteenth century*, New York: Norton

—— and Kunreuther, H. (1975) 'Cotton, corn and risk in the nineteenth century', *JEH 35*, 526–51

Wrigley, E.A. and Schofield, R.S. (1981) *The population history of England, 1541–1871: a reconstruction*, Cambridge, Mass.: Harvard University Press

Yaney, G.L. (1972) *The systematisation of Russian government: social evolution in the domestic administration of imperial Russia, 1711–1905*, Urbana: University of Illinois Press

Zajda, J. (ed.) (1981) *Education and society in the 1890s*, Melbourne: James and Nicholas

Zelnick, R.E. (1971) *Labour and society in Tsarist Russia: the factory workers of St Petersburg, 1855–70*, Stanford: Stanford University Press

Zevin, R.B. (1975) *The growth of manufacturing in early nineteenth-century New England*, New York: Arno Press

Zirkle, C. (1969) 'To plant or not to plant: comment on the planter's problem', *AH 43*, 87–90

Zlotnick, M.D. (1979) 'Muscovite fiscal policy: 1462–1584', *RH 6*, 243–58

Zuckerman, M. (1970) *Peaceable kingdoms — New England towns in the eighteenth century*, New York: Knopf

Index

261